COMMUNICATING IN GROUPS AND TEAMS
STRATEGIC INTERACTIONS

FOURTH EDITION

Joann Keyton and Stephenson Beck

North Carolina State University | North Dakota State University

cognella® | ACADEMIC PUBLISHING

Bassim Hamadeh, CEO and Publisher

Todd R. Armstrong, Senior Specialist Acquisitions Editor

Abbey Hastings, Associate Production Editor

Miguel Macias, Senior Graphic Designer

Alexa Lucido, Licensing Coordinator

Kassie Graves, Director of Acquisitions and Sales

Jamie Giganti, Senior Managing Editor

Natalie Picotti, Senior Marketing Manager

Cover image copyright © 2013 by iStockphoto LP/kali9.

copyright © 2013 by iStockphoto LP/kali9.

copyright © 2014 by iStockphoto LP/PeopleImages.

Printed in the United States of America.

ISBN: 978-1-5165-1928-6 (pbk) / 978-1-5165-1929-3 (br)

BRIEF TABLE OF CONTENTS

CONTENTS

CHAPTER 9
FACILITATING GROUP MEETINGS   162

A PREFACE FOR INSTRUCTORS

Teams and groups are a basic component of society and the economy. The overwhelming majority of college graduates will work in teams during school and in their future employment. Employees are often asked to lead and facilitate groups, which may involve managing a variety of technological advances and diverse populations. Not surprisingly, employers identify teamwork skills and collaboration as two of the most important skills they *expect* technical school, two-year and four-year college graduates to bring to the workforce. Of course, teamwork is not reserved solely for employment. Outside of their work life, college graduates are the most likely population to volunteer in their nonprofit and civic communities. Whether working in fundraising, directing or being involved in community service, or completing tasks as a member of a nonprofit board or city council, teamwork is a required skill for effective and successful outcomes.

Empirical research has demonstrated that college students are not apprehensive about working in groups and teams, but they do *dislike* working in teams. To remedy this problem, instructors can't simply talk about group concepts and characteristics. Instead, course instruction must be focused on two areas: the actual behavior, and *why* that behavior is important or effective. This is why a communication perspective is the best way to teach effective group member behavior. A communication perspective emphasizes the creation and management of messages, as well as the reception and perception of meaning. It directly examines communication as the foundation of all group activity. Additionally, it challenges students to glean explanation and interpretation from interaction. A host of individual-level outcomes, such as identity, commitment, and satisfaction, are all subjective creations based on group interaction. Thus, a direct focus on interaction is not only the foundation of group communication scholarship, but also the best way to engage students in the learning experience.

To emphasize the strong and unique perspective owned by group communication scholars, the first chapters of this book create a communicative framework for the investigation of groups and teams. Part of that framework is elaborating on the strategic and contextual nature of group interaction. This starting point positions our book differently from many others in the discipline. We do not simply define what communication is, but show how through our goals and purposes we adapt messages in desire of certain outcomes, while realizing that as soon as we utter our messages to other group members we lose all control of meaning and interpretation. In the first chapters, we also spend considerable time elaborating on how the fundamental characteristics of groups directly influence, and are influenced by, communication. In other words, we take seriously our focus on groups from a communication perspective, and spend considerable effort establishing this view.

Communicating in Groups and Teams: Strategic Interactions is based on three components to assist instructors in teaching group communication. First, the material presented is based on scholarly research findings from the field of communication and related disciplines. The book is skills based—and our skill recommendations are based on rigorous and current research. Second, to emphasize the group over the individual, the book describes and explains group communication concepts with examples based on typical group interactions. That is, dialogue in the book allows students to watch group dynamics unfold. Third, the book is structured around five key elements of groups that can be used to evaluate group effectiveness.

FEATURES TO ENHANCE LEARNING

This book contains a number of features to enhance student learning:

- *Putting the Pieces Together* **boxes.** The five core elements in defining a group are used as a structure for evaluating group effectiveness. The five elements are group size, interdependence of members, group identity, group goals, and group structure. These elements are introduced in Chapter 2 and integrated in every chapter as a special feature so that students become more aware of how communication inhibits or facilitates group success.

- **Skills grounded in a solid research base.** The best advice for communicating in groups is drawn from group research and theory, which has identified the most effective processes and results for group interaction. Thus, the skills presented and suggested in the text have been tested—many of them in the field.

- **Extensive use of realistic examples.** In addition to describing what is happening in groups through the use of extensive examples, this text provides transcripts of group dialogues so students can see the communication process unfold. Group dialogues also provide an opportunity to suggest and test different communication approaches. Using the dialogue examples in this way can help students analyze how the group's conversation might have proceeded differently if alternative communication strategies were employed.

- **A wide range of group types.** The text speaks to students' experiences by providing information about a wide variety of groups, including family and social groups, work teams and high-performance task groups, civic and community groups, and discussion and decision-making groups. Whether students' experiences are with groups that are formal or informal, personal or professional, task oriented or relationally oriented, they need communication skills to build and maintain relationships that support effective problem solving and decision making.

- **Four types of pedagogical boxes emphasizing more advanced learning**

  - *Message and Meaning* boxes display transcripts from groups and teams that have been part of our research, or transcripts that are publicly available.

  - *Theory Standout* provides an in-depth look at group communication theories that are introduced in this book. Featuring theories outside of the narrative provides a closer examination and invites questions about the theory-research link.

  - *Skill Builder* provides students an opportunity to test, develop, and practice their group communication skills through exercises and activities.

  - *Nailing It! Using Group Communication Skills for Group Presentations*: In talking with professors who do not teach the group communication course, we found that a primary concern was that students who had taken a group communication class had difficulty transferring group skills to developing group presentations in other courses. To address this issue, we have developed this feature to help students transfer what they are learning to the development of group presentations.

- **Other in-text learning aids**
  - Chapter previews: At the beginning of each chapter, there is an overview for students about what information and skills they will be learning and practicing in the chapter
  - End-of-chapter summaries and discussion questions and exercises
  - Glossary
  - Extensive list of references for further study

ORGANIZATION OF THE BOOK

To provide a foundation, Chapters 1 through 3 describe the importance of groups and teams, and how communication is basic to our understanding of these social and task forms. At the same time, we do not dismiss that individuals in groups have individual goals that may or may not be congruent with group goals. Our model, the five-piece group puzzle, is introduced in Chapter 2 and provides a structure for the remaining chapters, as well as an analytical tool for identifying key strengths and challenges of group interaction. Chapter 3 describes and explains the contextual influences that affect group interaction across group types: boundaries, time and space, diversity, and technology. Each of these influences is present in some way in every group interaction.

Chapters 4 through 8 describe and explain the core group processes for which each group member is responsible: sharing information, participating in decision making, building relationships, managing conflict, and providing leadership. These processes are interaction opportunities and problems that are regular and dynamic aspects of group interaction. Increasing students' skills in these areas will help them maximize their group interaction efforts.

The concluding Chapter 9 helps students participate in, navigate, and facilitate group meetings. Whether in the role of leader or member, students should be able to facilitate their group's interaction to help the group stay or get back on track. Armed with specific principles, procedures, and feedback techniques, students can make more informed choices about how to help their group.

RESOURCES FOR INSTRUCTORS AND STUDENTS

As group communication scholars and teachers, we develop our own Instructor's Manual materials. While we appreciate a publisher's preference for a portal linked to their brand, we also argue that Instructor's Manual materials should be regularly updated. Thus, we offer a two-pronged approach to Instructor's Manual materials. The main portal, with the password protected, with the following components are found on the Cognella site:

- *Instructor's Manual:* Outlines of learning objectives and a teaching manual suggesting active in-class and field learning exercises, as well as methods for evaluating group communication in the classroom and group assignments. This manual also includes the teaching philosophy that was a foundation for this book, syllabus examples for the group communication course, methods of obtaining feedback from students about the course and their learning experiences and expectations, chapter-by-chapter teaching resources and exercises, and suggestions for term-long group projects.

- *Test Bank:* An extensive print and computerized test bank, including multiple-choice, matching, identification, and essay questions, and identifying the pedagogical objectives addressed by each question.

- *PowerPoint:* Effective and clearly structured PowerPoint slides that avoid the trap of summarizing the chapters in PowerPoint format, as is often typical of such slides accompanying existing textbooks.

A second Instructor's Manual website—with regularly updated resources for instructors and students—will be linked directly from the authors' personal webpages (joannkeyton.com; stephensonbeck.com). Doing so allows us to update web resources quickly, as well as take advantage of current events that are group or team focused.

ACKNOWLEDGMENTS

During the development of this text, we received excellent feedback and encouragement from three reviewers: Dr. Mary Beth Asbury, Middle Tennessee State University; Dr. Linda G. Ward, University of Texas of the Permian Basin; and Dr. Cindy Peterson, MidAmerica Nazarene University. We appreciate the time they took to thoughtfully consider our approach to teaching the group communication course. Another group of communication professors provided feedback on the completed book manuscript. These reviewers were: Dr. Michelle R. Bahr, Bellevue University; Dr. Michael P. Pagano, Fairfield University; Dr. Tennley A. Vik, Emporia State University; and Marissa L. Wiley, University of Kansas.

Communication scholars who provided feedback on the earlier editions of this book include: Carolyn M. Anderson, Laurie Arliss, Dale E. Brashers, John O. Burtis, Marybeth Callison, Elizabeth M. Goering, Randy Hirokawa, Michael E. Holmes, Michele H. Jackson, Virginia Kidd, Bohn D. Lattin, M. Sean Limon, Michael E. Mayer, Mary B. McPherson, Renee A. Meyers, Marshall Scott Poole, Barbara Eakins Reed, Vanessa Sandoval, Kristi Schaller, Matthew W. Seeger, Nick Trujillo, Lyn M. Van Swol, and Clay Warren.

Studying and teaching group communication is our life's work. We thank the many group and team scholars who are part of our international network. They inspire us and hold us to a high standard in conducting research and in presenting our research findings. They are also a lively bunch and are fun to hang out with.

From Joann: I want to thank my personal network, who sustain me and allow me to say "I have a deadline" and not hold it against me. They are also the first to check to see if I need anything while trying to meet those deadlines.

From Steve: I want to thank Sarah, Joshua, and Whitney for their support and love. I'd also like to thank my colleagues who are willing to put up with me.

ABOUT THE AUTHORS

Joann Keyton (BA, Western Michigan University; MA, PhD, Ohio State University) is Professor of Communication at North Carolina State University. She specializes in group communication and organizational communication. Her current research examines the collaborative processes and relational aspects of interdisciplinary teams, participants' use of language in team meetings, the multiplicity of cultures in organizations, and how messages are manipulated in sexual harassment. Her research is field focused and she was honored with the 2011 Gerald Phillips Award for Distinguished Applied Communication Scholarship by the National Communication Association.

Her research has been published in *Business Communication Quarterly, Communication Monographs*, *Communication Research, Communication Studies, Communication Theory*, *Communication Yearbook, Journal of Applied Communication Research, Journal of Business Communication*, *Management Communication Quarterly, Small Group Research, Southern Communication Journal,* and numerous edited collections including the *Handbook of Group Communication Theory and Research*, the Sage *Handbook of Organizational Communication*, and the Oxford *Handbook of Organizational Climate and Culture*.

In addition to publications in scholarly journals and edited collections, she has published three textbooks for courses in group communication, research methods, and organizational culture in addition to coediting an organizational communication case book. Keyton was editor of the *Journal of Applied Communication Research*, Volumes 31–33, and founding editor of *Communication Currents*, Volumes 1–5. Currently, she is editor of *Small Group Research*. She is a founder of the Interdisciplinary Network for Group Research.

For more information, contact Joann at jkeyton@ncsu.edu or www.joannkeyton.com

Stephenson J. Beck (BA, Brigham Young University; MA, University of Illinois at Urbana-Champaign; PhD, University of Kansas) is Associate Professor of Communication at North Dakota State University. His research focuses on group communication and communication strategy. His current research investigates meeting facilitation, conflict management, and decision-making communication. His research endeavors involve studying a variety of group contexts, including breast cancer support groups, nonprofit boards, first responder teams, juries, city councils, data analyst teams, organizational teams, special education teams, and military teams.

His research has been published in *Small Group Research, Group Dynamics, Journal of Applied Communication Research, Business Communication Quarterly, Communication Yearbook, Personal Relationships, Communication Studies, Journal of Family Communication,* and *Cancer Nursing*, and he has authored several contributions to edited books. He is a member of the editorial board of *Small Group Research.*

For more information, contact Stephenson at stephenson.beck@ndsu.edu or www.stephensonbeck.com

CHAPTER 1

SITUATING YOUR EXPERIENCES IN GROUPS

After reading this chapter, you should be able to:

- ◀ Describe the role of groups in your life

- ◀ Explain the importance of groups to the functioning of society

- ◀ Describe the types of groups to which people belong

- ◀ Describe group communication

- ◀ Explain the role of interaction, messages, and meanings in group communication

- ◀ Identify individual and group goals accomplished in groups and teams

A basic part of who we are as individuals is based on our interactions with others. When young we are surrounded by parents, siblings, or other family members, and our experiences with them represent a large portion of our lives. These family relationships and interactions become the first opportunity for us to learn how to communicate with others (Socha, 1999). During this early period of life, you learn how to interact with individuals holding authority, share with those who want what you have, and persuade others to agree with you. These developmental milestones are encouraged by parents. For example, parents may arrange for you to play at the park with friends. The main function of these group experiences is to allow you to learn how to interact and get along with others. Although typically unstructured, such play dates are likely your first experiences in creating and managing relationships and sharing toys with peers.

Gradually, these social interactions expand to other types of groups. When we go to elementary school, we are surrounded by classmates. This setting was likely your introduction to task-focused work groups. For example, teachers often put children into small teams or pods to learn and practice reading and math. Desks are placed into clusters and the classroom is designed for students to gather around and learn together. These types of learning groups also facilitate social development, which help young students learn how to cooperate and help one another.

As students enter middle school, they participate in extracurricular activities, such as clubs and sports, which often involves working with other students to perform in band or choir, put on a play, or compete in robotics tournaments. In high school, working in groups centers around problem-solving tasks in the classroom and more complex performing groups, such as cheerleading, football, and ice hockey. Friends form cliques, which increases the intensity of friendship groups, as well as heightens the distinction of insiders from outsiders. At home, kids play online multiplayer games, which are designed for teams of players from around the world to work together to accomplish a quest.

Upon graduation from high school we continue to encounter groups and are likely to work in teams. Fraternities and sororities evolve around groups of students, and fast food or retail jobs are often team oriented. Grocery stores, assembly lines, and construction crews are often based on work shifts where individuals regularly interact and perform in groups. Many organizational structures are situated around working in teams, which are designed to pool resources and expertise in ways to improve product quality and quantity. When important projects or decisions are required by an organization, temporary or ad hoc committees are formed to handle the situation. As adults, we also belong to groups and teams in our personal and community lives. Book clubs, religious study groups, community service projects, and bowling leagues are all based on the concept of a team. We also depend on support groups when struggling with illness, addiction, or other personal problems. In these settings, group discussion helps us to manage these difficulties.

In addition, there are groups of which we are not members that have significant influence on our lives. Groups at local, state, regional, national, and international levels address societal issues, from local political advocacy groups to the United Nations Security Council. Government hearings and committees address a host of important issues through group debate and problem solving. Although there are certain key individuals in all levels of society who are considered leaders, each of these leaders surround themselves with teams to accomplish goals and objectives.

In groups, we decide, inform, relate, entertain, and socialize. We conduct many fundamental human behaviors and fulfill interpersonal needs with our behavior in groups. Groups are not just something we are forced in to for classroom projects. Rather, groups are so central to the human experience that we often fail to recognize our continual presence and participation in groups, even though groups influence the very norms and culture of society.

GROUPS ARE FUNDAMENTAL TO SOCIETY

In other words, groups are a basic and fundamental part of society, and greatly influence how we communicate with each other (Gastil, 2010; Poole, 1990). Group work is more than simply optional activities in which we endeavor; group interaction is the human experience. Social acts, or communication from one person to another, are a result of our need to seek out opportunities to be with and converse with others. Of course, some of us feel the need to be included much more than others. Due to pressures and anxiety associated with group communication, some of us would prefer to avoid groups. Even if this is the case, groups are so central and fundamental to how we view and participate in the world that they cannot be avoided. Whether it is through families, work, school, government, religion, nonprofit organizations, or play, we spend a good portion of our time in or preparing to be with others in groups.

Types of Groups

Despite the number of groups to which one belongs, one group is never quite like another. When groups and teams were first considered by researchers, they often focused solely on **task-oriented teams**. Common examples of these teams are work groups and management teams. The purpose of these project teams and work groups is to accomplish work tasks, and it is generally assumed that group interaction should be task focused and geared toward planning, debating, or implementing group decisions. However, more recently scholars have also focused on **relational groups** (Keyton, 1999), such as support groups, fraternities/sororities, and social groups. This focus on relational groups also highlights that all teams, whether primarily task or relationally oriented, have a relational dimension. Even members of a work team must learn how to get along, especially given conflict and debates about important task decisions. Thus, even though some groups may have an overarching task or relational focus, every group is goal directed and has both task and relational dimensions that are played out through interaction.

Some groups are created for the sole purpose of a task. For example, a student organization might determine to conduct a fundraiser, and assign a five-member group to

create the event. These individuals may have known each other from prior interactions, but there is a chance that none of them have worked together. Once this group plans, organizes, and implements the fundraiser, the group tenure will be over and they will return to their original student organization functions. Due to the short duration of the group, relationship development may be truncated and leadership structure may be formally and quickly determined and implemented.

However, some groups are ongoing. Fire and emergency medical personnel may work together on a regular basis to handle emergency situations. Experiences among team members in the present will directly influence team behavior in the future. As a result, individuals may be more conscious of relational development, knowing that preserving good relations may lead to positive results over time. Negotiation of roles may change during the life span of the group. The hiring of additional members may require a great deal of effort to acclimate new members to the norms of the established group. Behavior in this type of group may vary drastically from groups that are quickly created for a short-term purpose. Of course, there are many group types that fall between one-time groups and long-term groups.

Due to the different group types and task, group behavior can vary greatly. A social support group functions differently than a work group, which functions differently than a family. However, there is also similarity across these various groups. Groups have fundamental characteristics that make a group a group (see Chapter 2). Groups have formal or informal leaders who influence the flow of conversation. Some degree of common understanding among group members is required for successful group decisions. Groups that work together over time develop routines and norms that guide group interaction. Although these group characteristics can be manipulated and abused to the dismay of group members (e.g., social loafing, groupthink), these same characteristics can benefit a group in terms of leadership, diversity, and relational development.

GROUP COMMUNICATION

Of course, there are many ways to investigate and learn about groups (e.g., social psychological, sociological, management). However, this book examines groups from a *communication* perspective. In order to analyze groups from a communicative perspective, it is important to know what it is we mean by communication. **Communication** is the process of symbol production, reception, and usage; conveyance and reception of messages; and the meanings that develop from those messages (Keyton, Beck, & Asbury, 2010, p. 472). A communicative approach means we are examining symbols, messages, and meanings. All communication is strategic in that we combine symbols into messages in order to accomplish a specific purpose. We use messages to convey meaning to others, and other group members use our messages as evidence of what that meaning is. Unfortunately, the exchange of messages can lead to different interpretations by group members, causing miscommunication.

Interaction and Messages

In this book, we want to investigate groups by examining the processes members undertake to accomplish their task or relational goals. Process, another name for interaction, is the focus of how we study groups. Without interaction among its members, a group would cease to exist. So, while it might be interesting to study how different compositions of group members result in ineffective group outcomes, or whether face-to-face groups outperform online groups, we take these questions one step further: How do these different aspects of groups affect how groups communicate?

Thus, interaction is the foundation of all group endeavors. But due to the multiple opportunities for miscommunication, group interaction is much more complex than one-to-one or dyadic communication. For example, let's say that Sam was charged with researching a problem his sales team was having with one of its customers. After conducting the necessary research, Sam presents his information to his team members, explaining how and why the problem is significant and that it will require group members to work together to resolve the problem by next week's deadline. Since other group members have worked with Sam before, they are aware that when Sam says they will work "many hours," he means everyone will have to work an hour later each evening to get the project done. However, Tonya is new to the group, and when she hears "many hours," she is worried that they will need to work late into the night to get the project done. She may prepare her schedule differently as a result. Thus, some group members had a high level of shared understanding about the task due to their previous experience. Unfortunately for Tonya, her lack of shared experience prevents her from understanding Sam's message as he intended. Since group interaction is heard and interpreted by several individuals simultaneously, there is an increased opportunity for miscommunication and diverging perceptions of interaction. Although you may know some members very well and other members less well, all members may hear the same messages but interpret them in different ways.

Additionally, all messages are **strategic**. When we say strategic, we are referring to how speakers adapt their messages so that they will accomplish their goals (Kellermann, 1992). If you want to go out to eat with a good friend, you could probably say, "Hey, do you want to grab something to eat?" However, if you want to ask the same question of your supervisor, you may alter how you ask the question: "I was wondering if you would like to go to Café Rio for lunch on Wednesday?" Both of these messages are designed to arrange a lunch, but based on the people involved and the context of the relationship, the messages are very different (one informal, the other formal). This is what we mean by strategic—we adapt our messages so that they will best accomplish our goals. As a result, our messages may differ in terms of formality, brevity, complexity, and sincerity. And importantly, even the most elementary of messages, for example, "Will you please pass the salt?", are adapted to accomplish a specific purpose. But since these communicative processes are largely subconscious, we tend not to overly think about these adaptions in regular conversation.

Such message adaptions are true in groups as well, although the process is a bit more complicated. With multiple individuals, our adjustments have to be more complex or conscious. If your group contains close friends and superiors, you may err on adapting your messages more formally as a way of acknowledging the greater value placed on your superiors' opinions. If a deadline is approaching, your messages may be less nuanced and diplomatic, and instead become quite brief and direct. Communicating in a group context requires members to assess the situation and adjust messages accordingly. However, the situation may be difficult to assess. There may be quite a few unknowns. For example, how are people interpreting my messages? How are most group members siding on the decision? Is group member silence a good or bad thing? If the group is meeting quite regularly, it may be easier across conversations to evaluate how members' opinions are evolving.

Fortunately, from a communication perspective, we have a powerful piece of evidence for evaluating group member messages—the message itself. We can analyze how verbal and nonverbal messages are adapted in order to understand individual intent. For example, if a group member addresses the group leaders as "sir" or "ma'am" in a polite but serious way, we can assume that the group member has interpreted the group climate as very formal. The evidence is in the message itself. Thus, one of the important implications of using a group communication perspective is that we can investigate messages to understand meaning and influence on group goals and tasks.

Meaning is also extracted from the way messages follow one another. That is, messages are interdependent (Beck & Keyton, 2012). Certainly, it is impossible to predict what

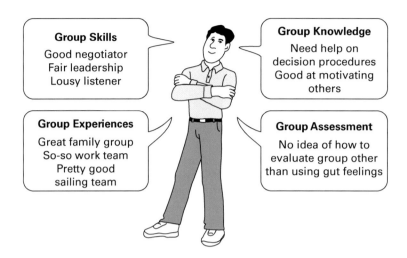

Figure 1.1   You may be good at some aspects of group communication but poor at others.

message a group member will use after another group member speaks. That's because communication is improvised in the moment of conversation. Still, the interdependence of messages that comprise group conversation allows for new ideas to be created, information to be shared, and problems to be solved.

Finally, messages are also multidimensional in that they can influence the conversation in multiple ways. At the simplest level, messages can be distinguished as task messages or relational messages. Since many groups have an overarching group goal, task messages are those messages designed to accomplish the task. This can involve sharing information, planning, coordinating, debating, deciding, and any activity behavior that is in line with accomplishing the group goal. Relational messages are those in which we show antagonism toward or friendly acceptance of others in the group. These types of messages influence the social fabric of the group. Upon completion of a project, June tells Grant that he did a good job on his part of the presentation. Such a comment shows clear support toward Grant and will benefit the relationship between the two, as well as the group as a whole. Both task and relational messages are required for a group to function successfully.

Although task and relational messages are often presented as distinct from one another, many messages contain both task and relational aspects. For example, Amber has been working on a project that she needs to report on to her boss, Katherine. When she stops by Katherine's office, Katherine says, "I don't have time to deal with that now." This message can be interpreted in multiple ways. It can be interpreted in terms of task (i.e., Katherine is busy) or relational (i.e., Katherine doesn't care about me). Even though the intent of the Katherine's message may be very task oriented (she may have a very busy day or an important deadline that she needs to meet), Amber may not use a task-oriented frame to interpret the message and may be very upset by Katherine's comment as a result. The multidimensionality of messages provides listeners several ways to interpret interaction and for group member interpretations to differ.

GROUP AND INDIVIDUAL GOALS

Since group members are adapting their messages to accomplish an array of individual and group goals, all in consideration of context, groups tend to be a very complex and messy forum for communication. Each group member has multiple individual goals (Hollingshead, Jacobsohn, & Beck, 2007), and goals vary across participants. Additionally, group members' perception of the group goal may also be different, especially if the goal has not been discussed in depth.

Importantly, individuals are often trying to accomplish more than one goal—some of these goals may be group oriented, others may be individual oriented (Wittenbaum, Hollingshead, & Botero, 2004). Because there are many goals, not all of them will align. For example, Eliza has a great idea for a fundraising project her team has been assigned. This idea will help the team accomplish their purpose in a high-quality manner with low costs (group goal). In addition, Eliza would really like to be promoted to group leader when the current leader retires next month (individual goal). She knows that if her idea were selected, it would help her appear very leader-like and increase her chances of getting the promotion. To accomplish both her individual and group goal, Eliza successfully persuades the rest of the team to support her idea. In this example, the individual and group goals were aligned with each other, and thus Eliza was not required to prioritize her goals. However, when goals diverge, such prioritization may be complex and difficult.

GROUP SKILLS FOR LIFE

Group interaction is the mechanism that creates many of the tensions and dynamics of groups. As will be outlined in this book, group interaction is the foundation for group identity, interdependence, and structure. It creates and fixes conflicts, leads to group decision making, and is the foundation on which members develop group relationships. Since groups are brought together to take advantage of group members' skills and talents, the ability to work in groups is essential to accomplishing the group's purpose.

As you proceed through this book, you will learn skills associated with being an effective group member. According to the National Association of Colleges and Employers (2015), teamwork is the one of the top skills desired by employers. Being able to work effectively with others in a group will also be useful in your social and community life. Our hope is that by reading this book and applying the concepts described, you will be a more productive employee and member of society. Importantly, since groups are commonplace throughout society, becoming a functional and dynamic group member will increase satisfaction and enjoyment in many aspects of your life.

In addition to learning skills, another objective of this book is to help you analyze and understand the groups or teams of which you are a member or for which you are responsible. By being able to analyze group activities, the interactions among members, and the environment in which a group operates, you will discover what's unique about a particular group and what are the most effective ways to participate in the group.

There are no magic formulas for group interaction or set procedures that work in every group setting. Each group is different, so your approach to each group must differ as well. This book is a guide for your exploration of groups, based on theory and research studies. From the theories contained in this book, we can identify the skills needed for effective and successful group interaction. By developing your group communication skills, you will be able to develop practical and viable solutions to the group interaction problems you encounter.

FORMAT OF THE BOOK

Groups are like individuals—no two are alike. The better equipped you are to analyze what is happening in and around the group, the more successful and satisfying your group experiences will be. To guide you through your investigation of group communication, this book is organized into three parts.

Chapters 1 through 3 provide the foundation for the remainder of the book. These chapters describe the importance of groups and teams and how communication is basic to our understanding of these social and task forms. At the same time, we do not dismiss that individuals in groups have individual goals that may or may not be congruent with group goals. Our model, the five-piece group puzzle, is introduced in Chapter 2 and provides a structure for the remaining chapters, as well as an analytical tool for identifying key strengths and challenges of group interaction. Chapter 3 describes and explains the contextual influences that affect group interaction across group types: boundaries, time and space, diversity, and technology. Each of these influences is present in some way in every group interaction.

Core group processes that occur in every group are described and explained in Chapters 4 through 8. These core processes are sharing information, participating in decision making, building relationships, managing conflict, and providing leadership. Each of these processes is an interaction opportunity, and each is a regular and dynamic aspect of group interaction. At the same time, these processes can create interaction problems that group members must address. Increasing your skills in these core processes will help you be more effective in group interactions.

Many groups do their work in meetings. So, in conclusion, Chapter 9 will help you participate in, navigate, and facilitate group meetings. Whether in the role of leader or member, you should be able to facilitate group interactions to help the group stay or get back on track. Armed with specific principles, procedures, and feedback techniques, you will be able to make more informed choices about how to help your group.

At the beginning of each chapter, a bulleted list presents the essential ideas for that chapter. Previewing these ideas before you read the chapter can help you organize your learning. In preparation for evaluations (tests or applications), reviewing these points can help remind you what you have learned. At the end of each chapter, you will find a numbered list of discussion questions and exercises. Answering these questions and reflecting on the exercises are an effective way of remembering and applying what you have learned. It is also a helpful way to determine if your learning was meaningful while reading the chapter. Although the material in this textbook is useful we all sometimes read a little too quickly or casually when studying for classes. Use the questions at the end of the book as a way of assessing your reading and preparation for the next class.

Throughout the book, you will notice words or phrases that are set in boldface. These words or phrases are part of the vocabulary unique to the study of communication or group communication. Each word or phrase is defined the first time it is used in a chapter. These definitions are also compiled in a glossary at the end of the book. Throughout the book, you will also find in-text citations that point you to the reference or scholarly source from which we developed our ideas. These citations comprise the References, which are at the end of the book.

Additionally, we use four features to develop your expertise about group communication. First, **Message and Meaning** boxes display transcripts from groups and teams that have been part of our research, or transcripts that are publicly available. Group interaction is not scripted in advance like a television show. Group conversation takes twists and turns based who says what, and these transcripts will draw your attention to the complexity of messages and meanings in group interaction. The second feature, **Theory Standout**, provides an in-depth look at group communication theories that are introduced in this book. Perhaps you will use one of these featured theories as a basis for a classroom assignment. The third feature, **Skill Builder**, describes how to develop a group communication skill. Whether you believe you are a novice or an expert, this boxed feature will help you identify ways to evaluate and further develop your mastery of this skill. The fourth feature, **Nailing It!**, helps you apply what you're learning to group situations you'll experience while in college. Some of these will be social groups; others will be task or decision-making groups. And, important to your classwork, some of these groups will be required to develop and give a group presentation.

DISCUSSION QUESTIONS AND EXERCISES

1 Think of a group you belong to now. Using the concepts presented in this chapter, how would you describe that group to someone unfamiliar with that group?

2 Reflect on one of your childhood groups. Compare that experience with one of your adult group experiences. What has changed? What is similar? Why?

3 Review the table of contents for this book. Thinking about your current level of group skills, and develop three lists: (a) group skills and knowledge that you have now, (b) group skills and knowledge that you'd like to learn, and (c) group skills and knowledge that you've mastered and could share with others.

4 Thinking to the future as you pursue your education or a career, what types of groups do you expect to be a member of? Be a leader?

Image Credits

CHAPTER 2

GROUP COMMUNICATION FUNDAMENTALS

After reading this chapter, you should be able to:

- Name the characteristics essential for defining a group

- Recognize the ways in which members socially construct the group through their interactions

- Develop an understanding for thinking about a group as a process

- Explain ways in which group communication is complex and messy

- Explain why both task and relational communication are required in group interactions

WHAT IS A GROUP?

We all have different past group experiences, which lead us to have different expectations and desires for group work. In fact, individuals may disagree on what a group is and is not. Are two people having dinner together a group? What about five people waiting for a bus on a street corner? Would you consider the 50,000 fans in a football stadium a group? And what about your friends who text or send photos to stay in touch during the day? How exactly is a group differentiated from other forms or contexts of interaction? First, let's consider what a group is.

Characteristics for Defining a Group

Five characteristics are central to the definition of groups: group size, interdependence of members, group identity, group goal, and group structure. In addition to defining what a group is, these characteristics are a good place to start developing an understanding about how members of a group interact effectively. These characteristics can help you isolate group interaction problems and understand why they develop. As you read in more detail about each of the characteristics, you will come to understand why a **group** is defined as three or more people who work together interdependently on an agreed-upon activity or goal. Each person identifies themselves as members of the group, and together they develop structure and roles, based on norms and rules, as they interact and work toward their goal.

Group Size

One of the primary characteristics of a group is **group size**. The minimum number of members in a group is three; the maximum number depends on the other characteristics, discussed shortly. Communication among two people, or a dyad, is labeled as interpersonal communication, and different from group communication. The interaction of three people differs significantly from the interaction of two, because the introduction of the third person sets up the opportunity to form coalitions. As an example, **coalition formation** occurs when one member takes sides with another against a third member of the group. This type of 2-to-1 subgrouping creates an imbalance of power, one that can only occur when at least three group members are present. A coalition creates interaction dynamics that cannot occur with two people. Of course, once a group expands beyond three members, different types of coalitions can occur. Three members can contest the ideas of one member who refuses to be persuaded, or a group can break into multiple subgroups or coalitions, each promoting its own view.

Introducing a third group member also allows **hidden communication** to take place. These hidden interactions are often attempts to build alliances, which underscore the role of relationship building as groups work on tasks. For example, let's say that Nancy and Michelle meet on their way to a meeting; Jeff is waiting for them in the conference room. Nancy takes this opportunity to brief Michelle on the background of the project and provide feedback and evaluations on her previous interactions with Jeff. Jeff does not have access to this hidden interaction, but Nancy's musings to Michelle will certainly affect the interaction among these group members. In this case, there was no strategic attempt to manipulate Jeff, but Nancy and Michelle's interaction still affected the group. Naturally, the larger the group, the more these hidden interactions are likely to occur. The size of a group has an impact not only on how members interact with one another but also on how roles are assumed (or assigned) within the group and how interactions are regulated.

What happens when a group is too large? It may be more difficult for members of larger groups to decide who takes what role because many members may have the skills necessary for various roles. Also, larger groups typically have more difficulty in scheduling time to meet with one another as a group.

Research has demonstrated that increased size can produce diminishing returns. In other words, bigger is not always better (Bettenhausen, 1991; Hare, 1982; Wheelan & McKeage, 1993). Although the addition of group members can expand the pool of skills and talents from which to choose, it can also increase problems with coordination and motivation. There is a point at which groups become too large and members become dissatisfied, feel less cohesive with one another, and perceive less identification with the group. Why? The larger the group, the fewer opportunities each member has to talk, and as group size increases, logistical problems in coordinating so many people may negatively influence what a group can accomplish. Thus, increased group size affects group productivity because members have less opportunity to participate. Because of their size, large groups require more attention to group norms and group roles. Even more problematic is the fact that group members are more likely to accept the illusion that someone else is responsible for accomplishing the group's task and so fail to do their own part. As a result, there are greater demands on group leadership in large groups. But large groups can be effective—if the goal is clearly identified for all group members, if members share a consensus about the goal, and if they recognize and fulfill their roles.

Relationships also are affected when a group is too large. For example, twenty members are probably too many to deliberate on a problem and make recommendations in one written report. Having twenty people write together is difficult! Additionally, when group members feel as if they are not needed to produce the group's outcome, or if their individual efforts are not recognized, they become apathetic and feel distant from the group. This form of detachment is known as **social loafing** (Comer, 1995). Social loafers are group members who do not perform to their maximum level of potential contribution. Rather, they use group members as a shield they can hide behind while still reaping the same benefits as other group members who work to make the group a success. The opportunity for social loafing increases as the size of the group increases (Lam, 2015).

What happens when a group is too small? Members of smaller groups may find that no one in the group possesses a critical skill or certain knowledge essential to the group's activity. For complex tasks, three members may be too few to effectively reach group goals. When there are too few members and there is too much work to do, group members are likely to become frustrated, and even angry, about the task and toward the group. In smaller groups, members may also feel pressured to talk more than they feel comfortable.

As you can see, there are problems when there are too many or too few group members. Thus, group size is most appropriately determined by the group's task or activity. In essence, group size should be restricted to the number of members necessary to effectively accomplish the group's goal based on the nature of the task, especially because smaller groups develop into more productive groups more quickly (Wheelan, 2009).

The maximum number of group members depends on the other four characteristics of groups. Rather than limiting or expanding group membership to some arbitrary number, we need to consider issues such as group goals, task complexity, and interaction opportunities to identify the appropriate number of group members. Of course, some groups and teams (juries, sports teams) have specific size limits or standards, which group members cannot change.

Interdependence of Members

A second critical characteristic of a group is the interdependence of group members. **Interdependence** means that both group and individual outcomes are influenced by what other group members do (Bonito, 2002). Members must rely on and cooperate with one another to complete the group activity, because they are attempting to accomplish something that would be difficult or impossible for members working as individuals to achieve. Through their interdependence, group members mutually influence one another.

For example, members of a softball team are a group. It's impossible to play effectively without members in the roles of catcher, pitcher, and shortstop. Each member of the softball team fills a specific role that functions interdependently with those of other players. Moreover, how well one role is fulfilled affects how another role is fulfilled. Even if the team has one outstanding hitter, the team will not win very often if other members don't also hit well or if there aren't any members who specialize in defense. Not only do these team members have to fulfill their specialized roles and depend on one another, but they have to communicate with one another. It is not enough to identify the necessary roles and to assign members to them; individuals in these roles have to be actively engaged and interacting with one another.

As another example, consider a project team at a digital gaming company that has been given the task of developing a multiplayer online game. This task can be seen as a **superordinate goal**—that is, a task or goal that is so complex, difficult, or time consuming that it is beyond the capacity of one person. To be successful, group members with different skills must work interdependently to achieve the group's goal. Team members are interdependent as they share ideas in the early stages of the project; later they can test various ideas with one another before engaging expensive resources. Such interdependence is likely to save their organization time, energy, effort, and money; it is also likely to create a better game.

The communication within groups also illustrates the interdependence of group members. Let's look at a student group concerned about course and faculty evaluations. Jennetta asks the group to think of ways to improve the evaluation process. Her question

MESSAGE AND MEANING

As is typical of many support groups, members of the Bosom Buddy breast cancer support group went around the circle to check in with one another. Here is Claire's check in and how other support group member responded.

CLAIRE: My sister, who lives in Michigan, called, and her middle daughter is the one that I told you had breast cancer—and now her husband has come up with a lump in his breast. And, they're going to do an ultrasound and they're trying to figure out what's going on. But, I thought, God, that's kind of a double-whammy. You know, he's gone through this with his wife and now he's facing the possibility that this is happening to him, too. And, you know, you don't generally think in terms of men having that, so you're not looking for it. My sister said it doesn't appear to be attached to anything. I said, "Well, that's good, because, you know, frequently it goes to the bones, the rib cage." And women have a little more breast tissue, so it can, you know, be growing there more before it gets to the rib cage than for men. She was asking me if I had heard of that, and I said, "Oh, yeah." While I was doing Reach to Recovery, I worked with three different men who had had breast cancer. And all of them, at that point, were successfully treated, but—so it does occur.

MAXI: Terrible, terrible.

TINA: Do you know the percentage?

FAYE: Is the rate for cure for men as high as the rate for women?

CLAIRE: You know, that's a really good question, and I'm not sure about that.

TINA: But I suspect it might not necessarily be high, because … you're not looking for it.

MAXI: And they don't get mammograms …

TINA: That's right, and also because you're right there on the rib cage … you know, you're right there on the rib cage, so it could go to the bones and then into the lung. So, I don't know, but that's a really good question. We should find that out.

Return to Maxi's comment, "Terrible, terrible." Who is she empathizing with? Claire? Claire sister's daughter? Claire sister's daughter's husband? What is she empathizing about? Next, notice how Tina asks a question to begin the informational phase of the discussion. Does her informational query create a different type of empathy?

prompts group members to respond with ideas that she writes on the board. When they finish, Jackson comments about one trend he sees in the list. Sara asks him to elaborate. As Jackson and Sara continue their conversation, Jennetta circles the ideas they are talking about and links them together while she gives affirming nods to indicate that they should continue talking. Pamela, who said very little during the idea generation process, now says, "But the ideas you are circling are ones we as students can do little about. What about working through student government to develop an independent evaluation process that could be published in the student newspaper?" Jennetta, Jackson, and Sara turn to Pamela expectantly. Their silence encourages Pamela to continue talking: "What I'm saying is that the ideas on the board are attempts to fix a system that is not under our control. So, why not develop an independent system that students control?" Jackson replies enthusiastically, "Great idea, Pam."

Notice how the verbal and nonverbal messages in this group depend on one another to make sense. Jennetta first invites members' participation, and they all generate ideas. The list they generate motivates Jackson to make an analytical comment, which is further encouraged by Sara's question. Although Pamela initially says little, her action has an impact on other group members' communication by giving Jackson and Sara more opportunities to talk. Pamela's interjection into the conversation startles the others, and their conversation stops. Her acute observation reminds them that she has not been ignoring what's going on; rather, her assessment helps them see that they may be wasting their time.

In this example, the communication itself was interdependent. One statement can only make sense when it is placed before and after other strings of the conversation. Each individual in the group is influenced by what others say (and don't say). The group's success depends on the extent to which the verbal and nonverbal messages make sense together.

Group Identity

A third defining characteristic for a group is group identity. Group members must know and act as if they are members of this particular group. In essence, **group identity** means that individuals identify themselves with other group members and the group goal. Group identity is fully achieved when members behave as a group, believe they belong to a group, and come to like the group—both its members and its tasks (Henry, Arrow, & Carini, 1999). Group identity fosters cooperation (Jackson, 2008). Without this type of identification, group focus and interdependence will weaken.

Unfortunately, many times people are identified as a group when they have little or no expectation that group interaction will occur. Such gatherings or collections of people are more appropriately called **groupings**. Throughout our lives, we are constantly identified by the groupings people assign to us. For example, others often label us by where we live (e.g., Midwesterner, in a big city), what type of work we do (e.g., lawyer, franchise owner), and the hobbies we pursue. But these characteristics do not necessarily put us into groups where we interact and interdependently work on tasks and activities with others. At the same time, individuals may join particular groups because they want to be identified and interact as members of the group (e.g., a fraternity or community chorus). Simply doing so will not result in group interaction opportunities unless the individuals are motivated to talk to others.

Remember that, just because individuals have some reason to be together or some surface connection seems to exist among them, group interaction may not occur. Simply being identified with others who share similar characteristics doesn't create a group. Group members can only develop identity with one another, and distinguish their membership in this group from memberships in other groups, when they communicate with one another in the beginning of the group and throughout the group's history (Zanin, Hoelscher, & Kramer, 2016). When group members identify with one another and the group's goal, they adopt the norms and values of the group, increasing group members' motivations and abilities to work together effectively.

Group Goal

Identity, then, is a necessary but not sufficient characteristic for a group. We also need a fourth characteristic: group goal. A **group goal** is an agreed-upon task or activity that the group is to complete or accomplish. This goal may be long term and process oriented (such as a family functioning as a social and economic unit), or it may be short term with specific boundaries and parameters (such as a youth group holding a car wash to raise money). Regardless of the duration or type of goal, group members must agree on the group's goal to be effective (Larson & LaFasto, 1989). That does not mean that all group members have to like the goal, but it does mean that there is clarity on what the goal is and that it is perceived by members as being worthwhile.

Having a group goal gives the group direction and provides members with motivation for completing their tasks. A group's goal should be cooperative. This means that, as one member moves toward goal attainment, so do other group members. A group goal is cooperative when it integrates the self-interests of all group members. Groups that are having trouble have often lost sight of their goals—sometimes because of distractions and other times because of external forces (a change in deadline or objectives). Groups that cannot identify why they exist and what they are trying to achieve are doomed to failure.

For example, as a student in the class for which you are reading this textbook, your goal is probably to get a good grade. But getting a good grade is your individual goal, not a group goal. Each student in the class may have this same goal, but it is not a shared, consensual goal that motivates interaction and activity. If it were, everything you did in preparation for class would be designed to help you, as well as other students, achieve the *group good grade* goal. Thus, agreement on a common goal among individuals, not similarity in individual goals, defines individuals as members of the same group. Group goals create cooperation, whereas individual goals often create competition (Van Mierlo & Kleingeld, 2010).

Group Structure

The final defining characteristic of a group is its structure, or how the team members are organized along with the tasks and resources needed to accomplish the group goal (Lafond, Jobidon, Aube, & Tremblay, 2011). Whether informal (a group of friends) or formal (a parent-teacher organization), some type of structure must develop. **Group structure** tends to develop along with, or to emerge from, group rules and **norms**—patterns of behavior that others come to expect and rely on. For example, a group of friends—Pat, Emily, Donna, and Greg—meet for social activities every Friday night. If the group does not set plans for the next week, Pat takes it upon himself to text everyone to get suggestions. No one has appointed him to this role; he does it naturally in reaction to the other group members' lack of initiative. Pat has assumed the role of the group's social organizer, and the group has come to depend on him to play that role. His role playing has created a certain structure in the group, and that structure has become a norm. Group members expect him to take the lead concerning their weekly activities.

In more formal settings, a group may elect someone to record what happens in the meetings as a way of tracking the group's progress and keeping an account of details. Again, the person taking on the recorder or secretary role is providing structure for the group, as well as behaving in a normative pattern. Thus, both the recorder's actions and the record of the meeting provide structure for the group. Anytime a group member takes on a formal or informal role, group structure is created. Likewise, any discussion or outcome that provides direction for the group is considered group structure. Suppose your family decides to visit Disneyland on vacation. That decision creates structure for your family discussions in the future because now your interactions will center around the logistics of traveling to California and planning your vacation.

To be viable, groups must have some form of structure, but the structure does not have to remain constant throughout the life of the group. Much of a group's structure is provided by **group roles**, or the functions group members assume through their interactions. Roles are not necessarily fixed. Formal roles—those filled through appointment, assignment, or election—are likely to be more permanent. Informal roles—functions that emerge spontaneously from the group's interaction (such as the group member who eases tension in the group)—may change as the talents of group members become apparent or are needed by others.

Integrating the Pieces of the Puzzle

The five characteristics that define groups—group size, interdependence, group identity, group goal, and group structure—can provide a foundation for analyzing the effectiveness of a group (see Figure 2.1). The following example will lead you through this analysis.

Like most students assigned a group project, Gayle, Rebecca, Sean, Jim, and Sonya wait too long to begin work on their assignment. Now, pressed for time, each member has other obligations and, quite frankly, more pressing interests and motivations. Still, the group has to produce what the professor expects in order to receive 20 percent of

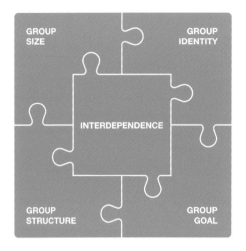

Figure 2.1

their course grade. Meeting once to get organized, Rebecca, Sean, Jim, and Sonya each assume responsibility for one area of the project, and Gayle agrees to take responsibility for integrating these parts. The group gives itself two weeks before reconvening to turn in finished materials to Gayle, who will pull it all together before the oral presentation to the class. Due to the members' late start, there will be only a few days between the group's second meeting and the oral presentation, putting extreme pressure on Gayle to integrate the project's parts and get it back to the other members so they can perform effectively during the presentation. These members are juniors and seniors, and they have done this type of group project many times in the past. They know they can pull it off.

This group is probably similar to other groups you've been in. Given their deadline, the decisions they have made about dividing up the workload may make sense. However, there may be some problems with these decisions as well. Consider the following questions:

Group Size

1 If Gayle asks her roommate for help, is her roommate part of the group? Why or why not?

2 If Sonya becomes sick and cannot perform her part of the project, is she still part of the group?

3 Would it help if the group had more members?

Interdependence

1 Does it make sense for one individual to integrate everyone's work?

2 What are the disadvantages of breaking up work in this manner? What if Sean's part of the project conflicts with the other members' parts?

3 Is this a superordinate goal? Why or why not?

Group Identity

1 Does this group have an identity? How would they know?

2 As the leader of the group, what can Jim do to enhance group identity?

3 Do the members even need a group identity, given their time constraints?

Group Goal

1 The goal was given to the group by someone external to the group. How will this affect group members' perceptions of the goal?

2 What are the boundaries of this goal? Does it align with individual goals?

Group Structure

1 Are these the only work roles the group needs to consider?

2 Is the group structure developed ideal for the project?

3 Does this project require a more formal structure to be successful?

Using the five defining characteristics of a group can help you understand what factors may be inhibiting your group. If you were in charge of this group, which of the five characteristics would be important for you to work on? Knowing, for example, that identity is weak in your group, you might want to suggest that group members spend some time getting to know one another before beginning work on the task. Or if the group goal is not clear and agreed upon by everyone, it will be helpful to spend a few minutes talking specifically about what the group is trying to accomplish. When one or several of the defining characteristics are weak or missing, the sense of groupness may be too fragile for the individuals to function effectively as a group.

To summarize: We have defined a group as three or more people who work together interdependently on an agreed-upon activity or goal. They identify themselves as members of the group, and they develop structure and roles, based on norms and rules, as they interact and work toward their goal.

Due to the defining characteristics of groups, each group takes on a life of its own. Each is unique. What we as individuals bring to group interactions is a unique compilation of all our past group experiences, good and bad. Your set of expectations resembles no one else's set of expectations, and members of the group bring different expectations to the same group experience. As a result, we live in a world of constant ebb and flow of group interactions in our personal, social, and professional lives that overlap and affect one another. It is to our benefit to understand these interactions and influence them. Not only are groups charged with completing tasks and activities, they also provide us with opportunities to develop and maintain relationships, to learn about ourselves, and to enhance our personal and professional skills. And all of this is accomplished through communication.

INTERDEPENDENCE OF TASK AND RELATIONAL DIMENSIONS

At this point, it should be obvious that a group is really a process. A group is not simply its number of members, its effectiveness, or its type of task or activity. A group is created through interaction among group members as they establish roles and relationships while they work toward their mutual goal or activity—and that process is both complex and messy. For example, group members need to meet together in order to construct role relationships and generate group identity, but most groups seldom have all members meeting together for all interactions. Likewise, in any group or team, there are likely to be multiple goals at multiple levels—group, subgroup, and individual. Finally, all group interactions are not likely to be friendly or produce positive outcomes.

Despite our best efforts, groups are not always effective, fun, or productive. When a difficulty occurs, it is often a signal that a core group characteristic—group size, interdependence of members, group identity, group goal, or group structure—is deficient, at risk, missing, or out of balance for that group's task or activity. That is, the group's size is too large or too small, group identity is too weak or too strong, interdependence of members is too loose or too strong, agreement and enactment of the group goal is under- or overemphasized, or the group structure is too rigid or too loose. Moreover, groups are not objects in containers. A group's relationship to its context is fluid and complex, which can create challenges for group members to address and resolve.

Part of the challenge is to balance the **task dimension**, or what a group does, with its **relational dimension**, or the social and emotional interactions of group members from which roles and relationships emerge. All groups have both task and relational dimensions. Groups with a strong task focus must also pay attention to the relationships that develop among group members, and even groups that are primarily social or relational have some task to perform. In these types of groups, the task may be as simple as members being there for one another, or it may be more specific, such as providing a place for members to explore their feelings. Regardless of a group's primary focus, both task and social dimensions are present, and they are inseparably interdependent (Fisher, 1971).

 THEORY STANDOUT

Task and Relational Messages

Early in the study of groups and teams, Bales (1950) identified both task and relational dimensions as the two central dimensions of group process. Watzlawick, Beavin, and Jackson (1967) went one step further and posited that all messages have both relational and task content. How can one message have both task and relational content? Think about a recent group interaction you have had. Did you use a short phrase or one word, such as "okay," to indicate your agreement? Did your "okay" mean that you agreed with your team members? Did the nonverbals that accompanied your "okay" indicate how you felt about your agreement?

Messages are complex. They can have more than one level of meaning. Most of the time, our verbal and nonverbal messages are in agreement. But sometimes, we use a verbal message to indicate agreement, and at the same time use a nonverbal message to indicate that we're not happy about having to agree. Moreover, how a message is evaluated by other group members depends on what messages occurred before and after the focal message.

Theoretical contributions by Bales and Watzlawick, Beavin, and Jackson encourage us to carefully consider what messages are and what messages do. Both task and relational messages are central to the study of group communication.

This two-dimensional aspect of groups is important because a group that concentrates solely on work without attending to its members' social or relational needs becomes boring and ineffective. Likewise, a group that focuses solely on having a good time can become tiresome if that social interaction does not lead to new information or provide opportunities to perform meaningful activities. The most effective groups are those that keep each of these dimensions in balance relative to their purposes and the needs of their members (Tse & Dasborough, 2008).

The task and relational dimensions are interdependent—that is, they work together. But this does not mean that group members use task and relational messages equally. Rather, all groups use more task messages—even groups with primarily relational or social goals. Why is that? Simply, talk does something; it is a **performative act** (Grice, 1999). For any group to achieve its goal, group members must exchange task messages which are interspersed with relational messages. For relational messages, we can analyze the frequency of positive relational messages to negative relational messages to understand the emotional tone or social climate of the group. For example, in community theatre groups, members of the casts and crews rated their relational communication with their peers as more important than task-oriented communication from the theater-group leaders (Kramer, 2005). However, a theater production would not have occurred if task messages were not also exchanged among group members.

Satisfying Task and Relational Dimensions of Groups

The balancing of task and relational group needs may depend on the nature of the group. A group's level of formality may determine the necessary frequency of task and relational messages. Some groups form deliberately; others emerge from spontaneous interaction. When groups form deliberately (e.g., work groups, neighborhood council), someone decides that a collection of individuals should accomplish a purpose or goal. Most problem-solving or decision-making groups (such as city councils) and social action groups (for instance, Stop Hunger Now) are examples of deliberately formed groups—it would be impossible for fewer people to accomplish their goals. These groups tend to have many task-oriented messages.

Other groups form spontaneously. Generally, individuals come together in these groups because of the satisfaction they expect to gain from associating with one another. A group of friends at work is a good example of a spontaneous group. In these cases, group membership is by mutual consent—each member wants to be in the group, and each is accepted as a group member. Typically, these groups form when individuals communicate frequently and voluntarily with one another. Thus, group membership is based on attraction.

However, all groups must balance task and relational dimensions. For example, a group of activists (such as a local affiliate of Habitat for Humanity) needs members with the technical skills of recruiting new volunteers and seeking and obtaining funding, as well as members who are willing to teach others the skills needed for building houses. Members also need the relational skills of motivating members to continue to work on behalf of the organization and the ability to create a supportive environment for members. The challenge is to find the appropriate balance between the two sets of skills. The balance will vary depending on the type of group and its activities and goals.

A group deliberately formed for a short period of intense work on a complex project may prefer members with a balance favoring technical skills over relational skills. For example, the technical skills of a team of doctors, nurses, and medical technicians delivering quintuplets are more important to the success of the group's task than team members' interpersonal relations. The team works together for a very short time and then disbands. Roles and responsibilities within the team are highly defined, which helps the team work effectively in the absence of well-developed personal relationships.

In contrast, a team that expects to stay together for a long period may initially favor a balance toward personal and relational skills. This is because, over time, group members can help one another increase their technical proficiency if the relationships among group members are well developed. Let's say that a project team with members representing different operations of a food manufacturer is assigned to develop prototypes for new market initiatives. With representatives from manufacturing, marketing, quality control, and food sourcing, the new product development team has six months to develop at least four products for consumer testing. Since the project is long-term and complex, it will be important for workers to work well together. If members possess the ability to work well with one another, they can also rely on one another to help fill in the technical expertise they may lack as individuals.

For instance, Jerry, the representative from manufacturing, knows very little about marketing. Initially, he relies heavily on Shanna's marketing expertise. Jerry asks Shanna lots of questions, requests marketing reports to read, and talks with her over lunch about marketing initiatives that have worked for other products. As the team works on product development, Jerry learns enough about marketing from Shanna to give informed opinions and ask appropriate questions. This process is enhanced because Jerry finds it easy to approach Shanna, and Shanna appreciates Jerry's willingness to learn about marketing.

Most spontaneously formed groups favor relational over task skills. Because group membership is based primarily on individuals' personal attraction to one another, relational skills are more important. If group members cannot get along and form a cohesive group, attraction will decrease, and members will leave the group voluntarily. This does not mean that task skills are not important—merely that relational skills are more essential in these groups.

For example, Rea's running group started over lunch when the four women discovered their common hesitance to try running. The decision first to hire a coach for the group and then to run three times a week was a natural outgrowth of the women liking one another; forming the group was not based on anyone's technical skill in running. As the group continues to work with its coach, members become confident enough to give one another friendly advice about selecting running shoes, stride length, and breathing techniques. However, if one member consistently gives poor advice or advice that detracts from another's running performance or enjoyment of running, this member's technical skill or motivation will come into question and may even disturb the relational balance of the group.

Simply put, group members will find it necessary to talk to one another to accomplish their task or activity. However, groups cannot accomplish their objectives only through task-related communication. Even if members try to constrain their messages to task issues, they are delivering implicit messages about relational issues in the group. All messages have both task and relational ramifications for group members, even if a specific message is predominantly task or relational in nature. A group is a social context, and social influence will occur whenever members are communicating. In whichever way the task and relational dimensions are balanced, the messages sent create the climate within which group members accomplish their tasks and activities (Keyton, 1999).

 ## SKILL BUILDER

Interdependence is a defining characteristic of a group. But where does interdependence come from? Often interdependence is built into the task of the group. Sometimes being interdependent means performing similar activities, and other times quite different activities. For example, a softball team requires many different sets of skill expertise. Each member takes a turn at bat, a skill all players need. But when the team is playing defensively in the field, members play a unique position that works together with other positions.

Relational interdependence is created directly through your interaction with other group members. Providing nonverbal support (e.g., smiling; head nods; direct eye contact) and giving verbal support (e.g., "good play" or "nice hit") can help you develop or deepen relationships with other group members. Think of two different groups you belong to. What nonverbal and verbal communication behaviors could you use to build or increase relational interdependence with members of each group?

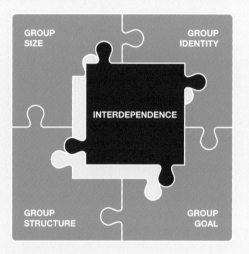

GROUPS OR TEAMS?

You have probably noticed that we do not distinguish groups from teams. That is purposeful. There is no rule for when *team* is more appropriate than *group*. These labels are often interchangeable, and there are other nouns that can be used as labels. For example, you are part of a family and a group of friends. You might belong to a book club, a soccer team, a rowing crew, or be a member of massively multimember online game (MMOG). You interact with others as a group if you are a member of a theatre troupe, a bowling team, or a cheer squad. Professionally, you may be a member of a sales team or work

crew. In professional, civic, and community settings, you may be a member of leadership council, or a ticket committee or subcommittee.

It does not matter what label is used. It does not matter if you communicate face-to-face or online. What does matter is the degree of interdependence among group members who create a group identity and group structure to support their group goal or activity. The size of a group matters to the degree that it enhances or impedes interaction among group members in accomplishing their goal.

SUMMARY

A group is defined as three or more individuals who identify themselves as a group and who can identify with the activity of the group. Five characteristics define groups: group size, interdependence of members, group identity, group goal, and group structure. Using these defining characteristics as avenues of analysis can help us understand the unique-ness of each group and the complexity of group interaction.

Clearly, it's more accurate to talk about a group as a process rather than defining a group by its number of members, its effectiveness, or its type of task or activity. The group interaction process is both complex and messy. Part of the challenge is to balance a group's task dimension, or what a group does, with its relational dimension, or the social and emotional interactions of group members from which roles and relationships emerge. All groups have both task and relational dimensions that should be balanced, based on the group's purpose and the needs of its members. Groups cannot accomplish their objectives only through task-related communication. A group is a social context, and social influence and messages about relational issues will occur whenever members are communicating.

DISCUSSION QUESTIONS AND EXERCISES

1 Think of a group you belong to in which members only communicate through technology. Now identify the group you belong to that is most diverse in its membership. Analyze these groups according to the five characteristics for defining groups.

2 Reflect on one of your childhood groups. Compare that experience with a current group of friends. What has changed? What is similar? What do you believe accounts for the differences and similarities?

3 Think of some past classroom group projects. What group characteristics made them effective? What group characteristics made them unbearable?

4 When groups are large, some members may think that their individual contributions will not be noticed and, as a result, decrease their level of activity in the group. When circumstances dictate that a group has many members, what strategies can group members use to control social loafing?

5 Think back to a group to which you belonged that was primarily task oriented. Compare that group with a group that is primarily relationally oriented. What are the similarities and differences in your assessments? Which group characteristics explain this?

 ## NAILING IT!

Using Group Communication Skills for Group Presentations

This chapter focuses on the five defining features of a group. Let's examine how these features can be used as your group develops its presentation. Your manager wants your team to give her a presentation about new ways to motivate customers to spend more in the store. The presentation is the group goal, or group task. Including you, there are five group members and you have worked together on the weekends for more than a year. You are accustomed to working together, and those working relationships are more positive than negative, so you have developed a moderate level of group identity. You know which team members you can rely on to help you close a sale, and which members are better at explaining the technical aspects of what you sell. This structure, and the interdependencies it creates, may work for selling. But will this same structure be the most beneficial for creating and delivering the presentation?

Let's start with the group goal and work backwards. You and your work group members agree that a good presentation has several components: developing the ideas to present, designing the presentation, and delivering the presentation. The group meets to brainstorm strategies for increasing sales, and everyone participates. Now those ideas need to be developed into a presentation. Two members have expertise in computer graphics, and one member is a skillful writer. These three group members work together to make a draft presentation for the group to approve. Along the way, the remaining two group members look at drafts and provide feedback. Now the presentation is completed and it's time to deliver it. One member wants the two members who did not directly participate in the design of the presentation to deliver it. Will it be effective for these two to share the presentation task? Or is it better to have the group member with the most effective presentation skills deliver the presentation to your manager? What if the most effective presenter is also one of the members who worked on the design?

As you can see, while group size remained constant throughout the process, group identity, group structure, and interdependence changed as group members worked on different aspects of this task. Groups that are flexible, yet involve all members in the group task, are likely to be the most effective.

Image Credits

CHAPTER 3

CONTEXTUAL INFLUENCES ON GROUPS

After reading this chapter, you should be able to:

- Use examples to describe how the bona fide group perspective illuminates the contextual aspects of groups and teams

- Distinguish between the contextual influences of time and space on group communication

- Describe different types of diversity found in groups and teams

- Explain ways in which individuals can overcome the challenges of diversity in group communication

- Explain the positive and potentially negative influences of technology on group and team interactions

BONA FIDE GROUP PERSPECTIVE

The five characteristics introduced in Chapter 2 (group size, interdependence of members, group identity, group goal, and group structure) are essential to defining a group. But these characteristics all occur within the group's context. The **bona fide group perspective** (Putnam & Stohl, 1990, 1996) illuminates the relationship of the group to its context or environment. The term *bona fide* was used to identify this perspective because many groups and teams studied by early scholars were ad hoc groups, or one-time groups. Group members had no history and no relationships with other members of the group.

Unfortunately, this is not a realistic view of groups or group dynamics. Rather, group members are influenced by their existing and previous group experiences, other members in these groups, the role and the importance of the group in members' lives, the way in which groups are set up by organizations or institutions, and what members expect from their group experiences. Thus, the bona fide group perspective focuses our attention on the way in which (a) groups have permeable and fluid boundaries and (b) the interdependencies between the group and its context (Putnam & Stohl, 1996; Stohl & Putnam, 2003), as well as the messages group members use in constructing and negotiating those boundaries and contexts in which a group works (SunWolf, 2008).

Permeable and Fluid Boundaries

The bona fide group perspective recognizes that group boundaries are generally stable but also permeable. In reality, a group's membership is seldom fixed. Additions are made to family groups through marriage, divorce, adoption, and death. Changes in organizational teams occur when employees leave the organization and new ones are hired. Even though we expect jury membership to remain stable, alternates are frequently required to step in when other jurors must be excused. Thus, while we often think of group membership as being static, it can be dynamic when group members are replaced, exchanged, added, or removed.

Thinking of group membership and its resulting boundaries in this way, it is easy to understand that groups are socially constructed through communication (Frey & SunWolf, 2005). Let's look at two examples. First, juries are the size they are because legal authorities debated the issues and made recommendations that became state and federal law. However, being named to a jury is not the defining feature. Rather, it is the interactions among jury members that move them from being *a* jury to being *this* jury. In essence, the jury as a group emerges through the interactions of members, not simply because they were assigned to the jury. When these jury members reflect upon and describe their experiences to others, they will point to specific interactions and specific relationships among jury members that caused them to agree that that defendant was guilty (or not).

In a second example, family members may agree that Sandra is a member of the family even though she is not related to any member. Rather, she was your mother's best friend who now lives on her own. Your family includes her as a member, inviting her to all family functions because they appreciate Sandra's thoughtfulness and helpfulness during your mother's illness. To signify her relationship to your family, you've taken to calling her Aunt Sandra. Communication between your family members and Sandra established a connection that encouraged your family to identify Sandra as a part of it and encouraged Sandra to think of herself as a member of your family.

Thus, group membership is perceived to be stable when you can identify who is in, and who is not a member of, the group. These identifications are made based upon who is communicating with whom and to what degree that interaction results in individuals identifying with a particular group. That is, individuals negotiate their identity with a group as their interactions construct the group. Of course, membership can change or be altered, permanently or temporarily.

PUTTING THE PIECES TOGETHER

Select two groups you belong to now or belonged to in the past. One group should have a relationally focused goal; the other group should have a task-oriented goal. For each group, answer these questions: How would you describe the task messages group members exchanged? How would you describe the relational messages group members exchanged? Which type of messages were more important? Why? Finally, how did the task and relational messages of group members help or hinder the group in developing its identity?

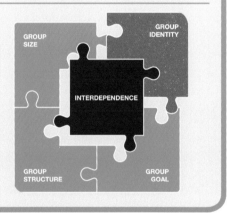

A Group's Interdependence With Its Context

Despite identifying with a particular group, members also participate in other groups. As a result, groups can interact with and influence one another. For example, if you are a member of several groups at work, you're likely to pass information from one group to another. Information gained in one group is taken—sometimes intentionally, sometimes unintentionally—to another group.

From the bona fide group perspective, a group is not a distinct entity with an environment that separates it from all other groups. Rather, groups are located within a fluid social context. The group is continually influenced by the environment in which it completes its tasks and by the social ties members have with other groups. The concepts of connectivity and embeddedness further explain how a group interacts with its larger social environment.

Connectivity is the degree to which several groups share overlapping tasks or goals. The more tightly coupled the groups, the more likely that change in one group will alter activities in others. For example, organizations are composed of many groups. A policy change developed and recommended by the human resources team is likely to affect the leadership teams of each division. A financial team may determine how much money the marketing team can use in their upcoming campaign. Although the teams have unique and specific goals, all teams function to meet the ultimate goal of producing the organization's products. When change occurs in one team, it is likely to affect other teams to which it is most tightly connected.

Connectivity increases in complexity when individuals participate in multiple groups. For instance, as a student taking several classes, it is likely that during any one term you are a member of several classroom groups. Although each group has unique membership and a goal specific to its particular course, you can use the information learned in one group in another. This information transfer is possible due to group members' multiple group memberships. Although information transfer is often viewed as a positive characteristic, it can be a negative when information learned in one group is used to the detriment of another. For example, Bryce is not thrilled to find himself in another group with Katerina.

In their statistics group, Katerina comes unprepared and seldom contributes anything meaningful. When Bryce learns that both he and Katerina have been assigned to the same group in their persuasive campaigns class, he immediately tells other group members about Katerina's substandard performance. Clearly this would influence how these members approach Katerina in their first team meeting

Another factor that contributes to complexity is **embeddedness**, which reflects the centrality of the group to its larger organizational structure. A group's position within the informal power structure or formal hierarchical structure affects its ability to obtain information and retain resources. Its position with respect to its environment also determines its degree of impact on the larger organization. For example, the student government group of your university is more deeply embedded within your university than any other student club or organization. Members of the student government have direct access to university officials; in fact, university officials may look to your student government as a primary source of student feedback and input. In contrast, a club such as Lambda Pi Eta (the communication students' honors organization) is affiliated with both the university and its national organization. To both the university and the national organization, the club is merely one student organization that competes with other organizations for attention and resources. Thus, its level of embeddedness in either the university or the national organization is shallower. In the university system, the student government group deals with issues more relevant to the university than the local Lambda Pi Eta chapter. In the Lambda Pi Eta system, one chapter is not likely to have more influence than any other local chapter.

When a group is characterized by high connectivity and high embeddedness, its boundaries are fluid. Information flows easily into and out of the group, making connections with other groups possible. Actually, it is the placement of a group within its environmental context that contributes to challenges, conflicts, and stresses group members are likely to face (Lammers & Krikorian, 1997). The more connected and the more embedded the group, the more pressures and influences it faces. When a group becomes highly embedded and connected, it may be difficult to clearly identify the group's membership.

For example, let's look at a biology study group. Five classmates meet every Thursday night to prepare for a biology test. But their interactions with one another are not limited to the Thursday night meetings. After biology class on Tuesday, the group meets quickly so Brandon can introduce a problem that involves the use of a specific lab instrument. No one in the group is sure how to use the instrument. But another student, Tom, overhears the conversation and offers to help. Because Tom is the instructor's lab assistant, members of the group consider Tom a reliable source of information. As the conversation about the lab instrument continues, Emily invites Tom to join this Thursday night's study group. Getting nonverbal agreement from the group, Tom says he will be there. Depending on how well the group interacts with Tom, he may become a regular member, and not simply a visitor. Suppose group members come to like Tom and value his contributions to the group, but Alex struggles in deciding whether to meet with the group or to play in a fraternity basketball league. Even though Alex was an original member of the group, his attendance depends on when basketball games are scheduled.

To clarify the concepts of flux and ambiguous boundaries, let's continue with the example. By the end of the semester, only two of the initial group members are left in the biology study group. Tom comes regularly now. Alex seldom studies with the group, but admits he could use an extra night of study before the final. He joins the group for this last session. To his amazement, almost half of the class is there, sitting in small subgroups going over different parts of the test material. Who is in this group? Who is not? What boundary separates this group from its environment?

INFLUENCE OF TIME AND SPACE

A part of a group's relationship to its context is the time and space of its interactions. The space a group works in, whether it is the physical space of a meeting room or the cognitive space provided by technology, influences how team members interact. Likewise, the time of day team members meet and how they use their time together also influences how members interact. Let's turn our attention first to time.

Time

Groups can have considerable histories or be of limited duration. While it is easy to think of groups that have short histories (e.g., jury, emergency task force) and long histories, (e.g., a book club that has been meeting for many years; a standing committee in a religious organization), not all group histories are this simplistic. For example, elections for city commissioners in some towns are held every two years, with three of the five commission seats up for reelection. If we measured the history of the city commission as a group, its duration would be two years. However, sometimes commissioners who receive the most votes are elected for four-year terms, while the commissioner receiving the least votes is elected for only two years. Thus, some commissioners can have considerably more experience in the group than others. This effect becomes particularly pronounced when a commissioner wins reelection many times. As another example, think of the board of directors of your local United Way. This group has considerable influence in your community, making decisions about how money is raised and how nonprofit organizations are funded. Yet any individual board member serves only a three-year term.

Another influence of time on groups is the frequency and duration of its tasks and activities (Lammers & Krikorian, 1997). One breast cancer support group, whose members are over 65 years old, has met every Monday night for one hour since 1989, while another group for younger women with breast cancer was established in 1999 and meets only once a month, but for two hours each meeting. The older women in the first group rely upon the companionship and social support of the group's members, as many are widowed. Their weekly meetings are highly social, with conversation turning to talk about vacations and grandchildren, not just methods of coping with their illness. The younger women, many of whom have children, meet less regularly but for a longer time so they can invite guest speakers to keep informed of the latest advances in breast cancer treatment and minimize the need for babysitters. Thus, frequency, or how often a group meets, and duration, how long a group meets, depends on the context of the group, the needs of members, and the task or activity the group undertakes. In turn, the length of time group members interact and the time between those interactions will influence group member relationships. Other dimensions of time influence how communication is structured in groups and teams (Ballard & Seibold, 2000, 2004). These include flexibility, linearity, pace, punctuality, delay, separation, urgency, and scarcity. **Flexibility**, or how rigidly time is structured, is apparent in how group members set deadlines. Flexibility is also seen when group members avoid setting a firm meeting schedule when they first meet. In some groups, the task they are working on will not allow a great deal of flexibility. A group's degree of flexibility can be discovered by asking these types of questions: Do group members set a rigid structure of deadlines? Or do group members allow each other to get the work done on their own time schedules? **Separation**, another dimension of time important to groups and teams, is the degree to which group members isolate their meetings from other interactions. To assess this dimension, we can ask these types of questions: How do groups and their members compartmentalize, or section off, their tasks? Do group members remove themselves from distractions by being in their own space? Or do group members welcome changes to their tasks? **Concurrency**, a third dimension of time, is based on how many tasks group members engage in. Do group members try to tackle several tasks at once? Or do group members take one task at a time and finish each task before starting another?

Time is not often talked about with respect to how groups work and group members interact. But communicating in groups does take time. Moreover, groups can develop a variety of ways of handling and expressing time as they work toward their goals. The three temporal dimensions described are just a few of the dimensions that provide context for group interaction. Groups and their members also vary by the following temporal dimensions:

- **Linearity**: Do groups create unique or special times for some events over others? Time is not only used to sequence events, it is also used to separate events. Teams expressing linearity will identify that their first meeting is to set ground rules, and the second team meeting is to focus on understanding their task.

- **Pace**: How fast are group members working? Is the tempo or rate of group activity fast or slow?

- **Punctuality and Delay**: Do group tasks have deadlines? Do group members respond promptly to each other's request for help?

- **Urgency**: Are group members preoccupied with task completion and task deadlines? Does the group treat every task as an emergency?

- **Scarcity**: How limited are the resources available to the group? Or does the group have adequate or unlimited access to resources?

- **Time Perspective**: Do group members talk about what needs to be done today, which is a present time perspective? Or do group members talk about upcoming activities and their long-term plans, which is a future time perspective?

Space

Like time, space is a contextual feature of and a contextual influence on group interaction. Some case studies drawn from research describe the different ways in which space influences group communication. In this first case, we can see how an interdisciplinary medical team at a geriatric oncology center engaged in two different types of conversation in the same work setting (Ellingson, 2003). In their formal, patient-centered conversations, team members requested information and shared impressions of patients. In this case, the presence of patients in examination rooms and the requirements of their tasks necessitated task-oriented messages. But when there was time between patients, conversations were used to build relationships among team members by talking about outside interests, such as families and vacations. Team members also bonded by complaining about their work schedules, the overbooking of patients, and the behavior of other clinic staff. Both the task-oriented and relationship-building conversations occurred in the same location—in the work space separate from the examination rooms. Although the space was the same, the presence of a patient in an examination room created a different perception of the context and, as a result, required a different type of communication among team members.

A second case describes the way in which interaction can become structured by the space in which it works. A twelve-person jury in Ohio was tasked with deciding the guilt or innocence of a defendant on two murder charges and thirty other offenses, mostly drug charges (SunWolf, 2010). After many days in the courtroom hearing testimony, the jurors were moved to a private, and very small, meeting room for their deliberations. With the other jurors seated around a long and narrow rectangular table, the jury foreperson sat at the head of the table. This seating arrangement in this small, enclosed physical space emphasized that the jurors look toward the foreperson during their deliberations. Imagine yourself in this situation. How would this physical space and close proximity to other jurors affect your interaction? Your display of physical and facial nonverbal cues? Your willingness to continue to deliberate when the others on the jury disagreed with you?

A third case of a group's use of space demonstrates how space influenced the interactions of multidisciplinary teams (Li & Robertson, 2011). If meeting rooms are outfitted with technology that is permanently placed, then presenters feel obligated to present from that fixed location even if it is not optimal to do so. When meetings are attended by many people, members who sit at the end, or at the periphery, of the meeting space may not receive eye contact from those seated more centrally in the space. As a result, the members sitting at the periphery of the space may not be called on for questions or for their opinions. When possible, space should be used so that all members have good visual access to all participants. Doing so promotes interaction among them.

Looking at groups from the bona fide group perspective, we are reminded that groups have permeable and fluid boundaries, are interdependent with their context, and are influenced by the time and space of their interactions. Most importantly, these characteristics exist because individuals construct any group and their identity in it through their interactions. If we were members of only one group at a time, then life would be simple and we could focus our attention on that group. But we are members of multiple groups, requiring that we negotiate multiple identities and manage many interaction relationships simultaneously.

As a result, multiple group memberships may create conflicting group identities for an individual. Or individuals may experience different interaction patterns or interaction roles when new members join an existing group. Moreover, the entrance and interaction of a new or temporary member can even cause group membership to change. Because individuals are members of multiple groups, an individual can serve as an implicit or explicit boundary spanner by taking information from one group to another, with the potential of creating communication exchanges between or among groups. When relationships between or among groups become established through interaction, they must coordinate or negotiate their actions and, at the same time, negotiate how they are different from one another. Thus, a member's sense of identity with a group, or sense of belonging, can shift, depending on the fluidity and permeability of the group's boundaries, the way in which the group is interdependent with its context, and the way in which group members use time and space to create a context for its interactions (Waldeck, Shepard, Teitelbaum, Farrar, & Seibold, 2002).

INFLUENCE OF DIVERSITY

Gender diversity and cultural diversity (racial, ethnic, nationality, language)—and even diversity based on profession, age, or length of membership in the group—are the primary ways in which group members distinguish themselves from one another. Individuals of any culture share common symbols, values, and norms, which result in a particular communication style with its own rules and meanings. When interaction styles are shared among group members, they perceive themselves similarly and as belonging to the same cultural group. However, when group members have different interaction styles, they are likely to attribute their differences to culture differences. Not only does this influence a group's member self-identity, it can also cause the group's identity to weaken or for subgroups to emerge (Larkey, 1996).

It is important to recognize that diversity is evident on many levels (Artiz & Walker, 2014). Obviously, team members may speak different languages or use different terminology and nonverbal symbols. Even when team members speak the same language, the cultural backgrounds of members can influence their language proficiency and language choices in both sending and receiving messages (Du-Babcock & Tanaka, 2013). Diversity can also be evident in how language is used interactively. For example, how group members initiate and respond to others, take turns, or shift to topics is influenced by the diversity of members in the group. Finally, diversity matters in how group members make decisions and assert leadership. For example, members who are from the United States display leadership by being decisive and task oriented. Alternately, group members from other cultures display leadership by being procedural or involving others in decision making. Thus, diversity matters in what is said, how something is said, and what processes develop from interaction.

The influence of diversity on groups is fairly complex for two reasons. First, while individuals from the same group (sex, gender, race, nationality) can share many interaction characteristics, there is also variation within any cultural group. Second, diversity influences individuals and the group as a whole. An individual group member's attitudes and cultural values can directly affect other members' communication behavior. In this way, each member of the group influences the perceived and real diversity in the group. There can also be a group-level influence when group members hold different cultural values. Thus, **heterogeneity**, or differences, in cultural values can influence a group's interaction processes and their performance as a group (Oetzel, McDermott, Torres, & Sanchez, 2012). We shouldn't be surprised that team members from different cultures bring different understandings of and practices for interacting in a group. That is, norms for communicating in a group vary across cultural groups. This is especially true for how group members share information and make decisions (Janssens & Brett, 2006).

 THEORY STANDOUT

More Than Cultural Differences?

Oetzel's (2005) theory of effective intercultural workgroup communication explores how self-construal, or how one defines oneself relative to others, is influential in intercultural communication. While Oetzel theorized about cultural differences as differences in geography, could the theory be applied to other types of cultural differences? Kirschbaum, Rask, Fortner, Kulesher, Nelson, Yen, and Brennan (2014) argue that cultural differences exist in groups of physicians in operating rooms. For example, when delivering a child, three physicians would be present: an anesthesiologist, a surgeon, and an obstetrician. Each physician has different tasks during the operation, and each relies on different professional norms for communicating with one another. After training that included the physicians practicing message strategies that were inclusive and responses that were inviting, physicians increased their scores on interdependent self-construal and reduced their scores on independent self-construal. As Oetzel et al. (2012) found, higher interdependence is related to a stronger positive interaction climate. And that was the case in the study of these interdisciplinary physician teams. In what other team settings can you imagine testing Oetzel's theory of effective intercultural workgroup communication?

These influences can be both positive and negative. For example, greater diversity among group members can result in changes in group membership, lower cohesiveness among members, and reduced problem-solving effectiveness by the group. Culturally diverse groups can benefit from the different perspectives group members bring, or they can allow their differences to fuel conflicts and prevent cohesion from forming (Watson, Johnson, & Merritt, 1998; Watson, Kumar, & Michaelsen, 1993). Thus, how a heterogeneous group handles its diversity is a key factor in task success.

The **theory of effective intercultural workgroup communication** (Oetzel, 2005) explains how the cultural differences among group members affect a group's task and relational communication, such as decision making and satisfaction, respectively. Let's look at the input factors of the model. First are the situational, or the contextual, features of the group. These include any unresolved conflict among members in the group or any unresolved conflict that exists historically among culturally different groups, the in-group/out-group balance among members, and members' status relative to one another. Together, these input factors can help or hinder the group in creating a common frame of reference for working together, as they represent deep-level diversity concerns. Individual differences among group members are the second input factor. These factors are self-construed, or how one defines oneself relative to others, and face concerns, which are an individual's beliefs about their image, reputation, and integrity. The third input factor is the composition of the group, or the group's diversity. These are issues of surface-level diversity, which are in contrast to deep-level diversity, which is based on broad differences among cultures and nationalities.

This theory reminds us of two valuable points. First, while there may be cultural differences, there are also differences within cultures. Second, culturally diverse groups can be more effective when encouraging equal participation, practicing consensus decision making, addressing conflict as cooperative rather than competitive, and engaging in respectful communication. These communication behaviors are the interaction climate, or the general tone, of the group that ultimately affects how well the group works together.

Although it is clear that cultural differences can influence group interaction, it is not apparent why this occurs (Oetzel, 2002). One explanation is that diverse groups can result in status differences related to ethnicity, nationality, sex, tenure, knowledge, and organizational position. Status anchored on these characteristics can affect member participation and result in negative group interactions because observable differences are used to assign group members to hierarchical positions within the group. As a result, group members are more likely to use biases, prejudices, or stereotypes in communicating with one another (Milliken & Martins, 1996). In this case, status is assigned to individuals simply because they possess or represent certain attributes.

Another explanation is that diverse groups must manage cultural differences, or the patterns of values, attitudes, and communication behaviors associated with specific groups of individuals. This explanation focuses on how differences are created through a group's interactions. These can influence relational communication, as well as member participation and turn taking, which ultimately can influence how well group members work together on their task.

Remember, though, that diversity issues go far beyond gender, race, ethnicity, and culture to include social and professional attributes and other demographic categories. In groups, we must be careful not to assume that diversity is based on a single dimension that seems to be the most obvious (Poncini, 2002). Not all of these types of diversity are equal, yet it is difficult to completely isolate one element of diversity from another. Thus, cultural diversity is really a combination of differences rather than a difference on any one dimension.

The type of group or group activity in which you are engaged creates a unique context in which diversity issues become salient. For example, your work group may be more sensitive to diversity in educational-level and political differences than to diversity in race and gender, especially if all group members are from the same department and have similar lengths of service with the organization. In this case, the differences that might exist due to race and gender are not as influential in the group because the group members know one another well and work on tasks regularly and effectively. In contrast, the cultural distance that can be created by race and gender differences may be maximized when members also represent different departments and are new to the group and its task. Group members in this situation have not had the chance to explore their differences and similarities or to develop as a group.

However, as group members gain more experience interacting with diverse others, group member participation is more equal, cooperation among group members is higher, and group members are more satisfied, which leads to fewer intercultural conflicts and prejudice (Larkey, 1996; Oetzel, Burtis, Sanchez, & Perez, 2001). As a result, task performance is enhanced when group members move from obvious surface-level or easily detectable differences to discussing different ideas or concerns relative to the task (Harrison, Price, & Bell, 1998). Moreover, there is evidence that groups with high levels of diversity have stronger beliefs about their abilities to complete the task. That is, when there are group members from many different racial and ethnic backgrounds, the group tends to avoid falling into majority/minority subgroups. As a result, communication is more effective, which facilitates group members' work on the task (Sargent & Sue-Chan, 2001).

INFLUENCE OF TECHNOLOGY

The increasing availability and variety of technology has resulted in more types of groups using technology as their primary method of communicating to accomplish tasks and other group activities. Some technologies can be used synchronously. For example, videoconferencing requires that group members coordinate their interaction as they meet in real time, although they do not need to be in one location. Alternately, other technologies are asynchronous. For example, email is asynchronous, as there are time intervals between messages among group members. Still other technologies can be used in both ways. For example, text messaging can be synchronous if all group members are attending to the interaction, or it can be asynchronous if group members only message one another infrequently on an as-needed basis. Technologies are appealing because they allow group members to work across distances—in both time and space. Today, some group members, like those in project teams at work who regularly complete complex projects, have never met in person. Interestingly, whether group members are situated around the corner or across an ocean, geographical distance among group members is not the prevailing reason for using technology. Rather, people use technologies, especially SMS (or text messaging), to enhance feelings of connectedness (Reid & Reid, 2010). As a result of these connections, people can create better working relationships, which lead to additional opportunities to become a group.

The use of technology does influence communication among group members. Technology mediates the group's interaction (Poole & Zhang, 2005). Simply, communicating through technology is not the same as communicating face-to-face. Why? Because technology leaves out or modifies social cues that we depend upon in face-to-face group interaction. Let's explore several issues group members should be aware of when communicating through technology. First, technology can eliminate or skew contextual information important to understanding messages. Second, technology can also impede the salience of information exchanged among group members. Third, groups that use technology for their interaction often do not share the cultural, social, team, or organizational norms that are more easily developed in face-to-face settings.

Technologies support a wide variety of group activities, including discussion, planning, generating ideas, and making choices, as well as collaborative document creation and

SKILL BUILDER

How Are You Using Technology in Groups?

Research (Lira, Ripoll, Peiro, & Zornoza, 2008) has demonstrated that when a group or team meets using technology rather than meeting face-to-face, group members become more effective at using the technology and develop new strategies for accomplishing tasks. Reflecting on your online group experiences, first identify which technologies you believe you use effectively; then, describe what new technique or strategies you've discovered for helping the group accomplish its task online. How would you teach others about using one of those techniques or strategies the next time you are a member of an online work group?

editing. Moreover, the use of asynchronous technology has spread from family and social groups to work and task groups.

Let's look at the use of SMS, or text messaging, in college classroom groups (Lam, 2012). Students were randomly assigned to a SMS-only or no-SMS group. The no-SMS group could use any technology except text messaging on their cell phones; overwhelmingly they chose email for 98% of their communication with one another. Here's what happened over the eight weeks in which students had to complete their group assignment: Members of the SMS-only group, who were to only use text messaging on their cell, communicated 40% more than students in the no-SMS group, especially in the first few weeks of working together. In the first four weeks of their interaction, the SMS-only group reported higher feelings of connectedness than members of the no-SMS group. However, as the groups continued to develop across time, that difference went away. With respect to how attracted students felt to their group, there was no difference after four weeks or after eight weeks. So, members of the SMS-only group communicated more, but this greater level of communication did not result in higher levels of feeling connected to other group members or more attraction to the group than it did with members of the no-SMS group. Another interesting difference is that members of the SMS-only group asked more questions and provided more answers; however, they also sent more off-topic messages to one another than the no-SMS group. The length limitations many people follow when they are texting likely created the increase in communication quantity, as well as the increase in the conversational question and answer sequences.

Could we consider groups like the student group above a virtual team? Yes. Members of the student groups were dispersed in time and space (Timmerman & Scott, 2006). Of course, group members are not limited to SMS or email technologies. Organizations routinely provide employees with teleconferencing, videoconferencing, and web conferencing systems, internal social networking tools, and project management systems in which team members can share documents and manage schedules to help team members communicate and collaborate. Each technology provides greater flexibility for team members in how they communicate. Each technology also creates a permanent, and often searchable, record of what group members communicated to one another. Some

MESSAGE AND MEANING

A few years ago, Nancy, Genevieve, Frankie, Kyle, and John worked as a group to develop a recycling center for five small rural communities. Each community wasn't large enough to warrant its own center. This five-person team developed the concept, presented it to each community, and received approval from each county to initiate the recycling center. In its 10th year, the center operates at a profit and keeps recyclable trash out of refuse stream. However, none of the team members are currently involved in the day-to-day operations.

A state environmental agency contacted Nancy asking her to check with the other team members to see if the team would present a panel discussion at a state recycling conference. The conference organizer wanted the team to explain how their idea came about, how the center was started, and what lessons could they pass along to other communities. Nancy sent this initial email:

> From: Nancy
> To: Genevieve, Frankie, and John
>
> Hi. The state environmental agency wants to know if we would put together a panel discussion for the state conference—some sort of retrospective. What do you think? I don't know if I have the bandwidth to take the lead on this, but I do think it could be of interest to the participants.
>
> Also, I don't have contact info for Kyle. Do any of you?

A few hours later, in a separate email, John lets Nancy know that he has Kyle's email and will see if it works, and then get back to her.

Another few hours later:

> From: Nancy
> To: Genevieve, Frankie, Kyle, and John
>
> Now we have Kyle in the loop (Hi Kyle!)! It's great to have us all together again! I have very fond memories of our time together. It seems like we all are interested in putting together a panel session for WeRecycle! on the history of the recycling center. I personally would love to participate, but with my new job, I'd prefer not to take the lead on this. Would any of you like to drive it?

An hour later:

> From: John
> To: Genevieve, Frankie, Kyle, and Nancy

Why not ask one the current volunteers to organize the panel and be the facilitator of questions to us?

Three days later:

From: Genevieve
To: John, Frankie, Kyle, and Nancy

Unfortunately, I'm in a similar situation as Nancy. I also have a new job. So, I can't take the lead on this. But, I do have some thoughts. To merit a presentation, I think there needs to be some new information that we could present. What data are there that demonstrate the impact the recycling center has had on the communities?

Another six days later:

From: Nancy
To: Genevieve, Frankie, Kyle, and John

Hi everyone. I conferred with organizer. He is interested in a fun retrospective, not an information session. He sees it as being during a lunch, or something like that.

Here are some of my ideas . . . we could do a slide show with pics, etc. Get creative. Perhaps we each could take the lead on a different aspect of the history of the center. Like the initial idea and meetings, the first years in operation, the formation of the board and nonprofit business, the meaning it has given our lives, and potential effects on the communities.

Your thoughts . . .

A day later:

From: John
To: Genevieve, Frankie, Kyle, and Nancy

I'm okay with that.

Another five days later:

From: Nancy
To: Genevieve, Frankie, Kyle, and John

Sounds like we're all in. Just need to hear back from Frankie!

Here's what we have so far . . .

Kyle: "I would be happy to do a short bit on the origins and what came before, and the barriers we had to overcome."

Genevieve: "I can talk about planting the seeds of what would become the recycling center. The "meaning in our lives" question is a significant one for me. My involvement changed me personally and professionally in so many ways . . . still seeing the impact today.

John: "When Citizens Try to Run a Nonprofit Organization" 😶

Frankie: (with a quizzical look on his face)

Nancy: I think it would be really cool to do a network map of who uses the recycling, including our community partners, but that would be work, which I have absolutely no time for. So instead, I could talk about the challenges of running the organization in terms of all we tried to do to develop a culture of collaboration. I could also talk about our winter board meeting where we all got snowed in!

After seven years of not meeting regularly, this team tries to reestablish itself to make a presentation about how they got the recycling center started. In the beginning, they regularly used email to stay in touch. Is email still the best technology to reunite the team? Some types of group communication are better suited for some technologies rather than others. What would recommend for this team?

technologies, like project email and management systems, also let group members send, receive, and store documents. As a result, reviewing the performance of virtual teams is easier.

The obvious advantage is that groups using technology are able to communicate, collaborate, and work on their goals regardless of temporal or geographic constraints. Simply, the group—and its members—have greater flexibility in determining when they work and meet. Group members may work asynchronously, as group members will not read or send messages at the same time. Group members can log on and communicate according to their own preferences and needs, and within their own timeframe. This type of asynchronous group communication has several advantages. Members do not have to compete for talking time when using technology that is textually based. They also have the opportunity to reflect on what is posted before responding. In general, group members have a greater opportunity to participate, as they are not closed out by powerful or talkative members. The asynchronous mode also allows any group member to introduce ideas into the discussion, as there are fewer opportunities for members to control the group's task or activity. These benefits of asynchronous communication are especially useful when a group is working on a less complex task, such as idea generation (Bell & Kozlowski, 2002).

Other groups use technology for synchronous communication, interacting at the same time even though they cannot be face-to-face. This type of group technology is effective for more complex tasks, as they require greater coordination. Increased coordination relies on feedback among group members. Thus, synchronous communication, especially technology with richer media, for example videoconferencing, is more effective for tasks that rely on greater interdependencies among group members (Bell & Kozlowski, 2002).

Trends in Technology

As new technologies develop, two trends are appearing (Darics, 2014). First, the line between synchronous and asynchronous communication is becoming blurred. When group members create norms for using technology such that time lags or gaps between messages are minimal or when the gap is only the few milliseconds required for the technology to send and receive messages, technology-based communication is more like talking over the telephone. The conversation is in real time; only the group members are distributed.

The second trend is that most group members are comfortable using many different technologies. Work or project groups, for example, will use instant messaging, videoconference, and email in addition to face-to-face meetings. Thus, visual, vocal, and physical cues available in the face-to-face setting are assumed to be presented when communicating through technology. As a result, a sense of copresence is present whether group members are meeting face-to-face or not. **Copresence** is the idea that a group member's behavior and messages are shaped by others in the group. That is, the sense of *being there* with the other group members when interacting face-to-face bleeds over to communication in which group members are not colocated (Flordi, 2005; Merolla, 2010).

The one disadvantage shared by all communication technologies is that each—some to a lesser degree than others—lack nonverbal cues. Some technologies lack visual cues; other technologies lack verbal cues. Video-based technology does not resolve this, as visual and verbal cues are degraded (e.g., the video is not clear, not all members can be heard when they talk, view of interactants is narrow or limited). Without these cues, it is more difficult for group members to appropriately contextualize their interaction (Baron, 2010). Many of the nonverbal cues available in face-to-face interaction are missing when group members communicate through technology. When nonverbal cues are missing, it is more difficult to clarify ambiguities and to accurately determine other members' interpersonal needs. As a result, group members who communicate through technology can find it more difficult to develop shared meanings with other group members (Berry, 2011).

Anonymity is a feature of some group-oriented technologies. Some technology-based groups can also work on their tasks without members knowing their identity. Interacting anonymously is common in online support groups and web forums in which participants work on solving problems. Regardless, groups that use technology are distanced by space, even if they are in the same building. Moreover, group members' communication is mediated by the technology (Bell & Kozlowski, 2002). This is not a moot point. Members must use and rely on technology-mediated communication to link them together as a group. In addition, groups must take the time to adjust to or learn about their mediated environment. Not doing so will negatively influence task completion and harm member relationships. Thus, groups who expect to work together on a task over a long period of time are better suited to using technology than groups for which the time horizon is very short (Walther, 2002).

Generally, a more complex task requires greater coordination among group members and more immediate feedback to ensure interdependence among team members. While there is little difference in task effectiveness on less complex tasks between groups that meet face-to-face and groups that meet virtually, groups perform better on complex tasks when they meet face-to-face.

Thus, two recommendations can be made when groups must work virtually. First, groups will have greater task success if the technology is rich enough to include both asynchronous and synchronous media, as well as easy methods for sharing documents, drawings, and other graphical information (Bell & Kozlowski, 2002). Second, technology can limit the development of relational ties among members of more formal groups. If possible, virtual groups should consider meeting initially face-to-face to help group members create a group identity with one another and develop agreement about the group's goal or task (Meier, 2003),

Another influence of the use of technology is that virtual teams often cross functional, organizational, and cultural boundaries. Because technology makes it easier for groups of people to meet, virtual groups often include members with different backgrounds, knowledge sets, motivations, and communication styles. Technology often makes communication in these groups more difficult because members have more trouble conveying meaning and in knowing when they are not understood. It is also difficult for groups using technology to form relationships and organize themselves (Kiesler & Cummings, 2002). To overcome these potential difficulties, groups can develop procedures or rules for interacting and creating linkages among members by assigning tasks to subgroups of members with different backgrounds (Bell & Kozlowski, 2002). Group members also need to address relationship development because groups using technology whose members have developed collective positive attitudes and beliefs about their group's ability to perform are more effective at their tasks (Pescosolido, 2003).

While groups that use technology to communicate have some special challenges, they are more like groups that meet face-to-face than they are different. Both types of groups have defined and limited membership, create a structure and group identity to work interdependently towards a shared goal, and need to manage their task as well as their relationships. The primary difference is that virtual teams are geographically dispersed for some or all of their interaction, making them rely on technology rather than face-to-face interaction (Berry, 2011). It is likely that face-to-face groups also use technology to some degree. Thus, virtualness is a matter of degree.

SUMMARY

The bona fide group perspective illuminates the relationship of the group to its context or environment. The perspective recognizes that group boundaries are generally stable, but also permeable and fluid when group members are replaced, exchanged, added, or removed. As a result, as group members communicate with one another, they socially construct or negotiate the group's boundaries. This perspective also acknowledges that a group is not a distinct entity within an environment, but is connected to or embedded in other groups in a fluid social context.

Time and space are two other parts of a group's context. Issues of time include: the length of a group's history, the frequency and duration of its tasks, how flexibly the group treats time, the degree to which group members are separated from distractions while they work, and the number the tasks worked on at one time. Issues of space include: group members meeting in formal or informal spaces, how members are seated relative to one another, and the group's use of technology to bring members together from around the block or from another country.

Diversity is a major influence on group member interactions. Some degree of heterogeneity exists in every group. Diversity can be based on gender, sex, race, ethnicity, nationality, language, age, profession, and length of membership in the group. These types of diversity can create both positive and negative influences. The theory of effective intercultural workgroup communication explains how diversity influences group decision making, as well as members' satisfaction with the group. It is important to remember that there may be differences within cultures, as well as diversity between cultures.

Some groups rely completely on technology to complete their goals. Even groups whose members can meet face-to-face will use some form of technology to work together. Some technologies are used synchronously; others are used asynchronously. Research has demonstrated that communicating through technology is not the same as communicating face-to-face. Technology can eliminate some contextual information that is important to creating shared understanding, skew information making it more difficult for all members to identify the important information, and diminish members developing and sharing relational and task norms. Technology continues to change, which creates new opportunities for group members to interact. Experts recommend that groups use technology that includes both synchronous and asynchronous channels of communication. Groups that will work virtually are encouraged to meet face-to-face the first time. Doing so will give group members an opportunity to create group identity and develop agreement about the group's goals.

DISCUSSION QUESTIONS AND EXERCISES

1 Watch a situation comedy. Identify the external factors that influenced the group of characters. For example, why are these characters interacting? What's their goal? Is the goal easy or difficult? Is the group working under time pressure? How well do these characters know one another? What other groups are the characters connected with? Use the bona fide group perspective to identify what made that interaction effective or ineffective.

2 How would you describe the influence of time when you are interacting in a group of friends? In a required classroom group? In your work team? In a sports team? Is the influence of time consistent or inconsistent? Explain the differences or similarities.

3 In a public space (e.g., library, shopping center, restaurant, park), observe a group conversation. How did that group mark their space boundaries? Use their space? Expand their space?

4 Recall a group situation in which there was cultural diversity. What evidence do you have that the distinctions you noted about group members were based on cultural differences? Evaluate the steps you took (or could take) to help the group overcome any cultural obstacles.

5 List the communication technologies that you are comfortable using when talking with a group of friends. Doing a group project at school? How does technology help or hinder those group interactions?

NAILING IT!

Using Group Communication Skills for Group Presentations

Reflect on an experience of developing and delivering a group presentation. How was time a liability as your group worked on the presentation? In what ways could technology have helped you overcome these time constraints? Is communicating through technology always a time saver over face-to-face group interaction? Why or why not? When developing a group presentation, encourage your group to develop a timeline, or a chronological list, of tasks that need to be accomplished in developing your presentation. Whether drawn by hand or with created with software, a timeline should include:

- a detailed description of each task,

- the group members responsible for completing the task, and

- the date each task must be completed.

These items are organized from beginning to end; as group members take ownership of different tasks, some tasks can be done in parallel. Each time the group meets, the timeline should be reviewed and revised as necessary.

Image Credits

CHAPTER 4

HOW WE COMMUNICATE WHAT WE KNOW

After reading this chapter, you should be able to:

- Explain why sharing information is central to group communication

- Describe how the alignment of individual and group goals may impede sharing information in groups and teams

- Describe team cognition

- Identify different types of ties in a communication network

- Differentiate between centralized and decentralized communication networks

- Identify when a faultline influences the creation of subgroups

S haring information is a primary way groups complete their work. Members may share information to inform, to persuade, or to create common ground. In this chapter, we explore how and why information sharing takes place in groups. First, we investigate information sharing itself, examining two theoretical frameworks that differ in their views of how groups communicate. Second, we investigate how sharing information influences team cognition, or the level of understanding shared across team members. Oftentimes team members believe they think about an issue the same way, when in fact they do not. Unfortunately, this may not be discovered by the group until it is too late. Last, we consider how communication networks form to facilitate the flow of information within and across groups.

INFORMATION SHARING

Oftentimes the information needed to make a decision is spread across group members. During discussion, information may be shared with fellow members in the hope that it will aid the group in making an effective decision. Not only are there differences in the distribution of information across the group, but the various resources and expertise of group members may lead to different interpretations of the information. For example, a marketing team receives information from a group member who is charged with identifying vendors. He learns that it will cost $100,000 to advertise a product. The marketing team member in charge of the budget looks at this information and worries about the high cost. The member in charge of advertising looks at this amount and believes it is not enough based on budgets from similar projects. Other members of the team look at this number and doubt its accuracy. Even though everyone is looking at the same information, different interpretations abound. This is not uncommon in teams. However, this does make it more difficult to create a common understanding of an issue.

 THEORY STANDOUT

Motivated Information Sharing Paradigm

Research aligned with the motivated information sharing paradigm suggests that group members have both individual and group goals that drive their interaction (Hollingshead et al., 2007; Wittenbaum, Hollingshead, & Botero, 2004). Although the individual and group goals may contradict (what is best for me vs. what is best for the team), that isn't necessarily the case. Sometimes individual goals naturally align with group goals, or at least oftentimes they don't directly conflict. Additionally, group members may be able to work toward an individual goal while disguising the attempt as a move toward the group goal. The recognition of both individual and group goals creates an environment where group members are strategic in how they communicate to their groups.

Thus, groups often try to align individual and group goals so that members are incentivized to work for the betterment of the group. If group members see other members as threats to their individual goals, then they may not communicate in a way best for the group. Joint group reward is one such way that this is accomplished. What are other ways that leaders can align individual and group goals?

Hence, the sharing of information is not always straightforward. As mentioned in Chapter 1, group members communicate in a strategic way, in hopes of accomplishing their purpose. Group members who possess important information potentially hold power and influence over the group (see Chapter 7). The way information is presented may make one option more appealing than another. At the same time, the sharing of information is essential to group functioning. How groups share information has been debated over the years, and two perspectives on information sharing have emerged.

Cooperative Information Sharing

The **cooperative information sharing paradigm** investigates how group members share information when trying to make a decision (Stasser & Titus, 1985, 1987). Central to this model is the **hidden profile**, which is a research technique used to study information sharing. In the hidden profile experiment, information is distributed among members of the group. Some of the information is shared by all group members, meaning that every member has the same information. Additional information is unshared, in that only one group member has a specific set of information. If all members decide to share the information that they uniquely hold, then the correct choice should be discovered and selected. However, if all the unshared information isn't shared, then the group won't make the right decision. To uncover the best decision (or hidden profile), all the information must be shared among group members.

Unfortunately, research has shown time and time again that team members rarely discover the hidden profile. In fact, group members readily share *shared* information, but rarely share *unshared* information (Reimer, Reimer, & Czienskowski, 2010). For example, a group is discussing whether to select option A or B. Cindy has some unique information about option B that would discourage the group from selecting it, and some positive information about option A that everyone already knows. Research suggests that Cindy is more likely to share the positive information than the negative information because it is already shared by others. Perhaps Cindy is doing this because she is afraid that no one else will support her unique information. Perhaps Cindy shares common information so that she appears supportive and the information can be confirmed by others, making her look credible. Either way, relying on information that everyone already knows can prove problematic when trying to determine the correct decision.

Researchers have explored a variety of ways to encourage group members to share unique information, including considering various group member characteristics, such as apprehension, (Henningsen & Henningsen, 2004), altering the group structure (van Swol, 2009), and altering when group members receive information (Reimer, Reimer, & Hinsz, 2010). However, in general, groups are often ineffective when it comes to discovering the hidden profile that exists in the information that is distributed among them.

Motivated Information Sharing

After more than two decades of focusing on the cooperative information sharing paradigm, Wittenbaum, Hollingshead, and Botero (2004) critiqued the model and offered an alternative: the **motivated information sharing paradigm**. This paradigm uses a communicative lens to explain why groups are ineffective at sharing necessary information. First, these scholars argued that some of the premises behind the cooperative information sharing paradigm were faulty. In other words, groups and group members really do not act in a way consistent with the assumptions of the model. For example, they argued that Stasser and Titus' approach did not consider contextual factors. The hidden profile assumed that group members had all the information necessary to make a decision, all the information was objectively and concretely understood, and group members were all united in their focus on the group goal. In fact, this rarely happens. Most of the time, groups do not know if they have all the information necessary to make a decision, and sometimes must engage in information searches to discover more information. Even though members may do their best to share information objectively, this is very hard to do. Why is this the case?

Group members consider individual goals simultaneously with the group goal, and sometimes these two types of goals do not align. For example, let's say that Stephanie has a good idea for an upcoming project. During a meeting, she introduces the idea and shares information pertaining to it so the group can successfully accomplish the group goal. However, Stephanie may also have a desire to be promoted within the group, and wants to be featured in the group's presentation. This may change her delivery of the message; she may be more prone to deliver it in a way so that she receives more credit for it. She may even be more critical of other group members' ideas so that her idea looks better. Of course, individual goals may be in harmony with or contradictory to the group goal. However, since individuals adapt their communication in accordance with both individual and group goals, Stephanie's creation of her message may be quite complex, and could be at odds with her group goal. Individuals may have more than one goal, which can cause individual team members to be distracted from the team goal (Hollingshead, Jacobsohn, & Beck, 2007).

Our tendency to not share unique information and our complication of balancing multiple individual and group goals when communicating creates a potentially complex social situation for sharing information. Effective group facilitators will look for opportunities to not only encourage members to share unique information, but to minimize any perceived risks of doing so. In addition, group members can use the messages of other members as evidence for their personal goals. For example, if someone becomes defensive when a decision option is critiqued, it may be that an individual goal (e.g., to be promoted, to be right) has been hindered. Analysis of the interaction may lead a group member to recognize other group members' interests and adapt their messages accordingly.

TEAM COGNITION

One reason group members share information is to increase the level of understanding across group members. **Team cognition** refers to the level of knowledge or information commonly shared and expressed by group members (Beck & Keyton, 2012). An easy way of conceptualizing this is to think of yourself in a new group. Although you may not know anyone in the group, it is still probable that you share a basic level of understanding of what behavior is appropriate. For example, you would probably not start yelling at another group member or start sharing very intimate information about your life. These discussions would be awkward and surprising, and would likely alienate you from other group members. Even if groups or group members are new, there is a common understanding about decorum and meeting behavior based on culture and context.

In addition, creating a common understanding about issues is important for groups. One of the reasons we share information is to create common talking points for group members. When sharing information, discrepancies may arise. This is because when groups share information, their communication becomes evidence of how they are thinking (Keyton, Beck, & Asbury, 2010). It is not only the message content that suggests differences in perceptions, but also nonverbal behavior. For example, Brett may come to a meeting believing her sales team should aggressively seek customers for their new product. She sees it as opportunity to move the company forward and help the team make a name for itself. However, when she arrives at her team meeting she remains silent for the first part of group discussion, where several of the more experienced group members give reasons why an aggressive sales strategy would be risky. With this new information, Brett reconsiders her view of the product. Since she hasn't spoken up, many might interpret her silence as support for what the experienced group members are saying. She may reassess her position based on explicit messages from these team members—namely, that it's not worth the risk, or by more subtle cues, such as a questionable facial expression, sarcasm in a team member's voice, or even silence. Brett will use these communicative cues from others as a way to understand how the group is viewing an issue.

 SKILL BUILDER

Having all team members on the same page is vital for group functioning. But oftentimes team cognition is difficult to assess. How does a group know if all members understand an issue the same way?

Unfortunately, group members usually don't know until it is too late. For example, in an undergraduate class a group was assigned to present on a topic in the next class period. All group members thought it would be beneficial to arrive early to class to make sure they were prepared. Most of the group showed up 30 minutes before class time, expecting to have a rehearsal of the entire presentation. However, one class member showed up five minutes before class and said, "I'm glad everyone showed up a few minutes early to make sure we are all ready and prepared to present. I've been practicing all day and am ready to go. How is everyone else doing?" Clearly, the last class member had a different understanding of what "showing up early" meant than the others. How could the group have been more aware of their expectation differences ahead of time? What is the best way for groups to assess team cognition?

What can you do to help your team members share information ? Importantly, the only ways that group members can know what other group members are thinking is through communication (de Vries, Van den Hooff, & de Ridder, 2006; Park, 2008). First, examine the attitude you display in the team. Do you willingly share information? If you do, you can create a norm of reciprocity. That is, your willingness to share information can encourage other team members to share information. Second, do you display enthusiasm for the group and what the group is working on? When you are enthusiastic, this will enhance other members' eagerness to share information. Third, are you willingly sharing information? If you remain silent in a conversation, members of the group tend to assume that you don't have a belief that severely contradicts the course of conversation. This is how **false consensus**, or the belief that group members are all in agreement when they are not, can emerge. When team members do not encourage and promote opportunities for everyone to share their beliefs and information, groups can be dominated by a few very vocal members.

GROUP COMMUNICATION NETWORKS

As group members regularly communicate about issues, certain channels of communication become routinized within the group. This can also occur for communication that moves across groups. This **communication network**, or a structure of who talks to whom, is the interaction pattern or flow of messages between and among group members. A network creates structure for the group because the network facilitates or constrains who can (or will) talk to whom.

A network is a social structure that consists of group members and the relationships or ties among them. While we generally think of who talks to whom, or communication ties, there are other types of ties among members (Katz, Lazer, Arrow, & Contractor, 2005). **Formal ties** describe who reports to whom or any other power-laden relationship. **Affective ties** describe who likes or trusts whom. **Material ties** describe who gives resources to whom. **Proximity ties** describe who is spatially close or electronically linked to whom. Finally, **cognitive ties** describe who knows whom. In a group, it is likely that describing the network among group members would look different based on which set of ties or relationships you were examining. Thus, the terms *communication, formal, affective, material, proximity*, and *cognitive* describe the nature of ties or relationships you have with other group members.

Ties or relationships among members in a network can further be described by their communication attributes. For example, ties can vary in direction. That is, communication may flow one way, from one group member to another group member. Or communication can flow between group members, with each person sending and receiving of messages. Ties can also be described based on the content of the communication, the frequency of the interaction, and the medium or channel used for communication among group members.

Network ties are described as strong or weak, based on the intensity and reciprocity in the relationship. You probably have stronger ties with your family and friends than you do with members of your work group because ties in groups where your relational needs are met require a greater amount of trust than ties in work groups, which may be temporary or situational. Of course, it may be helpful to have some weak ties, which require less relationship maintenance and effort but still allow you access to a variety of resources. Similarly, ties can be described as being positive or negative. Identifying a tie as strong or weak and positive or negative is really your evaluation of the importance of the tie to you.

Networks in groups and teams are multiplex, meaning that relationships among group members can be described or evaluated across a number of these dimensions. Moreover, describing group relationships according to one type (i.e., formal ties) will reveal a different network than describing relationships according to a second type (i.e., proximity ties). Creating a **sociogram**, a type of visual representation of the group members' relationships, for any particular type of tie reveals the number and pattern of network ties among group members. Because a sociogram reveals the network among group members, it is easy to determine if subgroups or cliques exist. Figures 4.1 displays two sociograms for a baseball team based on formal and affective ties. Notice both the similarities and the differences in the interdependence of member relationships in the two different networks.

Network theory can help us understand the importance of thinking of groups as networks (Wellman, 1988). One proposition of network theory proposes that group members' behavior can be predicted by the nature of their ties to one another. That is, group members tend to use their existing networks to get information, seek resources, and request support. Thus, a network presents a set of opportunities if a group member is well connected, but can also act as a constraint if the member is connected only weakly to just a few other members. While networks are comprised of sets of relationships between two members, another proposition suggests that every two-member relationship must be considered relative to how that particular relationship is situated within the larger network of the group. In other words, the pattern of all of the relationships are important, not just a specific relationship between two group members. How members are connected influences the flow of information and resources. That is, a member who is connected to only one other group member could still receive most of the information distributed in the group if the person he or she is connected to has relationships with all of the other group members.

Networks emerge among group members because they are working interdependently on a task or activity. Ties between members are based on both relational (i.e., affective) and task (i.e., formal) dimensions. Simply put, what group members talk about and how group members talk to one another creates structure for the group, and different structures will emerge based on the nature of the ties among members. In the case of the baseball team, the group's activity influences who talks to whom in a group. If you are the catcher for your softball team, you will talk to the pitcher and infielders more frequently than you will talk to the outfielders. By virtue of your position on the team, you must talk to the pitcher to plan your approach to opposing batters and to the infielders to coordinate your team's defense. A primary way to evaluate networks is to examine their centralized or decentralized structure.

Decentralized Networks

Most groups use a decentralized network that allows each group member to talk to every other member. There are no restrictions as to who can talk to whom. This pattern is decentralized because group members communicate without restrictions, and it is typical of most group interactions. Although a **decentralized communication**

(a)

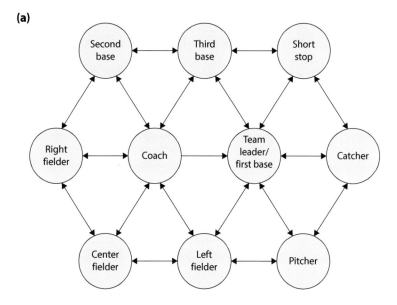

(b)

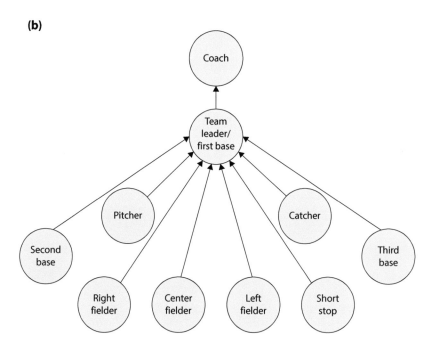

Figure 4.1 (a) Decentralized network of baseball team based on affective ties;
(b) Centralized network of baseball team based on formal ties

network is helpful for certain group tasks, such as discussions, problem solving, and decision making, it may slow down other types of group activities. A decentralized network is good for building group and team cohesiveness. For example, the affective network of the baseball team in Figure 4.1 is decentralized. The team has been together for a several years. Although there are formal positions of coach and team leader, nearly everyone is the same age, as the team comprises individuals who played baseball in college and now play as a team in an amateur adult league. Team members take frequent road trips together, and for many players the team has become their primary social outlet. Thus, team members get along well with one another and communicate frequently about topics other than baseball.

An open, or decentralized, network provides the most input, but it can also produce **communication overload**—too much or too complex communication from too many sources. When overload occurs, messages may compete or conflict, causing stress and confusion. Sometimes in discussions, groups may need a facilitator or coordinator to monitor turn taking so that everyone has a chance to be heard. Still, when a group works on a complex task or activity, a decentralized pattern is more effective (Brown & Miller, 2000).

Centralized Networks

Any type of network that imposes restrictions on who can talk to whom is **centralized**. The constraints might be real or perceived. For example, a real constraint is that members of the baseball team are asked to bring issues about uniform repair to the team leader. If they can't be resolved there, then the team leader takes the issue to the coach. A perceived constraint is that a relatively new member of the team feels uneasy about asking the team leader for new equipment. There is no rule or policy to suggest that he can't make this request, but he doesn't because he believes other players are not making similar requests.

When networks are centralized, some members may experience **communication underload**—too infrequent or too simple messages. Group members in an underload situation often feel disconnected from the group. A centralized network can develop if the leader of the group controls the distribution and sharing of messages in the group. From this central and controlling position, the member in the role of leader talks to other group members individually. Group members do not talk with one another; they communicate only with the leader. This type of pattern often develops when there is a strong, domineering leader. If this is the only communication pattern within the group, members are likely to be dissatisfied with the group experience. This pattern also restricts the development of a group identity and weakens the interdependence of group members.

In the case of the baseball team, a formal centralized network may be appropriate for the team's task. Usually, one person (i.e., the manager) is in charge of making decisions for the team. Of course, players can provide feedback to their manager, but during a game a manager cannot take into consideration everyone's viewpoints. Instead a manager may limit conversations to his coaching staff when making decisions. This allows the manager

to respond more quickly to situations that require immediate attention. Centralized networks prevent communication overload, especially when time is of the essence.

Evaluating Your Group's Network

Most groups think they use a decentralized or open network in which group members are free to talk to whomever they want. But as roles and norms develop in groups, a structure may be created that affects who talks to whom and who talks most frequently. Status and

---

 MESSAGE AND MEANING

Instead of holding a meeting, Jeff has decided to text his team requesting feedback on how large the marketing budget should be for the project. Within 10 minutes, he received the following responses:

JIM: $200,000

FRED: It really depends on whether you want to prioritize this project over Project B.

SARA: Shouldn't we first see how much the ads will cost?

JIM: Or we could probably run it at $150,000.

SARA: Jim also brings up a good question. Which project are we prioritizing? I meant to say Fred. Fred brought up the question.

FRED: $150,000 is way too low.

CAL: What do you think, Jeff?

JIM: I don't know anything about Project B. I think $150,000 may be what the clients are thinking.

SARA: You should check out the last marketing report from the downtown office.

ALLIE: I'm a little behind on this conversation. Is Project A our next project?

JEFF: Let's hold off on this topic and meet sometime next week.

Within a few minutes Jeff had received 11 texts about several different aspects of his question. He was overwhelmed with the information and couldn't control the flow of conversation. What type of communication network did they have for this team? What characteristics of their communication helped you determine the network type? Will holding a team meeting resolve the network problem? When is texting an appropriate communication medium for groups?

power differences among members also affect a group's communication network. As a result, some group members will end up talking more, some will be talked to less, and some will talk only to specific other members.

One way to examine the effectiveness of a group's network is to examine which members hold which knowledge or expertise. This is a first and necessary step, but simply knowing who has what knowledge is not sufficient. A group's knowledge network is only beneficial if group members have developed strong communication ties to share that information. Finally, member expertise and their communication ties must match the task interdependency of group members (Yuan, Fulk, Monge, & Contractor, 2010).

A second way to evaluate group network is look for **faultlines**, or characteristics or attributes of diversity that are salient for a particular group and its task (Lau & Murnighan, 1998). Faultlines can divide members into subgroups because group members commonly communicate more frequently with members who they perceive to be similar. For exam-

PUTTING THE PIECES TOGETHER

Group Size, Interdependence, and Group Structure

Reflect on a group or team you belong to now. How much of the overall group communication do you contribute? Twenty percent? Fifty percent? How does group size influence your amount of communication in this group? The way that group members interact influences the roles that group members take. For example, is the most talkative member of your group the leader? Why or why not? If you wanted to become the leader of the group, how would you have to interact?

Some group members may have expertise in different areas of the group task. How do you know which members are experts? How do members communicate their expertise?

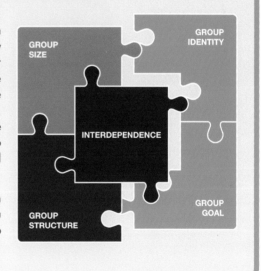

ple, a work group is discussing their organization's new early retirement and family leave policies and the impact of these new policies on the workplace. Older members or female members may create subgroups in the larger discussion, as age and gender are salient to the topic because older group members will easily identify with the potential of retirement and female employees may identify with the potential of taking family leave. When faultlines like these occur in a group discussion, subgroups can emerge. One way to avoid or decrease these types of demographic faultlines is to create relational ties among members on other dimensions. In this case, providing employees with a common goal for their unit that requires the skills and talents of all group members will encourage them to create a network that minimizes these differences.

So, which network should your group use? This depends on several factors. Although the task or activity of the group is often the primary determinant (Hirokawa, Erbert, & Hurst, 1996), do not forget about the effects of a communication network on a group's social or relational development. On the one hand, centralized networks place a heavy burden on the person at the center of the network. At the same time, a centralized pattern limits the opportunity for group members to get to know one another, to develop relationships within the group setting, and to create a group identity.

On the other hand, decentralized, open communication networks may slow the group's work on the task. Yet members communicating in this fashion are generally more satisfied with the group and its activity and are more committed to the group. You can ask yourself these questions to determine which communication network will work best for your group situation. More than likely, multiple networks will be required to satisfy both the relational and task dimensions of your group.

1 What is more important to the group right now—working on this task or developing relationships and commitment to the group?

2 How difficult is the task? Is it simple or complex?

3 To what extent do all group members need to develop leadership and followership skills? Or are roles and functions specifically set in this group?

4 Have demographic faultlines created subgroups? What other networks could be facilitated if subgroups are hindering group success?

SUMMARY

Group members share information to accomplish group tasks. Early research investigated why group members were often unsuccessful in their attempts to share information. The motivated information sharing paradigm explains that other factors also influence information sharing, such as the presence of individual goals or not having access to all necessary information. These other factors may lead group members to adjust their messages in ways that inhibit pursuit of the group goal.

One of the reasons members share information is so that members form a common understanding of issues. There may be differences in how members view an issue, but these differences are unlikely to be made known unless the group discusses them. Thus, member interaction is a great way of determining if other members have the same understanding. Without interaction, there is no way of knowing if agreement across the group is really false consensus.

As group members communicate within and outside the group, patterns of interaction are formed. These patterns may be based on a variety of characteristics, such as through hierarchy, proximity, or past relationships. The type of network a group needs is based upon the nature of the task they are trying to accomplish. For example, groups that have tasks requiring flexibility and creativity (i.e., design team in an advertising agency) are best managed by the use of decentralized networks. However, groups that have tasks that must be efficient or are urgent (i.e., emergency medical providers) may prefer centralized networks. Group member knowledge expertise or faultlines may also influence group communication networks.

DISCUSSION QUESTIONS AND EXERCISES

1 Have a conversation with your friends or coworkers. Ask them about instances in which their groups or teams had problems sharing information. Can they identify why such a problem existed? How did they become aware that information known to some group members was not being shared with everyone in the group? Did the unshared information have a positive or negative effect on the group?

2 Team cognition is a difficult concept to explain. Can you draw a picture to help explain this concept to others?

3 Observe a group in action, for example, a civic or governmental group, or a student, sorority, or fraternity council, or watch a situation comedy that features

 NAILING IT!

Using Group Communication Skills for Group Presentations

Developing and delivering a group presentation is a complex group goal. How well you and other group members share information during the developmental process will make a difference between a well-developed and cohesive presentation versus one that is disjointed.

First, to share information effectively, it is necessary to meet as a team—and meeting face-to-face may be helpful to communicate both verbal messages and nonverbal cues. Second, make a list of the type of information the group will need for the presentation. It is highly unlikely that one group member will have all the expertise or information the team needs. Assigning information-gathering tasks to all members helps to ensure that the group will have the information required for the presentation. Perhaps, the group will make information-gathering assignments based on types or sources of information (e.g., information from the web, scholarly journals, popular press books, or interviews). Or, perhaps your presentation topic is easily divided into different topics (i.e., environmental concerns about water quality, air quality, and soil quality).

Third, as you discovered in this chapter, there is a tendency for group members to not share information each member uniquely holds. To overcome that tendency, the group should make a plan for sharing information with one another. One way is to hold group meeting where the only item on the agenda is to make short informational presentations to one another. Holding a group meeting for this purpose only is a good strategy, as it allows group members to identify gaps, overlaps, or inconsistencies in the information gathered. Further, it allows group members to ask questions, which can help to uncover potentially unshared information.

group interaction, and create their communication network. Identify the type of communication network that emerges in the group interaction. After evaluating the strengths and weakness of the network, what suggestions would you make to the group and to individual members for changing the network structure?

Image Credits

CHAPTER 5

DECISION MAKING

After reading this chapter, you should be able to:

- ■ Explain why decision making is a core group activity

- ■ Describe the steps of functional decision making and identify them when they occur in group interaction

- ■ Distinguish between majority and minority group behaviors

- ■ Describe and explain these decision-making techniques to others: brainstorming, nominal group technique, consensus, voting, and ranking

- ■ Compare these decision-making techniques and select the most appropriate for a particular group decision

I n order to accomplish a group goal, members must make decisions about a variety of issues. Often, the first decision is to decide on a meeting time and location. Making decisions about group composition and leadership structure are also important. Of course, decisions pertinent to the purpose of the group can be quite difficult. In fact, groups and teams are often created because individuals do not want to make difficult decisions.

Thus, decision making is central to group and team interaction. In order to explore this topic, we first investigate two theories of decision making. Then we consider several techniques that have proven beneficial to improving communication during decision making. Last, we investigate several decision-making principles that are the foundation of successful group interaction.

GROUP DECISION-MAKING THEORIES

Functional Theory of Decision Making

When group communication scholars use a functional approach, they are speaking of three primary functional assumptions (Wittenbaum, Hollingshead, Paulus, Hirokawa, Ancona, Peterson, Jehn, & Yoon, 2004). The first assumption is that groups are goal oriented, something emphasized in Chapter 1. The second assumption is that group performance can vary and be evaluated; in other words, groups do not always succeed given the difficulty of tasks. This assumption also points out that a group's success can be measured. Third, group performance (or its effectiveness at decision making) is a product of interaction among group members, which is based on (a) internal inputs, such as group size and member composition, and (b) external circumstances, such as time pressure. A group's interaction reflects both of these. Obviously, the goal of task-oriented groups is to find the solution or decision. According to the **functional theory of group decision making**, these are the five critical functions in decision-making and problem-solving activities (Gouran & Hirokawa, 1983; Hirokawa, 1982):

1 thoroughly discuss the problem,

2 examine the criteria of an acceptable solution before discussing specific solutions,

3 propose a set of realistic alternative solutions,

4 assess the positive aspects of each proposed solution, and

5 assess the negative aspects of each proposed solution.

A function is not just a step or a procedure. Each function represents a type of interaction required among group members to make a decision. The functions do not have to be completed in order, but when the five functions are not accomplished, a group diminishes its chances of making good decision.

For the first step, group members need to achieve an understanding of the problem they are trying to solve. The group should deliberate until all members understand the nature and

MESSAGE AND MEANING

The jury has deliberated all day. After making decisions about a defendant's guilt or innocence of double murder, the jury still has 25 counts to deliberate. Each of these counts is about drug possession or drug trafficking.

JUROR 1:   Can I say something . . . I am willing to work here until 10 o'clock tonight if we have to, to finish this. Maybe in another hour or so, we can have some food brought in. Pizza or Chinese—I don't care. Whatever anybody wants. Let's just grind away at this.

JUROR 2:   I mean I think we need to listen to the tape. It's gonna take time.

JUROR 3:   Hopefully, they're [the audio tapes] readily accessible.

JUROR 2:   You know I mean . . .

JUROR 3:   The simple fact is that if we won't get into the hotel room till 11. Then we're gonna have to get up again at 7 o'clock and I don't want to do this. Perhaps we should wait until tomorrow.

JUROR 4:   I don't think it's gonna take till 10. Obviously, the sooner we get to these tapes, the better off we are. So instead of debating this, let's just get these tapes going. You have to take a break, go take a break for 15 minutes. It will, it will take them 12 minutes to get the tape ready for us. And then we're back in here.

JUROR 1:   As far as I'm concerned, I'll stay here all night.

[SEVERAL JURORS SPEAK AT ONCE]

JUROR 1:   Because then by the time they order the food,

[SEVERAL JURORS SPEAK AT ONCE]

JUROR 5:   I want to leave.

[SEVERAL JURORS SPEAK AT ONCE]

JUROR 2:   . . . it will be 8:30. I do not want to stay here any longer.

JUROR 3:   I don't want to stay here till 9 o'clock at night, for 12 hours. I don't want to do it, period.

JUROR 6:   Let's eat dinner here and leave at 7 and resume tomorrow.

JUROR 1:   I don't care if we stay later than that late. But I don't want to stay until 12 o'clock at night, 10 o'clock at night.

[SEVERAL JURORS SPEAK AT ONCE]

JUROR 4:   By 8 o'clock, if there're two verdicts left, I'll stay until they're done just so we can get it over with. But if they're still several verdicts to go, I'm not staying here, no way.

JUROR 1:   Well, you know we're all reasonable people here. Let's do the best we can and assess it when we get closer to a decision. It's only 5 o'clock. We're reasonable . . . listen, nobody wants to drag this out, obviously. But let's be reasonable about it.

Using the functional theory of group decision making, how effectively are jury members making this procedural decision about whether to stop deliberating for the day, or to stop for dinner and then continue to deliberate into the evening. How would you evaluate their abilities to 1) thoroughly discuss the problem, 2) examine the criteria of an acceptable solution before discussing specific solutions, 3) propose a set of realistic alternative solutions, 4) assess the positive aspects of each proposed solution, and 5) assess the negative aspects of each proposed solution? Is the functional theory of decision making appropriate for procedural decisions? If the jury were to effectively deliberate their current problem (whether to stop, or to eat and then deliberate further), what influence might that have on the remaining decisions they have to make?

significance of the problem, its possible causes, and the consequences that could develop if the problem is not dealt with effectively. For example, parking is generally a problem on most campuses. But a group of students, faculty, staff, and administrators addressing the parking problem without having an adequate understanding of the entire issue is likely to suggest solutions that will not actually solve the problem. The parking problem on your campus may be that there are not enough parking spaces. Or it may be that there are not enough parking spaces where people want to park. Or perhaps the parking problem exists at only certain times of the day. Another type of parking problem exists when students do not want to pay to park and park their cars illegally on campus and in the surrounding community. Each parking problem is different and so requires different solutions. When group members address this function—understanding the nature of the problem before trying to solve it—their decision-making efforts result in higher-quality decisions (Hirokawa, 1983).

Second, the group needs to develop an understanding of what constitutes an acceptable resolution of the problem. In this critical function, group members come to understand the specific standards that must be satisfied for the solution to be acceptable. Groups must develop criteria by which to evaluate each proposed alternative. Let's go back to the parking problem. In this step, group members need to consider how much students and employees will be willing to pay for parking. Group members also need to identify and discuss the type of solutions campus administrators and campus police will find acceptable. The group should consider if the local police need to agree with the recommendation. In other words, the group has to decide on the objectives and standards that must be satisfied in selecting an appropriate solution. Any evaluation of alternatives must be based on known and agreed-upon criteria (Graham, Papa, & McPherson, 1997).

Third, the group needs to seek and develop a set of realistic and acceptable alternatives. With respect to the parking problem, groups frequently stop generating alternatives when the first plausible solution is suggested. Look at the following dialogue:

MARTY: Okay, I think we should think about building a parking garage.

LINDSEY: Where would it go?

MARTY: I don't know. But there are all kinds of empty lots around campus.

HELEN: What about parking in the church parking lots?

LINDSEY: That's an idea, but I like the idea of our own parking garage better.

TODD: I like that, too. It would be good to know that whatever time I go to campus a parking spot would be waiting for me.

MARTY: Any other ideas, besides the parking garage?

LINDSEY: No, I can't think of any. I think we need to work on the parking garage idea.

TODD: Me, too.

HELEN: Shouldn't we consider something else in case the parking garage idea falls through?

MARTY: Why? We all like the idea, don't we?

If a group gets stuck in generating alternatives, as our parking group does, a brainstorming session or nominal group technique (discussed later in the chapter) may help. A group cannot choose the best alternative if all the alternatives are not known.

Fourth, group members need to assess the positive qualities of each of the alternatives they find attractive. This step helps the group recognize the relative merits of each alternative. Once again, let's turn to the parking problem. Students and employees probably will cheer for a solution to the parking problem that does not cost them more money. Certainly no-cost or low-cost parking will be attractive to everyone. But if this is the only positive quality of an alternative, it is probably not the best choice. For example, to provide no-cost or low-cost parking, your recommendation is that during the daytime, students park in the parking lots of churches and at night they park in the parking lots of office buildings. Although the group has satisfied concerns about cost, it is doubtful that those who manage church and office building properties will find this alternative attractive. Fifth, group members need to assess the negative qualities of alternative choices. By assessing positive and negative qualities separately, group members can avoid the tendency to provide an overall positive or negative evaluation when assessing an option.

When group members communicate to fulfill these five functions, they increase the chance that their decision making will be effective. This is because group members have worked together to pool their information resources, avoid errors in individual judgment, and create opportunities to persuade other group members (Gouran, Hirokawa, Julian, & Leatham, 1993). For example, the members of the parking group bring different information to the discussion because they come to school at different times of the day. Those who come early or late in the day have a harder time finding a place to park than those who come early in the afternoon. By pooling what each participant knows about the parking situation, the group avoids becoming biased or choosing a solution that will resolve only one type of parking problem.

In addition, as the group discusses the problem, members can identify and remedy errors in individual judgment. It is easy to think that parking is not a problem when you come in for one class in the early afternoon and leave immediately after. In your experience, the parking lot has some empty spaces because you come at a time when others have left for lunch. And when you leave 2 hours later, the lot is even emptier, making you wonder what the fuss is about in the first place!

Discussion also provides an opportunity to persuade others or to be persuaded. Discussion allows alternatives to be presented that might not occur to others and allows for reevaluation of alternatives that initially seem unattractive. Let's go back to the group discussing the parking problem:

MARTY: Okay, where are we?

HELEN: Well, I think we've pretty much discussed parking alternatives. I'm not sure.

LINDSEY: What about using the bus?

TODD: You've got to be kidding.

LINDSEY: Why not? The bus line goes right by campus and the fare is only 50 cents.

MARTY: Well, it's an idea.

HELEN: Well, what if the bus doesn't have a route where I live?

LINDSEY: Well, that may be the case for you, Helen, but I bet many students and employees live on or near a bus line.

MARTY: I wonder how many?

LINDSEY: Let's go online and get a copy of the entire routing system.

MARTY: Good idea, Lindsey. We were looking for parking alternatives and hadn't thought about other modes of transportation.

Groups that successfully achieve each of the five critical functions of decision making make higher-quality decisions than groups that do not (Hirokawa, 1988). However, the functional perspective is not a procedure for making decisions, because there is no prescribed order to the five functions. Rather, it is the failure of the group to perform one of the five functions that has a profound effect on the quality of the group's decision making. But do the five functions contribute equally to group decision-making effectiveness? An analysis across hundreds of groups indicates that the most important function is group members' assessment of the negative consequences of proposed alternatives.

Next in importance were thorough discussion and analysis of the problem, and the establishment of criteria for evaluating proposals (Orlitzky & Hirokawa, 2001). The functional theory of decision making continues to be the central theory of decision-making communication.

Majority/Minority Influence

Another avenue of group communication research is to investigate how different sub-groups argue for their respective positions in a group. One way to do this is to look at majority and minority subgroups and how they communicate to accomplish their respective goals. Early efforts on such influence focused on the differing purposes of each group. In general, majorities try to effect compliance through their control and use of resources, and by using their numerical advantage to enforce public compliance (Moscovici, 1976). Such influence may be used in a variety of different ways. For example, majority subgroup members could try to communicate more than other groups since there are more members to speak. They may try to threaten to be unhappy with or noncompliant to others' ideas, knowing that without the majority members supporting a position, it will likely fail, no matter if the leader feels differently.

On the other hand, minorities try to provoke or stimulate thought to encourage majority members to reflect on their attitudes and beliefs (Nemeth, Swedlund, & Kanki, 1974, Nemeth, 1986). Simply put, minority subgroups may be stubborn about their position, and attempt to make bold statements to lead others to second guess their beliefs. They can also make it very clear that if the majority wins, the minority will be very difficult throughout the rest of the process.

In terms of group communication, majority/minority influence has found three primary results (Meyers, Brashers, & Hanner, 2000). First, the majority subgroup is often victorious in winning the final result. This is not surprising given that most decisions are majority-rule, but it is an important finding nonetheless. Minorities know from the outset that they have a difficult mountain to climb to have any effect on the proceedings, let alone to convince others of their position. Second, argument consistency is important for both majorities and minorities to be influential (Bazarova, Walther, & McLeod, 2012). If either group moves away from their initial position, they are often considered weak or wishy-washy. For minority subgroups, this stubbornness is especially important when seeking concessions from the other side.

Third, majorities and minorities tend to trigger different thought processes in group members. Majority subgroups tend to encourage integration and convergence from others. Majority subgroups members may attempt to control the conversation and perhaps even minimize communication if it is clear that they hold the winning position. Minorities, on the other hand, try to spark discussion or conflicts, and sometimes the anxiety created by such behavior may lead others to want to reduce it, even if that means conceding on some points or ceasing to seek out helpful information Meyers et al., 2000.

A direct study of argument interaction (Meyers et al., 2000) found that majority subgroups used more convergence-seeking messages, or messages that encouraged group members to unite with a point of view. For example, members of the majority were more likely to agree with another person's position, or show support and understanding of others' viewpoints. On the other hand, minority subgroups used more disagreeing messages in their argumentation. If, for example, another group member said something that a minority subgroup member disagreed with, the minority member would be more prone to vocalize that disagreement. The findings by Meyers et al. (2000) support earlier findings, that majority and minority group members strive to accomplish different purposes in decision making.

DECISION-MAKING PROCEDURES

In order to facilitate the decision-making process, there are variety of communicative techniques that group members use. These procedures differ in many ways, including their level of formality (Schweiger & Leana, 1986), forcefulness, and participation. Procedures help members balance task and relational dimensions of their group and develop agreement among members (SunWolf & Seibold, 1999). In this section, we focus on five: brainstorming, nominal group technique, consensus, voting, and ranking.

Brainstorming

Brainstorming is an idea generation technique designed to improve productivity and creativity (Osborn, 1963). Thus, the brainstorming procedure helps a group to function creatively. In a brainstorming session, group members first state as many alternatives as possible to a given problem. Creative ideas are encouraged; ideas do not have to be traditional or unoriginal. A central component to brainstorming is that all ideas be accepted without criticism—verbal or nonverbal—from other group members. Next, ideas that have been presented can be improved upon or combined with other ideas. Finally, the group evaluates ideas after the idea generation phase is complete. The group should record all ideas for future consideration, even those that are initially discarded. A group member can act as the facilitator of the brainstorming session, but research has shown that someone external to the group may be more effective in this role. The facilitator helps the group maintain momentum and helps members remain neutral by not stopping to criticize ideas (Kramer, Fleming, & Mannis, 2001).

This brainstorming procedure helps groups generate as many ideas as possible from which to select a solution. Generally, as the number of ideas increases, so does idea quality. Members may experience periods of silence during idea generation, but research has shown that good ideas can come after moments of silence while members reflect and think individually (Ruback, Dabbs, & Hopper, 1984). So, it may be premature to end idea generation the first time all members become quiet.

When should a group use brainstorming? Brainstorming is best used when the problem is specific rather than general. Why? If the problem is too generally stated, suggestions will not be focused or helpful. For example, brainstorming can be effective for identifying ways to attract minority employees to an organization. But the problem—What does a group hope to accomplish in the next 5 years?—is too broad. Use a brainstorming session to break issues down into subproblems, and then devote a further session to each one. Brainstorming works best with smaller rather than larger groups. Brainstorming

THEORY STANDOUT

Persuasive Arguments Theory

In order to demonstrate the benefits and strengths of a communication perspective, it is also important to consider a noncommunicative theory on group decision making. Early research assumed that the process of group decision making largely consisted of group members making up their minds prior to meetings, meaning that communication during meetings was largely unimportant.

For example, **persuasive arguments theory** posits that instead of interaction being important, it was rather the cognitive processes of individual group members prior to meetings that led to interaction outcomes. In other words, group members make up their minds prior to a meeting. Thus, the real purpose of meetings is not to develop the correct solution, but to simply convince others to support premeeting decisions by group members. Since group members have made up their minds prior to group discussion, it becomes increasingly difficult to persuade other group members. One approach may be to present extreme arguments in order to shock others into supporting the prevailing view. This persuasive technique for group decision making, however, leads to **group polarization**, or the tendency for groups to gravitate toward decisions more extreme than any of the members would prefer individually.

Although a provocative way to view group decision making, group communication research suggests there is little data to support it (Meyers, 1989). Persuasive arguments theory minimizes the influence created in group discussion specifically, and communication, more generally.

Questions:

1. Do you make up your mind on issues prior to your group's discussion? Is this beneficial or harmful to group decision making?

2. Is suggesting extreme views to win a point ethical?

3. Are there differences in how group members talk when trying to discover the best solution as opposed to simply persuading other group members to agree with them?

also works best when group members are diverse in the knowledge they hold about the issue (Wittenbaum, Hollingshead, & Botero, 2004). Finally, members are more likely to generate a greater number of unique ideas if they write their ideas down before presenting them to the group (Mullen, Johnson, & Salas, 1991).

Brainstorming can help increase group cohesiveness because it encourages all members to participate. It also helps group members realize that they can work together productively (Pavitt, 1993). In addition, group members report that they like having an opportunity to be creative and to build upon one another's ideas (Kramer, Kuo, & Dailey, 1997), and they usually find brainstorming fun. However, groups do better if they have a chance to warm up or to practice the process (Firestien, 1990). The practice session should be unrelated to the subject of the actual brainstorming session. Practice sessions are beneficial because they reinforce the procedure and reassure participants that the idea generation and evaluation steps will not be integrated. Posting the five brainstorming steps so they are visible during the session helps remind participants of the procedure's rules.

Brainstorming can be done effectively in groups that meet face-to-face, as well as in groups that use technology to facilitate the process (Barki & Pinsonneault, 2001). Also note that groups do better at brainstorming—both in quantity and quality of ideas—if they have been through a practice round. One way to do this is to have group members use the brainstorming technique as a way to get to know one another better. For example, group members can be asked to "generate as many ideas as you can related to your area of expertise, age, sex, major, ethnicity, and geographical location" (Baruah & Paulus, 2008, p. 530). Practicing on the topic of major, groups members could brainstorm the types of jobs graduates with communication degrees could apply for. Notice that brainstorming is a procedure for generating ideas, and not for making decisions. As a result, brainstorming by itself cannot satisfy the five critical functions of group decision making. However, it is especially effective in helping a group seek and develop a set of realistic and acceptable alternatives and in coming to an understanding of what constitutes an acceptable resolution, and moderately effective in helping group members achieve an understanding of the problem.

Nominal Group Technique

The same basic principles of brainstorming are also applied in the **nominal group technique** (NGT) except that group members work both independently as individuals and interdependently in the group. Thus, the nominal group technique is an idea generation process in which individual group members generate ideas on their own before interacting as a group to discuss the ideas. The unique aspect of this procedure is that the group temporarily suspends interaction to take advantage of independent thinking and reflection (Delbecq, Van de Ven, & Gustafson, 1975). NGT is based on two principles: (a) individuals think more creatively and generate more alternatives working alone, and (b) group discussion is best used for refining and clarifying alternatives.

NGT is a six-step linear process, with each step focusing on different aspects of the problem-solving process. In Step 1, group members silently generate as many ideas as possible, writing down each idea. It's sensible to give members a few minutes after everyone appears to be finished, as some of our best ideas occur to us after we think we are finished.

In Step 2, the ideas are recorded on a flip chart by a facilitator. Generally, it is best to invite someone outside the group to help facilitate the process so all group members can participate. Members take turns, giving one idea at a time to be written on the flip chart. Duplicate ideas do not need to be recorded, but ideas that are slightly different from those already posted should be listed. Ideas are not discussed during this step. The person recording the group's ideas on the flip chart should summarize and shorten lengthy ideas into a phrase. But first, this person should check with the member who originated the idea to make sure that editorializing did not occur. When a member runs out of ideas, the member simply says "pass," and the facilitator moves on to the next person. When all members have passed, the recording step is over.

In Step 3, group interaction resumes. Taking one idea at a time, group members discuss each idea for clarification. If an idea needs no clarification, then the group moves on to the next one. Rather than asking only the group member who contributed the idea to clarify it, the facilitator should ask if any group member has questions about the idea. By including everyone in the clarification process, group ownership of the idea increases.

In Step 4, group members vote on the ideas they believe are most important. For instance, if your group generates 40 ideas, consider asking group members to vote for their top five. By not narrowing the number of choices too severely or too quickly, group members have a chance to discuss the ideas they most prefer. If time permits, let group members come to the flip charts and select their most important ideas themselves. This helps ensure that members select the ideas that are important to them without the influence of peer pressure.

 ## SKILL BUILDER

Which Procedures Will Help Your Group?

Think of three recent group experiences in which decision making was the focus of your group's activity. Which procedures do you believe might have been most beneficial for each group? Why? Could the groups have benefited from using more than one procedure? How might you have initiated the use of procedures in your groups? Would group members have welcomed this type of procedural assistance or resisted it? What strategy or strategies could you have used to get your groups to adopt decision-making procedures? What communication skills could you have relied on to help the groups adopt these procedures? Which communication skills will you use in your next group meetings to encourage the groups to adopt the procedures?

In Step 5, the group discusses the vote just taken. Suppose that, from the 40 ideas presented, 11 receive two or more votes. Now is the time for group members to further elaborate on each of these ideas. Direct the discussion according to the order of ideas as they appear on the flip chart, rather than starting with the idea that received the most votes. Beginning the discussion in a neutral or randomly selected place encourages discussion on each item, not just on the one that appears most popular at this point in the procedure.

With that discussion complete, Step 6 requires that group members repeat Steps 4 and 5. That is, once again, members vote on the importance of the remaining ideas. With 11 ideas left, you might ask members to select their top three choices. After members vote, the group discusses the three ideas that received the most votes. Now it is time for the final vote. This time, group members select the idea they most favor.

The greatest advantage of NGT is that the independent idea generation steps encourage equal participation of group members regardless of power or status. The views of more silent members are treated the same as the views of dominant members (Van de Ven & Delbecq, 1974). In fact, NGT groups develop more proposals and higher-quality proposals than groups using other procedures (Green, 1975; Kramer et al., 1997). Another advantage of NGT is that its specified structure helps bring a sense of closure and accomplishment to group problem solving (Van de Ven & Delbecq, 1974). When the meeting is finished, members have a firm grasp of what the group decided and a feeling of satisfaction because they helped the group reach that decision.

When is it best to use NGT? Several group situations can be enhanced by the NGT process (Pavitt, 1993). NGT is most helpful when proposal generation is crucial. For example, suppose your softball team needs to find new and creative ways to raise funds. Your team has already tried most of the traditional approaches to raising money, and members' enthusiasm for selling door-to-door is low. NGT can help the team identify alternatives because it encourages participation from all group members without surrendering to the ideas of only the coach or the most vocal players. NGT also can be very helpful for groups that are not very cohesive. When a group's culture is unhealthy and cohesiveness is low but the group's work must be done, NGT can help the group overcome its relationship problems and allow it to continue with its tasks. The minimized interaction in the idea generation phase of NGT gives everyone a chance to participate, increasing the likelihood that members will be satisfied with the group's final choice. Finally, NGT is particularly helpful when the problem facing the group is particularly volatile—for example, when organizational groups have to make difficult decisions about which items or projects to cut

PUTTING THE PIECES TOGETHER

Group Goal and Interdependence

Think about a group decision in which you participated and consensus was the decision-making procedure chosen by the group. To what extent did consensus decision making help the group achieve its goal? How did consensus decision making reflect interdependence among group members? Was consensus the most appropriate decision-making procedure for this group and this decision? In what way did the group's practice of consensus match the description of consensus given in this chapter? Considering what you know now about decision-making procedures, what three pieces of advice would you give to this group about its use of consensus?

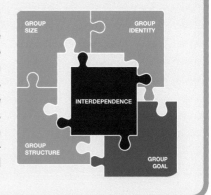

from the budget. The conflict that is likely to occur through more interactive procedures or unstructured processes can be destructive. The structured process of NGT helps group members focus on the task because turn taking is controlled.

With respect to the five critical functions of group decision making, NGT satisfies four. Because interaction is limited, especially in the idea generation phase, group members are not likely to achieve understanding of the problem. The discussion phase of NGT, however, should be effective in helping group members come to understand what constitutes an acceptable resolution to the problem, develop realistic and acceptable alternatives, and assess the positive and negative qualities of alternatives considered.

Consensus

Consensus means that each group member agrees with the decision or that group members' individual positions are close enough that they can support the group's decision (DeStephen & Hirokawa, 1988; Hoffman & Kleinman, 1994). In the latter case, even if members do not totally agree with the decision, they choose to support the group by supporting the decision. Consensus is achieved through discussion. Through members' interactions, alternatives emerge and are tested. In their interaction, group members consult with one another and weigh various alternatives. Eventually, one idea emerges as the decision that group members can support.

To the extent that group members feel they have participated in the decision-making process, they are satisfied with the group's interaction. That satisfaction is then extended to the consensus decision. Thus, when all group members can give verbal support, consensus has been achieved. To develop consensus, a group uses discussion to combine the best insights of all members to find a solution that incorporates all points of view. For example, juries that award damages in lawsuits must make consensus decisions—everyone must agree on the amount of money to be awarded.

Too frequently, consensus building is seen as a freewheeling discussion without any sort of process, plan, or procedure. But there are guidelines a group can use to achieve consensus. This procedure is especially useful for groups that must make highly subjective decisions (e.g., a panel of judges deciding which undergraduate should be selected as the commencement speaker, or the local United Way board of directors deciding how much money will be allocated to community service agencies) (Hare, 1982). Thus, consensus is a procedure that helps a group reach agreement. However, for consensus to work well, group members should discuss what they mean when they use the word *consensus*, as people have different conceptualizations of what consensus means and different feelings about its effectiveness (Renz, 2006).

To develop consensus, the leader or another group member takes on the role of coordinator to facilitate the group's discussion. This coordinator does not express opinions or argue for or against proposals suggested by the group. Rather, the coordinator uses ideas generated by members to formulate proposals acceptable to all members. Another group member can act as a recorder to document each of the proposals. Throughout the discussion, the recorder should read back statements that reflect the initial agreements of the group. This ensures that the agreement is real. When the group feels it has reached consensus, the recorder should read aloud this decision so members can give approval or modify the proposal.

In addition to following these steps, all group members need to be aware of a few basic discussion rules. First, the goal of the group's discussion is to find a solution that incorporates all points of view. Second, group members should not only give their opinions on the issue, but also seek out the opinions of other members. The coordinator should make an extra effort to include less talkative members in the discussion. Third, group members should address their opinions and remarks to the group as a whole, and not to the coordinator. Finally, group members should avoid calling for a vote, which has the effect of stopping discussion.

Consensus can only be reached through interaction. Although each group member should be encouraged to give an opinion, group members should avoid arguing for their personal ideas. It is better to state your ideas and give supporting reasons. Arguing about whose idea is better or whose idea is more correct will not help the group achieve consensus. If other group members express opinions that differ from yours, avoid confrontation and criticism. Rather, ask questions that can help you understand their points of view.

As the group interacts, it can be tempting to change your mind just so the group can reach consensus and move on to other activities. Be careful! Changing your mind only to reach agreement will make you less satisfied with the process and the decision. If the group has trouble reaching consensus, it is better to postpone the decision until another meeting. Pressing for a solution because time is short will not help group members understand and commit to the decision. If a decision is postponed, assigning group members to gather more information can help the next discussion session.

How well does consensus achieve the five critical functions of decision making? As a decision procedure, it is very effective in helping group members achieve an understanding of the problem they are trying to resolve, identify what constitutes an acceptable resolution, and develop a set of realistic and acceptable alternatives. Discussion leading to consensus allows more viewpoints to be discussed, so members are made aware of issues and facts they did not previously know. As a result, group members become more knowledgeable about the problem. Consensus discussions involve everyone, which results in a high degree of integration, as at least part of everyone's point of view is represented in the final decision. Thus, consensus can help achieve the first three critical functions. However, it is less effective in helping groups assess the positive and negative qualities of the alternatives presented.

There are a few disadvantages to using consensus. First, this procedure takes time. When not enough time is allotted, some members may opt out of the discussion process, allowing the group to come to a **false consensus**—agreeing to a decision simply to be done with the task. Thus, the extent to which consensus is effective depends on the voluntary and effective participation of group members. Second, consensus is usually not effective when controversial or complex decisions must be made. A group charged with making a decision that heightens emotional issues for members is likely to make a better decision with a more standardized approach that structures group inquiry. This is why the consensus procedure is not always effective in assessing the positive and negative qualities of the alternatives presented.

Voting

Voting, another decision-making procedure, is simply the process of casting written, verbal, or online ballots in support of or against a specific proposal. Many organizational groups rely on the outcomes of majority voting to elect officers or pass resolutions. A group that votes needs to decide on three procedural issues before a vote is taken.

The first procedural issue centers on the discussion the group should have before members vote. Members do not simply walk into a meeting and vote. Voting should be on clear proposals, and only after substantial group discussion. Here is a suggested procedure to follow in voting (Hare, 1982). Members bring items to the attention of the group by making proposals in the form of motions. Let's say that your communication students' association is making decisions about its budget. Karen says, "I move that we set aside part of our budget for community activities." But subsequent discussion among group members reveals two ambiguities. What does Karen mean by "part of our budget"? Twenty percent? Forty

percent? And what are "community activities"? Do they include teaching junior high students how to give speeches? With other members' help, Karen's proposal is made more specific: "I move that we set aside 20 percent of our budget for community intervention activities that help children appreciate the value of communicating effectively." Now, with a specific motion, Karen can argue for her proposal by stating its merits. Even with a specific proposal, she is going to receive some opposition or face more questions. That is okay because it helps all group members understand her motion more clearly. During this discussion, the group leader makes sure that all those who want to be heard get a chance to talk. However, the leader does not argue for or against any particular motion. To do so would put undue influence on the group. The group's secretary or recorder keeps track of the motions and identifies which ones receive approval from the group.

The second procedural issue is to decide how the vote will be taken. When sensitive issues are being voted on, it is better to use a written ballot. Similar ballots or pieces of paper are given to each group member. Written ballots allow group members to vote their conscience and retain their anonymity. Two group members should count the votes and verify the decision before announcing it to the group.

A verbal vote, or a show of hands, is more efficient when it is necessary only to document the approval or disapproval apparent in the group's discussion. For example, suppose your communication students' association has several items of business to take care of at the next meeting. Specifically, the association needs to elect officers, approve the budget, and select a faculty member for the outstanding professor award. The budget was read to members at the last meeting and then discussed. Although members will ask some questions before the vote, the group basically needs to approve or disapprove the budget. Because there is nothing out of the ordinary about the budget and little contro-versy is expected, it is okay to use a show of hands in this case.

However, electing officers and voting for one professor to receive an award can bring up conflicting emotions among group members. Both of these matters are better handled with written ballots. This ensures that group members can freely support the candidates and the professor they desire without fear of intimidation or retaliation.

The final procedural issue that needs to be agreed on before taking a vote is how many votes are needed to win or decide an issue. Most of the time, a simple majority vote (one more than half of the members) is satisfactory. However, if a group is changing its constitution or taking some type of legal action, a two-thirds or three-fourths majority may be preferable. Both the method of voting and the majority required for a decision need to be agreed upon before any voting takes place.

Voting can be efficient, but it can also arbitrarily limit a group's choices. Many times, motions considered for a vote take on an either/or quality that limits the choice to two alternatives. And a decision made by voting is seen as final—groups seldom revote. This is why having an adequate discussion period before voting is necessary. As you can see, voting is not the best choice when complex decisions must be made.

To summarize, the procedures for voting include the following:

1 Hold discussions to generate a clear proposal.

2 Decide how the vote will be taken—written ballot, verbal vote, or show of hands.

3 Decide how many votes are needed to win or decide an issue.

4 Restate the proposal before voting.

How well a group develops the discussion before voting determines how well the group satisfies the five critical functions of group decision making. Although voting is often perceived as a way of providing a quick decision, inadequate time for group discussion can severely limit the appropriateness or effectiveness of the proposals to be voted on.

Ranking

Ranking is the process of assigning a numerical value to each decision alternative so that group members' preferences are revealed. Groups often use a ranking process when there are many viable alternatives from which to choose, but the group must select the preferred alternative or a set of preferred alternatives. There are two steps to the ranking process.

First, each member individually assigns a numerical value to each decision alternative. In effect, rankings position each alternative from highest to lowest, as well as relative to one another. Usually, 1 is assigned to the most valued choice, 2 to the next most valued choice, and so on. These rankings may be based on a set of criteria developed by the group, for instance, how well the alternative fixes the problem or if the alternative is possible within the time frame allotted the project.

Second, after group members complete their individual rankings, the values for each alternative are summed and totaled. Now the group has a score for each alternative. The alternative with the lowest total is the group's first-ranked alternative. The alternative with the second-lowest score is the group's second-ranked alternative, and so on. This procedure, which helps group members come to agreement, can be done publicly so group members can see or hear the ranking of one another's alternatives, or the process can be done on paper so individual rankings are anonymous.

Just as with voting, the ranking procedure is most effective when the group has adequate time to develop and discuss the alternatives to be ranked. Compared to groups instructed to "choose the best alternative," groups that rank-order their alternatives do a better job, as all alternatives must be discussed for members to perform the ranking task (Hollingshead, 1996). Thus, the extent to which this procedure satisfies the five critical functions of group decision making depends on the quality of the group's discussion.

Although ranking decreases group members' feelings of personal involvement or participation, groups using this procedure report little negativity in decision making. Fewer arguments or conflicts are reported when ranking is used because it is more difficult for one or two individual members to alter a group's decision-making process. All members get to indicate their preference, and all preferences are treated equally. Thus, group members report feeling satisfied with the outcome (Green & Taber, 1980). Group members usually prefer ranking to voting for making a decision when more than two alternatives exist.

Comparing Procedures

Procedures help groups by managing their discussions and decision-making processes. In turn, this enhances the quality of decision making in the group by coordinating members' thinking and communication, providing a set of ground rules all members can and must follow, balancing member participation, managing conflicts, and improving group climate (Jarboe, 1996; Poole, 1991; SunWolf & Seibold, 1999). Most importantly, procedures help groups avoid becoming solution minded too quickly.

But which procedure is best? Sometimes the group leader or facilitator selects a procedure. Other times the group relies on familiarity—selecting the procedure it used last time regardless of its effectiveness. Rather than select a procedure arbitrarily, groups should select a procedure or a combination of procedures that best suits their needs and satisfies the five critical functions of group decision making. Table 5.1 summarizes the ways in which each procedure satisfies the five functions.

Table 5.1 The Ways in Which Various Procedures Satisfy Problem-Solving and Decision-Making Functions

	Understand the Problem	Understand What Constitutes Acceptable Resolution	Develop Realistic and Acceptable Alternatives	Assess the Positive Qualities of Alternatives	Assess the Negative Qualities of Alternatives
Brainstorming	Somewhat	Yes	Yes	No	No
NGT	No	Yes	Yes	Yes	Yes
Consensus	Yes	Yes	Yes	No	No
Voting	Depends on quality of group discussion before voting	Depends on quality of group discussion before voting	Depends on quality of group discussion before voting	Depends on quality of group discussion before voting	Depends on quality of group discussion before voting
Ranking	Depends on quality of group discussion before ranking	Depends on quality of group discussion before ranking	Depends on quality of group discussion before ranking	Depends on quality of group discussion before ranking	Depends on quality of group discussion before ranking

Before you select a procedure, you should analyze the type of task before your group. If the task is easy—for example, the group has all of the necessary information to make effective choices—the type of procedure you select will have less influence on the group's ability to resolve the problem or reach a decision. However, if the group task or decision is difficult—for example, members' decision-making skills vary, the group needs to consult with people outside the group, or the decision has multiple parts—the decision procedure selected will have a greater impact on the group's decision-making abilities. Generally, in these situations, the procedure that encourages vigilant and systematic face-to-face interaction will result in higher-quality outcomes (Hirokawa et al., 1996).

Regardless of which procedure your group selects, all members must agree to use the procedure if any benefits are to be achieved. Also remember that the procedure itself does not ensure that all members will be motivated and willing to participate. Decision procedures cannot replace group cohesiveness.

DECISION-MAKING PRINCIPLES

Regardless of the procedure or process your group uses, four principles seem to fit most group problem-solving and decision-making situations (Hirokawa & Johnston, 1989). First, group decision making is an evolutionary process. The final decision of the group emerges over time as a result of the clarification, modification, and integration of ideas that group members express in their interaction. A student government group may know that it needs to make a decision about how to provide child care for university students, but the final decision results from the group bringing new information to meetings and other group members asking for clarification and developing ideas. Thus, a group will have a general idea about a decision that needs to be made, but not necessarily its specifics.

Relatedly, the second principle is that group decision making is a circular rather than a linear process. Even when they try, it is difficult for group members to follow a step-by-step approach to group decision making. Group decision making is circular because group members seldom bring all the needed information into the group's discussion at the same time. For example, let's say that your group decides to hold a fundraiser on May 3, close to the end of the spring semester. In discussion, your group needs to make this decision first to secure a date on your university's student activities calendar. Now that the date is settled, your group can concentrate on what type of fundraiser might be best. But you have to take into consideration that it is late in the semester. Not only will students have limited time because of term papers and final exams, but their funds likely will be depleted. That information will affect the type of fundraiser you will plan. But wait! At that point in the semester, students really enjoy having coffee and doughnuts available in the early morning, after all-night study sessions. And your group can sell lots of coffee and doughnuts to many students for very little money. As you can see, this example shows how ideas and questions do not simply emerge in a linear fashion. Instead interaction evolves in its own way, and group decisions will continually adjust for these changes.

The third principle is that many different types of influence affect a group's decision making. Group members' moods, motivations, competencies, and communication skills are individual-level variables that affect the group's final decision. These are individual-level variables because each member brings a unique set of influences to the group. The dynamics of the interpersonal relationships that result in group member cohesiveness and satisfaction also affect a group's decision making. Finally, the communication structure or network developed in the group impacts information flows among group members. The quality of information exchanged by group members affects a group's decision outcomes.

Additionally, forces outside a group can influence decision making. An example of this type of external influence is the generally accepted societal rule about making decisions quickly and cost-effectively.

The fourth principle of group decision making is that decisions are made within a system of external and internal constraints. Few groups have as much freedom of choice as they would like. Groups are constrained by external forces, such as deadlines or budgets imposed by outsiders and the preferences of the people who will evaluate or use the group's decision. Internal constraints are the values, morals, and ethics that individual members bring to the group setting. These values guide what the group does and how it does it.

These four principles reveal that decision making may be part of a larger problem-solving process. Problem solving is the communication group members engage in when there is a need to address an unsatisfactory situation or overcome some obstacle. Decision making and problem solving are often used interchangeably, but they are different. Decision making involves a choice between alternatives; problem solving represents the group's attempts to analyze a problem in detail so that effective decisions can be made (SunWolf & Seibold, 1999). Hence, this problem: Groups often make decisions without engaging in the analysis associated with problem solving. For anything but the simplest matters, groups are more likely to make faulty decisions when they do not take advantage of the problem-solving process to address contextual details.

Research has demonstrated that groups using formal discussion procedures generally develop higher member satisfaction and greater commitment to the decision. Yet many groups try to avoid using procedures. This is because discussion and decision-making procedures take time, and groups must plan their meetings accordingly. Group members often are reluctant to use procedures because they are unaccustomed to using them or initially find them too restrictive. It is often difficult for groups to stick with a procedure once it has been initiated.

Procedures help group members resist sloppy thinking and ineffective group habits (Poole, 1991). When procedures seem unnatural, it is often because group members have had little practice with them. When all group members know the procedure, it keeps the leader from assuming too much power and swaying the decision process. In addition, procedures help coordinate members' thinking and interaction, making it less likely that a group will go off topic. As member participation becomes more balanced, more voices are heard, and more ideas are deliberated.

SUMMARY

Decision making is a primary activity of many groups. To a large extent, our society depends on groups to make decisions—decisions that affect governmental and organizational policies, long-term policies, and day-to-day activities. Family and other social groups also make decisions. Across the variety of group decision-making situations, group members need task, relational, and procedural skills. Generally, groups are better decision makers than individuals when the problem is complex, when the problem requires input from diverse perspectives, and when people need to identify with and commit to the decision.

Functional theory of group decision making advocates five functions as necessary for effective decision making: understanding the problem, understanding what constitutes an acceptable choice, generating realistic and acceptable alternatives, assessing the positive qualities of each alternative, and assessing the negative qualities of each alternative. Groups whose communication fulfills all five functions are more effective in their decision making because information has been pooled and evaluated.

Decision-making procedures can help groups stay on track, equalize participation among members, and balance emotional and social aspects with task issues. Groups can choose from a variety of decision-making or discussion procedures. Brainstorming is an idea generation procedure that can help groups be creative in thinking of alternatives. The nominal group technique also assists the idea generation process, although it controls the timing of communication among group members. Consensus is a technique with wide application in group decision making. In this procedure, one group member helps facilitate the discussion and makes sure that all members have the opportunity to express their points of view. Voting is a popular procedure when groups must make their final selection from a set of alternatives. Like ranking, voting allows each member to equally affect the outcome.

Each procedure can help groups be more effective, but some procedures are better suited to different aspects of the decision-making process. Groups can compare procedures for their ability to satisfy the five critical functions according to functional theory.

Regardless of the procedures or process your group uses, four principles seem to fit most group problem-solving and decision-making situations. Acknowledging that group decision making is evolutionary and circular, and that there are multiple influences on decisions made within a larger context of constraints, allows us to embrace rather than fight the process. No one person or procedure will make group decision making effective. It is the appropriate selection and combination of people, talents, procedures, and structures that strengthens group decision making. By monitoring your own performance and the performance of the group as a whole, you will be able to select the most appropriate decision-making or discussion procedures.

DISCUSSION QUESTIONS AND EXERCISES

1 For one week, keep a diary or journal of all the group decisions in which you participate. Identify who in the group is making the decisions, what the decisions are about, how long the group spends on decision making, and what strengths or weaknesses exist in the decision-making process. Come to class ready to discuss your experiences and to identify procedures that could have helped your group be more effective.

2 Using the data from your diary or journal (from the first item), write a paper that analyzes your role in the problem-solving and decision-making procedures your group uses and the ways in which your communication skills in that role influence your group's decision-making effectiveness.

3 Select someone you know who works full time in a profession you aspire to, and ask this person to participate in an interview about group or team decision making at work. Before the interview, develop a list of questions to guide the interview. You might include questions like these: How many decision-making groups or teams are you a part of? What is your role and what are your responsibilities in those groups and teams? How would you assess the effectiveness of your decision making? Is there something unusual (good or bad) that helps or hinders your groups' decision-making abilities? If you could change one thing about how your groups make decisions, what would it be?

4 Reflect on situations in which your family or group of friends made decisions. Using the five key components of a group—group size, interdependence of members, group identity, group goal, and group structure—describe how this social group was similar to or different from a work group or sports group to which you belonged. Selecting one decision event from both types of groups, compare the decision process in which the groups engaged. What task, relational, and procedural skills did you use to help the groups with their decision making? Which of these skills do you wish you would have used? Why?

 NAILING IT!

Using Group Communication Skills for Group Presentations

When deciding on how to present a group project, it will be important to incorporate everyone's input. There are many aspects of a group project that should be decided upon (e.g., who should present, should PowerPoint® be used, how do we grab the audience's attention). With all of these options to consider, what is the best approach for choosing a presentation format?

With help from Table 5.1, analyze which decision-making procedure would be most helpful when determining the format for your group's presentation. What is your rationale for making the selection? Is it possible that all procedures could be helpful?

Image Credits

CHAPTER 6

BUILDING RELATIONSHIPS IN GROUPS

After reading this chapter, you should be able to:

- Contribute to developing a supportive group communication climate

- Assist your group in developing cohesiveness

- Maximize your satisfaction in a group and help create satisfaction for other group members

- Maintain the trust of group members

- Socialize new members into a group

A group is a social context in which people come together to perform some task or activity. Just as group members work interdependently on a task or goal, they also create interdependent relationships. This chapter will explore the communication relationships among group members that help to form a group's communication climate and the degree to which communication contributes to cohesiveness and satisfaction among group members. The strength and resiliency of group member relationships is a critical factor in the equity and trust group members perceive in the group. Thus, how you build and maintain relationships with other group members will influence whether and how well the group completes its task.

GROUP COMMUNICATION CLIMATE

A group's **communication climate**, or the social atmosphere group members create, results from group members' use of verbal and nonverbal communication and their listening skills. Another way to think about group communication climate is to ask yourself: How do you feel about being a group member? Are you glad you are a member of this group or team? Do other group members communicate with you in a friendly manner? Assessing your group's communication climate will help you present your ideas and opinions in ways that make them more likely to be accepted. By paying attention to your presentation strategies, you are also likely to strengthen your relationships with others in the group and avoid unnecessary confrontation. Thus, a group's communication climate is the tone, mood, or character of the group that develops from the way group members interact and listen to one another.

PUTTING THE PIECES TOGETHER

Group Identity and Group Structure

A group's communication climate is a critical factor in how members identify with and structure their group. Of the six supportive communication climate dimensions—description, problem orientation, spontaneity, empathy, equality, and provisionalism—which of these is most important to developing group identity? Which of these are more important to how norms, roles, and communication networks develop in the group? How have the dimensions you identified been instrumental to the development of your relationships with other members in your groups?

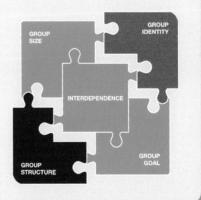

Early research on groups (Gibb, 1961) demonstrated that climates in groups range on a continuum from defensive to supportive. Not many of us would want to be in a group that has a **defensive climate**—a climate based on negative or threatening group interaction that discourages other members from communicating. Rather, a **supportive climate**, or a positive or encouraging environment, is more effective. But, not all groups and teams need the same level of supportiveness. For instance, counseling or support groups need a more supportive climate since they often include members who need encouragement to participate. An arbitration or legal group may not need as supportive of an environment, as lawyers are trained to stand up for their clients even if others disagree. All groups require a supportive climate, but groups do vary in the degree of supportiveness needed.

A group's supportive or positive communication climate is built on group members' use of six different types, or categories, of communication behavior: description, problem orientation, spontaneity, empathy, equality, and provisionalism.

Description

To arrive at a good idea, it is typical for group members to suggest many options for consideration. Not every idea is great, and when a group member suggests an idea that is considered less than ideal by other members, there is a tendency to evaluate the person rather than the idea. A more positive approach is to use **description**. Describing what is wrong with an idea gives the group member who introduced it the opportunity to clarify its presentation or to amend the idea for consideration by the group. Describing the idea may also encourage other group members to join in and help transform a poor idea into a better one. Thus, description is almost always preferable to evaluation because group members benefit when they know why an idea is rejected. **Evaluation**, or using language that criticizes others and their ideas, simply humiliates the person who offered the idea, and is likely to result in a defensive relationship and a defensive group climate.

Problem Orientation

To make the most of group situations, members need to exhibit the spirit of group participation and democracy. Taking a **problem orientation** approach, group members strive for answers and solutions that will benefit all group members and satisfy the group's objective. The opposite of problem orientation is **controlling behavior**. A group member using controlling behavior assumes there is a predetermined solution to be found. Alternately, asking honest questions like "Is the budget we're working with $250,000?" is a method for seeking collaboration on solving the problem. When group members adopt this attitude and it is reflected in their interactions, it is easier for them to cooperate with one another, and, as a result, develop group cohesion while completing their task.

Spontaneity

Group members who act with **spontaneity** are open and honest with other group members. These group members are known for their immediacy in the group and willingness to deal with issues as they come up. If a member is sincere and straightforward with others, the group members are likely to reciprocate that honesty and openness, which creates a more supportive communication climate for completing the group's task or activity. When a group member fakes sincerity or tries to hide motivations that could be hurtful to the group, the member is likely to be accused of being **strategic** or manipulative.

Empathy

We have all had bad days and not performed at our best in group situations. In a supportive group climate, other group members express empathy for our situation because we have expressed empathy for them. **Empathy** does not mean that other group members are excused from doing their assigned tasks; rather, it means that group members express genuine concern and are helpful if their help is requested. Empathic communication conveys members' respect for and reassurance of the receiver. Nonverbal behaviors are especially good at conveying empathy. For example, a smile, a kind gesture, and respect for someone's privacy are ways group members can express empathy for one another. However, when a group member reacts in a detached or unemotional way, the member is demonstrating **neutrality**. When group members react with a lack of warmth, other members often feel as if they are not important.

Equality

Groups are more likely to create supportive communication climates when **equality** is stressed. This does not mean that everyone does the same thing. Instead, it is important for group members to perform equitable work and to treat each other accordingly. Remember that trust and respect are earned and given incrementally. It is every group member's responsibility to work for trust and respect, and to give trust and respect when these are due. And because each group member must establish a relationship of trust with each other group member, creating a sense of trust within the group is a long-term, complex process. Using a respectful, polite tone and using the same kind of language to talk to different members will help in establishing equality. If members try to reinforce their **superiority**, or the belief that they are better than other group members, equality can be quickly diminished.

Provisionalism

To act with **provisionalism** is to be flexible. Rather than taking sides, provisional group members want to hear all ideas so they can make better, more informed choices. Provisionalism encourages group members to experiment with and explore ideas in the group. This creates an opportunity for group members to ask more questions, which can diffuse the dominance of one or two group members. Alternately, group members who believe they have all the answers or who *know* what another group member is going to say or do are communicating **certainty**. For instance, certainty is revealed by a group member who cuts off the attempts of other members to provide more information on a certain alternative.

Why does creating a positive or supportive group communication climate matter? First, when a group has a more positive or constructive communication climate, group members are more willing to seek and share information, which in turn creates members' commitment to the group (van den Hooff & de Ridder, 2004). A positive group communication climate is, simply, more open, which encourages group members to be more creative in working on their tasks or goals (Shin, 2014). It's not surprising then that a supportive communication climate is positively related to a group's performance (Liu, Hartel, & Sun, 2014).

Changing Group Climate

How can you help your group develop a more supportive climate? The important first step is to monitor your behavior and adopt more positive behaviors based on the six previously mentioned categories. The behaviors that create a supportive communication climate require you to assess the group situation, think about what you want to say, and evaluate your statements for their potential impact on other group members. Of course, you must follow through. Good intentions alone do not lead to a supportive communication climate. Use description rather than evaluation to assess the input of others. Create opportunities for all group members to participate. Be open and honest, but tactful. Express empathy for others in the group. Create a sense of equality through equitable assignments and responsibilities. Finally, be flexible and open. If you adopt some of these supportive interaction strategies, you will strengthen your relationships in groups and help your groups achieve more effective outcomes.

A second way to help your group develop a more supportive climate is to monitor your reaction to the interaction of other group members and respond to them in a more productive fashion. For example, an effective way to neutralize superiority is to respond with equality. It is every group member's responsibility to break destructive cycles in group interaction, and the development and maintenance of a defensive group climate is one such destructive cycle. Communication climate is changeable, but first group members must recognize what communication habits have been established and which ones should be changed. By using supportive communication, group members can create a more positive climate. When defensive strategies are present in a group, tolerating those behaviors can indirectly reinforce their use.

GROUP COHESIVENESS

Cohesiveness is the degree to which members desire to remain in the group. When the desire to be a group member is strong across all members, they are more likely to demonstrate cohesion and be committed to the group's task (Whitton & Fletcher, 2014). But cohesiveness is an elusive concept. Most people can sense when it exists within a group. But cohesion can manifest differently depending on the group or team context.

 ## MESSAGE AND MEANING

A nonprofit organization, FreeInternetForAll.net, was having their weekly team meeting. At the end of the meeting, Fred, the team leader, went around the room as he often did, asking everyone for a quick update on their work.

FRED: Alright. Joel, where are you at?

JOEL: Let's see. What did I do this week? Well, the big thing I did this week and that no one noticed, and, well, that's fine, I'll just deal with it, but ...

CHRISTY: Hey, if you do your job right, we shouldn't notice, right?

JOEL: Exactly, exactly. [laughter]

FRED: Yeah, if he's doing his job right, we shouldn't notice [laughter].

JOEL: That's right, not a big deal. But this week I created ...

Following this exchange, Joel proceeded to give the details on his accomplishment during the week. However, no one had previously seemed to notice that Joel had done something of significance during the week, and he decided to use a joke to inform the group. Do you think that Joel wanted others to recognize his work from last week? Was his use of joking and laughter a way of receiving recognition, or was it simply a funny way of giving his work report? Group members may have to think of creative ways to receive recognition for one's efforts, because by simply announcing a good deed the group member may come off as arrogant. However, the other group members communicatively interpreted it as a joke. Do you think they recognized that Joel wanted people to notice his work? The use of joking and laughter can be a tricky type of relational communication (Keyton & Beck, 2010).

There are three general ways that cohesiveness develops (Carron & Brawley, 2000). Some types of group are based on belonging. Family and friendship groups are good examples. Likewise, sorority and fraternity groups also display high cohesion because membership is controlled or invited. The sense of belonging that is driven by the feeling or desire to be a member creates cohesion. Second, cohesion can develop when groups are completing highly interdependent work that requires coordination. Volunteer groups building houses for Habitat for Humanity are a good example of this, as are work groups that meet regularly to finish complex projects on a tight deadline and within a tight budget. It takes everyone's skills and expertise to finish these tasks successfully. Third, cohesiveness can develop when individuals are attracted to a group. For example, individuals are drawn to community action groups or groups that espouse certain values or beliefs. Members are attracted because being a member of this group provides an opportunity to interact with others who share their beliefs and values.

Thus, group cohesion is a complex, multidimensional construct. Cohesion in one group may not look or feel like cohesion in other groups. As Pescosolido and Saavedra (2012) describe, "members of a hockey team may develop greater understanding of shared strategies and tactics over a season, members of a group therapy session may develop feelings of acceptance and a sense of belonging, and members of a business unit may develop a sense of shared responsibility and success" (p. 753). Thus, we distinguish between social cohesion, which is based on the quality of relationships among group members, and task cohesion, which is based on commitment to the group's task (Hackman, 1992).

Importantly, balancing social and task cohesion may be tricky in certain types of groups. Although online groups are commonplace, it may be more difficult to create social cohesion by communicating online. This is not to say that it can't happen, but it may require extra effort or longer periods of time to develop. Intentional efforts to communicate relationally (which may be more natural in face-to-face groups) may be required, such as an online session specifically devoted to getting to know one another or communicating via social media (e.g., tweeting with one another; becoming a Facebook friend). Online platforms may be better geared toward social (Facebook) or task (Google Drive) purposes, and combined, these platforms may improve both types of cohesion.

How group members communicate with one another is a good indicator as to whether cohesion exists. For example, when group members use the same or similar types of words at the same rate, especially words that provide structure for conversation, cohesiveness among members is higher. Prepositions (e.g., at, for, into), conjunctions (e.g., and, but, or), and pronouns (e.g., we, us) help speakers organize and present their thoughts in ways that generalize across content, context, or channel of communicating. Why is this the case? Communication requires coordination, and one measure of coordination is the degree to which group members use the same or similar words. In essence, when group members like one another they tend to use the same rates of prepositions, conjunctions, and articles. When a group member mimics the style of speaking of other group members, cohesiveness tends to be higher (Gonzales, Hancock, & Pennebaker, 2010).

One group member cannot build cohesiveness alone, but one member's actions can destroy the cohesiveness of the group. Although we say that the group is cohesive, cohesiveness actually results from the psychological closeness individual group members feel toward the group. Cohesiveness can be built around interpersonal attraction to other members, attraction to the task, coordination of effort, and member motivation to work on behalf of the group (Golembiewski, 1962). That is, when group members believe that their task and relational needs are being fulfilled, they perceive the group as cohesive (Carron et al., 2004).

Sometimes people refer to cohesiveness as the glue that keeps the group together; others describe cohesiveness as the morale of the group. In either case, cohesiveness serves to keep group members together because of their attraction to the group. There are three specific advantages to building and maintaining a cohesive group. First, members feel that they are a part of the group. Second, cohesiveness acts as a bonding agent for group members. Members of cohesive groups are more likely to stick with the group throughout the duration of its task (Spink & Carron, 1994). This, in turn, creates more opportunities for norms to be developed and followed (Shaw, 1981). Third, cohesive groups develop a "we" climate, not an "I" climate. In fact, one way to know if group members are close is whether they start using plural pronouns like "we" and "us."

Cohesiveness and Group Performance

Research has reportedly demonstrated that communication is the central binding force of team and group activities (Weick, 1969). When group and team members use cooperative communication practices, such as information exchange, opinion sharing, and agreement seeking, group cohesion is strongest (Bakar & Sheer, 2013). Simply stated: The more cohesive the group, the more likely the group is to perform effectively (Cohen & Bailey, 1997). This relationship between cohesiveness and performance is often reciprocal (Greene, 1989). When an ongoing group performs well, it is also likely that its members will generate additional cohesive feelings for one another or at least maintain the current level of cohesiveness in the group. Cohesiveness in a group can also affect individual group member performance. Members of groups with high task cohesiveness put more energy into working with and for the group (Prapavessis & Carron, 1997). In other words, individual members have greater adherence to the team task when the group's task is attractive to them. Thus, group members are successful because they have helped the group become successful.

However, the relationship between cohesiveness and performance is not a straightforward one. The degree of interdependence needed to perform a group's task affects the cohesiveness-performance relationship (Gully, Devine, & Whitney, 1995). When a group task requires coordination, high levels of interaction, and joint performances from group members, the cohesiveness-performance relationship is stronger. But when task interdependence is low, the cohesiveness-performance relationship is much weaker. An emergency response team of firefighters and medical personnel is an example of a group that requires a high degree of interdependence to successfully complete its task. The coordination and communication efforts during a rescue are very high. Thus, the more cohesive the group, the more effective the team will be in its tasks, because high cohesiveness also motivates individual group members to perform well.

Alternately, tasks with low interdependence provide less opportunity for members to communicate and to coordinate their actions. Even if cohesiveness develops, there is

less opportunity for it to be demonstrated and for it to affect group performance. A sales team is a good example of how low interdependence and low cohesiveness-performance interact. The salesperson approaches a client while the service manager makes the follow-up call. Back at the office, two administrative assistants talk the new client through the initial steps of filing forms and preparing documents. Once the goods have been delivered, the salesperson steps back in to say hello. This task has low interdependence because the steps of the task are not done simultaneously and because team members are responsible for unique tasks. Thus, cohesiveness is likely to be low in these situations.

What benefits can cohesive groups expect? Members of cohesive groups are less likely to leave to join other groups. For groups with long-term goals, this can be an especially important benefit because the group does not have to spend time finding, attracting, and integrating new members. More cohesive groups also exert greater influence over their members. Thus, norms are less likely to be violated because cohesiveness exists. In addition, this level of influence encourages group members to more readily accept group goals and tasks. Generally, there is greater equality in participation in cohesive groups because members want to express their identity and solidarity with the group (Cartwright, 1968).

Can a group ever be too cohesive? Yes. Some groups can develop such a high level of social cohesiveness that new problems appear. For example, giving constructive criticism to one another becomes difficult when social cohesion is high. Other problems associated with high social cohesion are: (a) the group's focus on socializing overshadows their work on their task or goal, (b) group members feeling isolated because they feel left out of a social clique that is developing in the group, and (c) a general reduction in commitment to the group's task.

When a group develops very high levels of task cohesion, other problems develop. These include: (a) working on the task overshadows the development of group member relationships; (b) communication among group members can be taken the wrong way, as social relationships are not well developed; (c) focusing on the goal or tasks diminishes enjoyment normally associated with it; (d) the development of perceptions that some members are overly serious about the task, and (e) group members feeling too much pressure about their performance and the group's goal achievement (Hardy, Eys, & Carron, 2005).

What group members consider to be the optimum level of cohesiveness will vary depending on the group's task or activity and the type of attraction group members hold for the group. When cohesiveness is based on interpersonal attraction, groups are more susceptible to **groupthink**, a condition that occurs when group members' desires for harmony and conformity results in dysfunctional and ineffective decision making. When cohesiveness is based on task attraction, groups are less susceptible to these deficiencies (Mullen, Anthony, Salas, & Driskell, 1994). When your group has strong interpersonal relationships and cohesiveness is high, the group leader or facilitator may want to take extra precautions to prevent groupthink from developing.

GROUP MEMBER SATISFACTION

Closely related to cohesiveness is satisfaction with the group. **Satisfaction** is the degree to which you feel fulfilled or gratified as a group member; it is an attitude you express based on your experiences in the group. When your satisfaction is high, you are likely to feel content with the group situation. As an individual group member, you perceive some things about the group as satisfying (such as being assigned to the role you requested), but you may also perceive some group elements as dissatisfying (for instance, having to meet too frequently).

The types of things that satisfy individuals in group settings are quite different from those that cause dissatisfaction (Keyton, 1991). As long as the group is moving along its expected path, group members are likely to be satisfied. This occurs, for example, when group members feel free to participate in the group, when they feel that their time is well spent, and when their group interaction is comfortable and effective. Alternatively, dissatisfaction develops when group members spend too much time on activities that do not contribute to task completion, when the group lacks organization, and when members display little patience. Thus, dissatisfaction is more likely to result from negative

THEORY STANDOUT

Satisfaction and Dissatisfaction

The word *satisfaction* is frequently used as group members' evaluation of what is happening in their group or team. But satisfaction is more complicated than that. According to Keyton (1991), satisfaction is a global factor, as well as situationally bound. When a group is moving along as expected, satisfaction is a positive and global affect evaluation. When a group is not moving along very well, then group members start to anchor on specific negative things that dissatisfy them. Thus, what dissatisfies us in a group or team is not simply the opposite of what satisfies us. Take a look at these statements and see if you agree. For example, Keyton suggests that group member participation is expected. Therefore, participation does not help in developing satisfaction. But, when members do not participate, dissatisfaction occurs.

Global Satisfiers

1. Everyone seems genuinely interested in getting something accomplished.
2. Group members can provide constructive criticism to others.
3. Group members interact well with one another.

Global Dissatisfiers

4. Not everyone in my group is participating.
5. It is difficult for my group to come to a decision.
6. My group gets sidetracked by distractions.

Situational Satisfiers

7. There is diversity of ideas among my group members.
8. The individual personalities of the group members do not clash.

Situational Dissatisfiers

9. My group has too many people making the decisions.
10. Interaction roles have not been established.
11. My group can come to an agreement, but getting there is frustrating.

Think of two very different groups and evaluate each group on the 11 items above. Do you see evidence that some things satisfy or dissatisfy you regardless of the group? Do you see evidence that what satisfies and dissatisfies you in one group does not in the other?

assessments you make about the group as a whole (such as the perception that the group is in chaos) than from an evaluation of your individual interaction opportunities.

As with cohesiveness, your satisfaction with the group is partially based on communication behaviors, task elements, or a combination of both (Witteman, 1991). The use of verbal immediacy behaviors by group members results in higher group member satisfaction (Turman, 2008). Examples of verbal immediacy behaviors include: asking questions that invite other group members to give their opinion, encouraging others to respond, using other members' first names, and engaging in interpersonal interaction before and after the group meets. With respect to group tasks, when you are satisfied with the activity of the group, you try harder to communicate more effectively. As a result, you are satisfied with communication within the group.

How a group handles its conflict also affects member satisfaction. Members of groups that identify viable solutions to conflict have greater satisfaction than members of groups that avoid conflict. Thus, even groups that experience conflict can have a satisfying group experience, especially when group members use these behaviors to: (a) make direct statements about the conflict rather than try to avoid it, (b) work to find a solution by integrating the ideas of all group members, and (c) demonstrate flexibility, which demonstrates goodwill toward other group members. Note that it is how group members handle conflict that influences group member satisfaction, not its absence. Finally, group members who are satisfied are more likely to attribute credit to other team members rather than to themselves (Behfar, Friedman, & Oh, 2016).

Improving Cohesiveness and Satisfaction

Building cohesiveness and satisfaction in a group cannot be accomplished alone. But there are some tactics you can undertake as an individual to help the process along. For example, you can adapt and monitor your communication so that your interaction encourages positive climate building in the group. Your interaction should be more supportive than defensive. You can encourage your group to celebrate its successes; this creates a history and tradition for the group. But do not wait until the project is over; each time the group accomplishes some part of the task, recognize the achievement. If you facilitate or lead the group, adopt a reward system that encourages all members, and not just a few, to participate. Basing rewards on group output rather than individual output builds cohesiveness. To make this work, however, group goals must truly be group goals. Additionally, group members should have input in developing goals. Each time the group gets together, group members should be aware of how their communication and activities contribute to the pursuit of these goals.

There are three cautions in developing closeness in groups. First, groups that are not cohesive and in which members are not satisfied are unlikely to produce positive outcomes. But high levels of cohesiveness and satisfaction among group members do not always lead to acceptable output (McGrath, 1984). Cohesiveness in a group can be so high that members overlook tasks in favor of having fun. Cohesiveness can also insulate a group, making it less able to fully explore its task or options. Instead of making a group more vigilant, overly high cohesiveness among group members can make the group susceptible to faulty thinking. With respect to satisfaction, group members may be satisfied because they like one another and as a result become focused on the relational aspects of the group while minimizing their attention to tasks.

Many people want to believe that cohesiveness and satisfaction are so tightly related that, as one increases, so must the other. This is the second caution. If group members become overly cohesive, they may start to reject or ignore their task. For instance, if you are attracted to a genealogy group because you want to learn more about how to research your family's history, you will probably not be very satisfied if the group regularly focuses its conversations on other topics. Although the cohesiveness of the group might enhance the discussion of any topic, your satisfaction with the group may actually decrease because you are not accomplishing your goal.

The third caution involves group size. When a group becomes too large, creating greater complexity than can be handled by the communication structure of the group, there are fewer interaction opportunities among group members. This diminishes cohesiveness and satisfaction. Both cohesiveness and satisfaction develop from the opportunity for members to interact on a regular basis. Moreover, developing cohesion and satisfaction is worth the effort. When group members are comfortable enough with one another, they perceive each other as friendly peers and colleagues, and, as a result, disclose more personal information with one another. In turn, these group members experience greater cohesion and satisfaction. As importantly, they are more favorable toward the group and learn more as they work on their task (Myers et al., 2010).

TRUST

You have probably heard that trust is earned, that trust is not automatic or given freely to others. **Trust** is a group member's positive expectation of another group member, or a group member's willingness to rely on another's actions in a risky situation (Lewicki, McAllister, & Bies, 1998). In other words, when we trust someone, we expect that they will be helpful, or at least not harmful. Thus, trust resides in one group member's relationship with another group member, is based on previous experience with one another, and develops over time as relationships unfold and confidence builds. When you trust another group member, it helps you predict how this group member will behave or react.

Trust can develop early in a group's interaction, especially when group members have some history or familiarity with one another. At that point, however, trust is not very complex. As group members interact more, two other types of trust emerge: affective trust and cognitive trust (Webber, 2008). **Affective trust** is based on the interpersonal concern group members show for one another outside of the group task. This type of trust is enduring and significantly influences how interpersonal relationships among group members develop. Not surprisingly, affective trust is demonstrated through group members' commitment and communication to and with one another. Alternatively, **cognitive trust** is based on group members' assessments about the reliability, dependability, and competence of other group members while they are working on the task. Interestingly, cognitive trust only develops if group members develop a significant level of early trust and group members demonstrate reliability in their task performances for the group.

As you can see, trust is not easy to establish. Moreover, as a group member, trust is established with each group member, which is why establishing trust in group settings takes such a long time. Trust is also extended slowly and incrementally. For example, if Russ trusts Sonya a little, this will often lead Sonya to trust Russ a little in return. If Russ begins to feel comfortable with how his relationship with Sonya is developing (and Sonya is not explicitly communicating anything to the contrary), then Russ may extend a deeper level of trust to Sonya. Extending trust is risky, which is why we are unwilling to give full trust to new people in new settings. An individual's level of trust for all group members will collectively determine how the individual feels about the group as a whole.

 SKILL BUILDER

How Fragile Is Trust?

Reflect on one of your current group experiences. What is the level of trust in that group? Specifically recall behaviors you have used to help develop or maintain trust within the group. Have you done enough to reinforce trust among group members? What else could you do to strengthen the level of trust among group members? Consider the following: Do you always follow through on commitments you make to the group? Have you ever broken a confidence inside or outside the group? Do you ever withhold information from other members? Have you ever indicated that you would do one thing for the group and then did something else? Identify what you would do and communicate to sustain or enhance trust among group members. What communication skills are most central to sustaining and maintaining trust?

Trust is also multifaceted, based on honesty, openness, consistency, and respect (Larson & LaFasto, 1989). As you might suspect, it is difficult to trust a group member who is not honest. It is also difficult to trust a group member who is not open. Sharing part of yourself with the group by revealing personal or professional information helps others to get to know you. Not only must you share with others, you must also be receptive to receiving personal and professional information about other group members. Openness cannot be one-sided. Being consistent in your group's interactions helps others understand you as well. When you are inconsistent in your interactions with other group members, they could become hesitant around you because they are never quite sure how you will react.

Finally, trust is based upon respect. It is hard to trust someone who does not respect others or who acts or communicates in ways that do not deserve respect. In a group, our behaviors and interactions are always being evaluated by other group members. If you tell offensive jokes about someone when that person is not present, other group members might assume that you tell jokes about them when they are not around too.

How can you build trust in groups? First, be aware of your communication style in the group and work to minimize your apprehensiveness. This will increase your ability to develop positive interactions with others. Second, use the supportive climate interaction

characteristics discussed earlier. If you interact in a defensive manner, it is unlikely that others will extend trust to you. Third, use appropriate self-disclosure. We have all met people who tell us more than we want to know about them in our initial meeting with them. Extend only the personal and professional information about yourself that you believe will be perceived by others as positive contributions to the group. As group members warm up to one another, self-disclosure often becomes more personal. Remember, however, that in decision-making and other task groups, revealing too much personal information may be considered unprofessional. Moreover, personal information can be used against you—once you reveal it, you lose power over the information. Fourth, focus on developing a positive and collaborative climate with *all* group members. For instance, Devon may resist extending his trust to you because you treat Maggie more favorably than other group members. Finally, monitor your interaction behavior to ensure that you are not overusing defensive behaviors or behaving in such a way that other members label you as dysfunctional. Trust is seldom extended to group members who are perceived negatively. "Skill Builder Feature: How Fragile Is Trust?" explores the effect of lack of trust on group interaction. These recommendations will help you build affective trust with your team members. But it is not enough. You must also build cognitive trust by performing well and completing the tasks you agreed to in order to help the group be successful.

Socializing New Members Into Groups

Socialization is the process that new and existing group members go through when a new member joins a group. New members want to both fit in and to adapt to the group and its goal. New members also need feedback from other group members so they can reduce the uncertainties that being new in a group brings (Riddle, Anderson, & Martin, 2000). Even if the new members are joining a group for which they have task familiarity, they must be introduced to the other group members and become comfortable with their role in this particular group (Kramer, 2011).

Sometimes membership changes are temporary, as when a factory worker takes a 2-week vacation and is replaced by a utility person who floats among team assignments. At other times, membership changes are permanent. Members may leave the group for a variety of reasons (e.g., quitting, retiring, transferring), or they may simply grow tired of the group and drop out. Each of these membership changes is member initiated.

Membership change in groups can be critical because a change in the composition of the group also changes the cluster of knowledge, skills, and abilities within the group (McGrath, Berdahl, & Arrow, 1995) as well as the relationships among group members. Let's explore some of the issues surrounding membership change to assess its impact on groups (Arrow & McGrath, 1993). First, when membership change increases or decreases the number of members in the group, other aspects of the group—group roles, norms, and communication networks—must change as well.

For example, Kara's honors study group meets with its honors advisor to work on a research project. For over a year, the group—the professor and four students—has met in the professor's office. After much discussion about whether to add other students, the group decides that adding one more student will help lighten the workload of running the experiments. Unfortunately, the group does not think about how an additional group member will affect the group's meetings. The professor's office is crowded with stacks of books and computer printouts. There is a couch that can seat only three people, as well as a visitor's chair and the professor's chair. When the group with its new member meet for the first time, someone has to sit on the arm of the couch. This seating arrangement creates awkward dynamics among group members and impedes the group's ability to work together coding data. Certainly, the group could move to a new meeting location, but that would cause another disruption in the group. Although adding a member seems to be a gain for the group because it will lighten the workload, it also creates an unexpected negative consequence.

Second, it is important to know why there is a change in group membership. Group members react differently to situations in which membership change is member initiated, and not controlled by someone outside the group. You are more likely to accept a new member who persuades you to let her join than a member who joins because your supervisor says she must. Sometimes groups actually recruit new members because they need skills that group members lack. Does a group ever purposely change members? Yes. Sometimes a group member creates a logjam, making it difficult for the group to accomplish anything (Cohen, 1990). Groups can get stuck when strong, self-oriented individuals are in the leadership role, and groups can fail to meet their potential if there is a weak link. Changes to replace ineffective members are made deliberately to help the group out of its entrenched patterns. We expect professional sports teams to use this strategy, and we should want our groups to do the same.

The timing of a change in group membership is also important. Most of you expect that your membership in classroom groups will remain stable throughout the term or the course. What will happen to your group and how will you respond if 3 weeks after your group forms, your instructor adds a student to your group? Making changes after your group has formed and while members are developing a group identity and structure will likely be disruptive.

The frequency with which groups change membership influences the group's ability to chart a course for itself, and can reflect poorly on the group's leadership. For example, an executive team that cannot hold any person in the position of executive assistant for longer than 6 months makes you wonder more about the executive team and less about the individuals rotating through the administrative role. Groups that have regular turnover like this are often questioned about members' ability to work together. The assumption is that their inability to do so effectively drives off the executive assistants.

Fourth, it is important to know which members are leaving, because group members are not interchangeable. A group that loses an effective leader will experience disruption and frustration. Sometimes another group member can assume that role and take on new responsibilities; other times, however, a group role must be filled. For example, your relay swim team relies on the swimmer who can assess how the other teams are doing in relationship to your team and then really kick in for a quick finish. Thus, if you lose the member who normally swims the anchor or final leg of the relay, your group has a specific role to fill.

What is affected by changes in membership (Arrow & McGrath, 1993)? Obviously, membership dynamics and relationships will change. Any change in group membership will alter to some degree the interactions among group members. Not only does the structure and the process of the group change, but members' performance is also likely to be affected. The more interdependence among members of the team, the more the team will feel the effects of membership changes. And the more central the member is to the team, the more the team will feel the effects of the change.

Group members build a history together, and each group develops a memory of how and why it does certain things in certain ways. At the very minimum, a new group member will be unfamiliar with a group's habits and routines (Gersick & Hackman, 1990). These need to be explained, or the new group member will feel left out. And the new group member cannot share in the memory of the group—there is simply no way for the new group member to know what it feels like to be a part of this group (McGrath et al., 1995). Assumptions or existing knowledge that other group members use in making decisions simply are not available or do not make sense to the new group member.

Also, there is no guarantee that current members will be able to make the behavioral adjustments needed when a new group member enters. However, a group can overcome these effects by realizing that membership change actually creates a new group. The group must allow members time to resocialize and to reidentify the role structure. The challenges of membership change are (a) to initiate the new members into the team, (b) to learn from the new member's fresh perspective, and (c) not to sacrifice the pace and focus of the team (Katzenbach & Smith, 1993).

When group membership changes, socialization, or the reciprocal process of social influence and change by both newcomers and established members, occurs (Anderson, Riddle, & Martin, 1999). Group socialization is an ongoing process, but it becomes especially salient to group members anytime an established group finds itself creating or re-creating itself or its activities.

Obviously, group members do not join a group as a blank slate. Individuals bring knowledge, beliefs, and attitudes about group work with them, just as they bring their own motivations for joining the group and their own sets of communication skills. The socialization process really commences as an individual begins to anticipate what it will be like to be a member of a particular group. For example, you are thrilled that you were selected to be a member of your university's ambassador team but also a little concerned about how you will blend in with students who have already served on this team for several years. And even as you are anticipating joining the team, the existing team members also have anticipatory expectations about you. They might be wondering if you'll be able to devote the time these group activities demand. They might also be hoping that you'll live up to the performance level you claimed you could achieve in the interview.

The first day you meet with the ambassador team, you and the other members begin to adjust to one another, and to negotiate the formal and informal roles, norms, and communication networks of the group. There are many ways to introduce yourself to other group members. If you get there early, you can greet the other members as they arrive. Always be sure to introduce yourself to anyone you do not know well. When you do this, you help establish a friendly and supportive climate and create a sense of openness to which others will respond.

At your first meeting and in subsequent encounters with other group members, you need to continue to assimilate yourself into the group. One way to get to know others is to sit next to someone you do not know at all or do not know well. You can start a conversation by bringing up an easy topic (weekend activities, hobbies, your role in this group). The objective here is to create an opportunity for interaction that will help you get to know the other person. But the topic of conversation should not be threatening or invasive.

Now, as a member of the team, you are influencing the group, just as the group and its other members are influencing you. You are fully integrated, or assimilated, into the group culture when you and the other team members establish a shared group identity by working effectively and interdependently within the group's structures toward a common group goal.

Of course, current members should also help to welcome and socialize new members into a group. During a meeting, you can assimilate new group members by asking them to comment on what the group is talking about ("Michael, what do you think of this plan?"). This is especially important because as new members they may believe their opinions are not welcomed, given that they have little or no history with the group. Creating opportunities for new members to contribute to the group's task or activity also provides a mechanism for them to create interdependence with other group members, from which relationships flow.

SUMMARY

Working in groups means building relationships with others. You are likely to develop dependent relationships with some group members, but be careful. Dependent relationships create superior-subordinate interaction. Alternatively, interdependent relationships are those that are more equally balanced. When group members perceive interdependence with one another, they can use communication to resolve differences. Interdependence also creates a seamless communication flow among group members.

Group communication climate is the atmosphere group members create from the content, tone, mood, and character of their verbal and nonverbal messages. A group will develop a defensive or negative climate if group members send messages that are based on evaluation, control, strategy, neutrality, superiority, and certainty. Alternatively, a group will develop a supportive or positive climate if group members send messages that are based on description, problem orientation, spontaneity, empathy, equality, and provisionalism. While groups will vary in their need for a supportive climate, all groups require some level of supportiveness to maintain interdependence among members to accomplish the group task or activity.

When a group is cohesive, members want to remain in the group, whether they are attracted to the group's task or to group members. Group cohesiveness contributes to the development of interdependence. Cohesive groups often perform more effectively, but cohesiveness does not ensure good group performance. In fact, too much cohesiveness can actually interfere with the group's ability to critically examine alternatives. Like cohesiveness, satisfaction develops from interdependent relationships. Members are satisfied when they are fulfilled or gratified by the group, particularly when the group is moving along its expected path. When group members are satisfied, they are willing to work harder and be more committed to the group.

Trust is a group member's positive expectation of another group member, or a group member's willingness to rely on another's actions in a risky situation. Thus, trust resides in group member relationships, and is developed as relationships unfold over time and individuals build confidence in each other. Trust is based on honesty, openness, consistency, and respect. Group members must earn trust in one another through their interactions. Trust is fragile; once broken, it is hard to reinstate.

Building relationships with group members is particularly important when a new member joins an established group, thereby changing the group's cluster of knowledge, skills, and abilities, as well as the relationships among group members. Socialization, or the reciprocal process of social influence and change by both newcomers and established members, occurs any time membership changes in a group. Both new and established members are responsible for making the transition a smooth one.

DISCUSSION QUESTIONS AND EXERCISES

1 Think of a recent group experience, and write a short essay analyzing the communication climate within the group. Give specific examples to support your conclusions. Provide three recommendations for maintaining or increasing a supportive climate.

2 You've been asked to be a consultant to a team at work that is experiencing relational disharmony. What advice will you give this group for developing and maintaining positive and productive group member relationships?

3 Describe three things that you see as evidence of group member cohesiveness and satisfaction in one of your groups. Do these descriptions apply to all groups, only to groups like yours, or only to your group?

4 Think back to one group in which trust was high and to another group in which trust was low. Write a short paper responding to these questions: What accounted for the difference in level of trust? How did the level of trust affect the group's communication? How did one group build trust? What happened in the other group to erode trust?

5 Based upon your experiences in joining groups and teams, what advice would you give to a friend who is joining an established sports team? Changing teams at work? Welcoming a new member into the family? Would your advice be similar or different across these three contexts? Why or why not?

 NAILING IT!

Using Group Communication Skills for Group Presentations

Your group presentation is not fully developed because a group member has dropped out of the project and your supervisor recommends that Emma join your group. Because you are the only member of the group who knows Emma, you make a mental list of behaviors to welcome your new group member and to help her become socialized into your group. As other members arrive, you facilitate introductions between them and Emma. After introductions, you briefly describe the objectives, timeline, and audience for the group's presentation. Then you invite Emma to ask questions. You are careful not to answer her questions, which allows Emma to begin relationship building with the other group members. Finally, you ask Emma to talk about her strengths in developing and giving presentations. To your delight, Emma describes her experience with different types of data visualization tools—a skill no one else in the group possesses. As the meeting winds down, you feel confident that your group handled this membership transition well, and that rather than hurt the group's presentation, adding Emma is a bonus!

Image Credits

Figure 6.1: Adapted from: Copyright © Depositphotos/megastocker.

Photo 6.1: Copyright © Depositphotos/vilevi.

Photo 6.2: Copyright © Depositphotos/Blulz60.

CHAPTER 7

MANAGING CONFLICT IN GROUPS

After reading this chapter, you should be able to:

- Explain the advantages and disadvantages of group conflict

- Identify types and sources of conflict

- Recognize the relationship between power and conflict

- Identify five conflict management strategies

- Help your group engage in an effective conflict management strategy

- Avoid or respond to nonproductive conflict management strategies

Seldom do individuals—each with unique experiences, perspectives, knowledge, skills, values, and expectations—develop into a group or team without experiencing conflict. In fact, the more complex the group task or activity, the more likely conflict is to occur. Although most people don't like conflict, nearly every group experiences it. Conflict is inherent in group situations because incompatibilities exist among group members. At its worst, conflict interferes with task coordination, creates opportunities for dysfunctional power struggles, and disrupts the social network and communication climate among group members. At its best, conflict can help groups find creative solutions to problems and increase rationality in decision making.

DEFINING CONFLICT

In current society, we use the word *conflict* regularly, often not thinking about what it really means. Conflict results from incompatible activities (Deutsch, 1969). To be in a **conflict** means that at least two interdependent parties (individuals or groups) capable of invoking sanctions oppose each other. In other words, one party believes that the other party has some real or perceived power over it or can threaten it in some way, or that the other party will use that power, real or perceived, to keep it from reaching its goal. Generally, conflicting parties have different value systems or perceive the same issue differently, thus creating incompatibilities (Jehn, 1995).

Communication is central to conflict as it is through group members' verbal messages and nonverbal expressions that other group members understand that conflict exists. As a process, "communication shapes the very nature of conflict through the evolution of social interaction" (Putnam, 2006, p. 13). Thus, (a) communication within a group can cause conflict, (b) conflict develops from patterns of interactions among group members, and (c) communication among group members can resolve conflict.

PERSPECTIVES ON CONFLICT

There are three perspectives for understanding why conflict occurs in groups (Poole & Garner, 2006). An **instrumental perspective on conflict** is about a group's performance and outcomes. From this perspective, conflict can be productive or destructive. Productive conflict is that which helps group members figure out what the goals are and how to accomplish its tasks. Destructive conflict impedes the group and keeps the members from reaching their goals, as this type of conflict stems from relational problems, or the individual goals of group members. A **developmental perspective on conflict** treats conflict among group members as a natural part of the group's development and results from the typical challenges and dilemmas any group must work through to achieve their goal. In this perspective, conflict is productive if its emergence and the group's resolution helps the group move forward. Alternatively, conflict is destructive if a group does not allow conflict to emerge. Conflict is also destructive from this perspective if conflict does emerge, but group members get stuck in the conflict and cannot move forward. A **political perspective on conflict** situates a struggle for power as the source of conflict. When these struggles allow alternative points of view to surface, then conflict can be productive. However, if a conflict only reaffirms or strengthens the dominant member or members in the group, then the conflict is destructive. These three perspectives provide different vantage points for describing and analyzing conflict in a group.

Regardless of the perspective, conflict is a process that occurs over time or in a sequence of events (Thomas, 1992). A conflict starts when one or all group members realize that an incompatibility exists. Group members may then frame conflict by identifying what the conflict is over, who the conflict is with, and what the odds are for succeeding. The conflict continues with group members interacting, each trying to obtain his or her goal. Here is where a conflict can become really interesting, because no matter how well you think through a conflict strategy or how well you rehearse what you are going to say, you can never fully predict what the other person will say or do. Thus, you have to adjust your intentions and behaviors during the conflict management interaction.

Fortunately, most conflicts have an end. This occurs when each party is satisfied with what it won or lost or when those involved believe that the costs of continuing the conflict outweigh the benefits of continuing the conflict. Regardless of the outcome, it's important to realize that one conflict episode is connected to the next one. How you evaluate the outcome of the first conflict episode will affect your awareness of the next (potential) conflict. Suppose you are in a conflict with another person and believe that the two of you have reached a mutually agreeable decision. The next time you engage in conflict with that person, you will expect to again reach an agreeable outcome. Alternatively, if you believe the decision was unfair, you may harbor negative emotions that will influence your interaction the next time you have a conflict. In other words, your awareness of conflict in subsequent episodes is heightened by your sense of success or loss in the first one.

The feelings that result from conflict are the **conflict aftermath** (Pondy, 1967). In other words, each conflict leaves a legacy. If the conflict results in a positive outcome, members are likely to feel motivated and enthusiastic about the group, as they recognize that conflict does not necessarily destroy group relationships. However, if the conflict is resolved with some group members feeling as if they have lost, they may have negative feelings for other group members and even become hostile toward the group.

How important is conflict aftermath? Conflict aftermath affects group members' perceptions of their ability to work together. When the aftermath is negative, members are less likely to embrace conflict in the future. After all, they believe that they lost this time and do not want to lose again. For instance, Theo is distraught over his group's recent conflict episode because he feels as if he really didn't get a chance to express his viewpoint during the argument. "Man, that wasn't a good situation," he concludes. "Now nobody in the group gets along, and we were just given another project to complete." Theo's feelings—his conflict aftermath—will affect his interaction in the group. His motivation to work with group members, his trust of other members, and his interpersonal relationships with other members are all negatively affected.

But conflict can also create positive outcomes (Wall, Galanes, & Love, 1987). A moderate amount of conflict can actually increase the quality of group outcomes. Conflict can motivate members to participate and pay attention and can strengthen a group's ability to solve problems. When group members manage the conflict by satisfying their own concerns, in addition to the concerns of others, group outcomes are of a higher quality (Wall & Galanes, 1986; Wall & Nolan, 1986). Furthermore, when conflict is managed effectively by the group, high levels of trust and respect are generated (Jehn & Mannix, 2001).

Thus, conflict is an emotionally driven process, and group members experience emotion in positive and negative ways. When individuals are vested in the group or its activities, group members identify with the group. Emotions are more salient because group members' identities are affected when conflict occurs and threatens members' positions, ideas, or points of view. This, of course, can influence their relationships. Thus, conflict is emotionally defined, valenced as positive or negative, identity-based, and relationally oriented (Jones, 2000).

Is Conflict Always Disruptive?

Although we often think of conflict as being disruptive, conflict can be productive for groups (Deutsch, 1969). When conflict exists, groups are engaged and talking with one another. This means that stagnation is prevented and that interest in and curiosity about the group and its activities are stimulated. Conflict provides an opportunity for members to test and improve their abilities and to create solutions. This is not to say that groups seek conflict. Rather, conflict naturally occurs, and it is an important part of group functioning. Conflict about the group's task can keep members from prematurely accepting or agreeing on solutions. In fact, a moderate amount of task conflict improves a team's problem solving (De Dreu, 2006).

 SKILL BUILDER

Did I Do That?

Think about the last group conflict in which you were involved. At what point did you know that a conflict had developed? What cues led you to this conclusion? What was your role in helping to develop or establish the conflict? Did you say something that someone found offensive, inaccurate, or personal? Or did you neglect to say something when you should have spoken up? Did you behave in a way that demonstrated lack of interest in the group or in what the group was doing? Could you have changed your communication or behavior in any way to help the group avoid or minimize the conflict?

Although conflict can help groups generate creative and innovative solutions, many groups try to avoid conflict at all costs. Other groups deny that conflict exists and continue with their interactions as if nothing is wrong. Still other groups believe that conflict is disruptive and detrimental. Why do groups hesitate to engage in conflict, given that positive outcomes can be achieved? One reason has to do with the anxiety associated with conflict. When you compare the language and interaction of groups in conflict with that of groups not in conflict, distinct differences emerge. Group members in conflict actually change their verbal patterns. For instance, they become more repetitive and use simpler forms of language, speaking in habitual ways and repeating phrases without adding anything new to the conversation. In addition, their anxiety rises, which affects their ability to take the perspectives of others in the group. Look at the following example:

LUCY: Can we just get on with it?

JIM: Sure. I want us to vote for the incorporation.

ELLA: Right, as if the incorporation will do us any good.

JIM: Well, it will . . . the incorporation, I mean.

LUCY: Can you explain more about the incorporation plan, Jim?

JIM: Well, as you know, the incorporation plan will incorporate all of the surrounding towns into Plainview.

ELLA: If we incorporate, we'll be just like Plainview. No different, but just like Plainview.

LUCY: I've figured out you're against incorporation, Ella. But could someone please tell me what incorporation means?

In this case, the low levels of language diversity or redundancy—such as the repeated use of the word *incorporation* with no explanation of what it means—reinforce the disruptive nature of conflict (Bell, 1983). Anxiety is increased in conflict situations like this, affecting group members' abilities to take the perspective of others in the group. Although group members are using the same word—incorporation—there is no evidence that they have similar meanings for it. Because members take positions, they are not likely to have common ground, and misperceive what others in the group are saying (Krauss & Morsella, 2000).

Is Conflict Inherent?

Conflict occurs because one of three things happens (Smith & Berg, 1987). First, groups often need people with different skills, interests, and values to accomplish their goals. These differences alone can create conflict. Although group member differences may be necessary, they can also threaten a group's capacity to function effectively. To benefit from diversity, group members must become interdependent in a way that provides unity while preserving differences.

Second, groups have a natural tendency to polarize members in terms of how they communicate (Bales & Cohen, 1979). Friendly group members often feel that they are in conflict with members who are negative and unfriendly, and submissive group members sometimes feel opposed to members who are dominant, outgoing, and assertive. When differences in levels of group member dominance are great, conflict is likely to occur (Wall & Galanes, 1986). For example, both Yvonne and Joe are talkative, bold, and expressive. They usually initiate group conversations and occupy most of the group's talking time. In comparison, Marc and Wendy are more submissive. They really do not like to talk much, preferring to follow Yvonne and Joe's lead. But this does not necessarily mean that Marc and Wendy will go along with everything the other two suggest. Wendy, in particular, may become angry—but will not show it—when Yvonne and Joe decide what the group will do. As this example suggests, differences in ideas are often exacerbated when there are differences in levels of group member dominance. More dominant members take responsibility for the group, often without asking other members for their input or for agreement. More submissive members are less likely to take a vocal or overt stand against ideas, making it appear that they agree with more dominant members.

In addition, conflict is also likely to occur when there are differences in group members' orientation (Wall & Galanes, 1986). Some members may have a higher task orientation, whereas other group members have a higher relationship orientation. This difference in orientation affects how individuals perceive their group membership and the primary function and goal of the group. The task-oriented members think the other members are slowing them down, and the relationship-oriented members think the task-oriented members need to relax to allow group members to develop stronger relationships. Frequently, these group members will find themselves locked in a distributive conflict in which one side will win and the other will lose. Try the "Skill Builder Feature: Did I Do That?" to reveal your role in a group conflict.

Thus, group life is filled with many opportunities for oppositional forces to exist and many instances in which members perceive that opposition exists. This means that individuals in groups and groups as a whole will always be managing differences even as they are seeking a certain level of homogeneity (Smith & Berg, 1987).

Third, group members can experience feelings of ambivalence about their group membership, which can cause conflict. You may want to identify with others and be part of a group, but you also want to retain your individuality and be different. Thus, you feel both drawn toward the group and pushed away from it: "I'm like them; I'm not like them." The desire to be both separate from and connected to the group can result in individual-to-group conflict. For example, Jones is a member of a fraternity, and he values his affiliation with his fraternity brothers. He wears their logo proudly on a cap and a sweatshirt, and plays on their soccer team and captains their softball team. But Jones's fraternity brothers are notorious for waiting until the last minute to fulfill their service work as campus safety escorts. Because Jones lives in the frat house, he is called on frequently to take shifts when others do not show up. Lately, he has become resentful of others relying on him to take their shifts. "After all," Jones complains, "don't they realize I have a life of my own?"

Conflict can even be inherent in the most common of group tasks. For example, in a group brainstorming session, members produced 64 unique ideas for consideration. When group members voted on their top 5 ideas, 33 different ideas received at least one top-5 vote (Warfield, 1993). As you can see from this example, group members' different skills, interests, and values generated a substantial number of solutions for consideration. This is certainly one advantage of working in groups. However, with so many ideas capturing the interests of group members, conflict will surely arise as the different ideas are debated and discussed. According to the **law of inherent conflict**, no matter the issue or group, there will be significant conflict stemming from different perceptions of relevant factors (Warfield, 1993).

TYPES OF CONFLICT

As mentioned previously, conflict is not necessarily destructive. It may seem that way when you are involved in a conflict situation, but conflict actually can be productive for the group. Conflict is destructive if it completely consumes the group's energy and time, prevents members from working together, or escalates into violence. Alternatively, conflict can be productive if it exposes new ideas, helps clarify an issue, or alerts the group to a concern that needs to be addressed.

Is the conflict personal? **Relational conflict** is rooted in interpersonal relationships, emotions, or personalities (Jehn, 1995). Even when group members agree about the group's goals and procedures, this type of relational conflict can keep a group from accomplishing its task. For instance, when Angie refuses to listen to what Scott has to say because she thinks he is arrogant and that he thinks he is better than the rest of the group, the conflict is relational. This type of relational conflict is based on social or relational issues like status, power, perceived competence, cooperation, and friendliness, and it generally increases emotional responses. Effective groups are those that can experience conflict over ideas without tying the conflict to particular group members. When conflict is linked to a particular group member, it is personalized. This type of conflict is likely to be more dysfunctional because it is like a deep current running through the group, and it is often subtle. Typically, relational conflict is disruptive and can negatively influence team members' satisfaction with the group. Also important, the greater the relational conflict among team members, the less likely members will seek information from one another (Meng, Fulk, & Yuan, 2015).

Second, **task conflict** is rooted in issues or ideas, or disagreement about some aspect of the group's task (Jehn, 1995). For example, members disagreeing about the appropriateness of two alternatives or about the scope of their responsibilities are having task, or substantive, conflicts. Managed effectively, task conflicts help groups to be creative, improve their problem-solving abilities, and generate member satisfaction with decision making (De Dreu & Weingart, 2003; Yong, Sauer & Mannix, 2014). However, if group members perceive or are told that the group's performance is inadequate or ineffective, relational conflict is likely to develop (Guenter et al., 2016).

Third, **process conflict** occurs when group members have disagreements about which group member is assigned duties or given access to resources (Jehn, 1997). Coordination among group members is central to process conflict. If group members are having difficulty with time management, how work and responsibility are distributed among members, or how group members decide to approach their work, they are experiencing process conflict (Behfar, Mannix, Peterson, & Trochim, 2011).

When conflict erupts in a group, it is seldom the case that group members will be able to agree about the source or type of conflict. To be effective, groups must express some agreement about the type of conflict that is occurring (Pace, 1990) before they can move toward managing it. What can group members do when task or relational conflict occurs? Sharing more information among group members appears to strengthen group process and lead to better decision making (Moye & Langfred, 2004).

Another distinction concerning conflict is whether the conflict exists in a competitive or cooperative environment (Guetzkow & Gyr, 1954). **Competitive conflict** polarizes groups, with one side winning and the other side losing. When this happens, group members are likely to escalate the conflict and become defensive or even hostile toward one another. Alternatively, **cooperative conflict** occurs when the disagreement actually helps move the group along with its task or activities. In this case, the climate surrounding the conflict is supportive or positive. As a result, the group is more likely to find a mutually beneficial resolution to the conflict.

How important is the conflict? A third distinction is the centrality of the conflict to the group (Guetzkow & Gyr, 1954). How important is the issue to the members who are in disagreement or to the group as a whole? If the conflict is about a trivial matter (e.g., what type of paper to copy the agenda on; which room to meet in), then the conflict is not as salient, or important, to the group's objective. If group members are arguing about a critical feature of the group's project (e.g., the scope of the project or its budget), then the conflict is salient and has the capacity to create more dysfunction in the group.

Is the conflict over information? A **cognitive conflict** exists when group members disagree about information or the analysis of that information (Knutson & Kowitz, 1977). For example, when discussing a group project, Jacob says, "the instructor said that the most important part of the task is the class presentation." However, Dante says, "No, the teacher said the most important part of the project is the portfolio." One team member (or potentially even both members) has heard the information incorrectly or made an incorrect assumption about the information provided. In most cases like this, the conflict can be resolved when group members get more or better information. But it must be evidence or data from a valid source. It does not work to say "because I say so." To resolve a conflict over information, data must be available to all group members.

Is the conflict about expectations? **Normative conflict** occurs when one party has expectations about another party's behavior (Thomas, 1992). In other words, conflict occurs when someone evaluates your behavior against what that person thought you should have done. Sororities and fraternities often deal with normative conflict when a member ignores or breaks one of the house rules. For instance, Heidi turns in her sorority sister because she violated sorority house rules by bringing her pet to the house over the weekend. Heidi expected her sorority sister to know the rules and abide by them. Normative conflict can evoke an emotional response like blame, anger, or disapproval, and it is usually followed by sanctions intended to produce conformity to the formal rules or implied standards.

When group members disagree about the nature of the conflict, such issues need to be addressed before the group can resolve the primary conflict. Disagreements over these issues allow group members to perceive that incompatible goals exist. The more disagreement there is about the nature of the conflict, the more strain there will be on the group's interpersonal relationships. Group members who can come to agreement through interaction on the nature of conflict are more likely to build consensus and cohesiveness (Pace, 1990).

POWER

Central to all types of conflict is the use of power among group members. Why? It is unlikely that all group members are equally skilled or knowledgeable, and even more unlikely that all group members perceive that they have equal status. **Power** is the capacity to produce effects in others or influence the behavior of others (Burgoon & Dunbar, 2006). This influence, which results from social interactions or is created by the possession of or access to resources, is an issue in all types of groups (Lovaglia, Mannix, Samuelson, Sell, & Wilson, 2005). Think for a moment of your family group. Who has the most power? Your mom? Your dad? Your little brother? Now think of your work group. Who has the most power? The leader?

 ## MESSAGE AND MEANING

To use power, others must recognize and endorse your power (Clegg, 1989). If others do not, then whether you actually have power is debatable. The city commission in a medium-sized town was debating a rezoning issue amongst themselves. One of the commissioners was arguing that the city had made a plan for development, and that the city commission ought to adhere to it.

SALLY: Jack, do you have any comments on the proposed rezoning for this store?

JACK: I think we are missing a very important piece of information as we talk about this issue. Five years ago, we created a resource plan. This was an important plan that was supposed to guide the city commission in decision making over the next decade of development. And I've heard no one on this commission referring to it as we discuss this issue.

SAUL: Jack, that plan is outdated. We all know this. We aren't referring to it because it is worthless.

JACK: But I think it is still helpful . . .

In this circumstance, Jack presented information that no one was using. He hoped that this new information, a formal report that the city commission had funded a few years earlier, would hold considerable weight in the debate. After Saul's comment, can Jack have any influence by using this plan? Can someone simply refuse to endorse someone's comments (like Saul did) and reduce an argument to nothing? Why? What must Jack do to be persuasive along this line of argumentation?

Power is not inherently good or bad. Having access to power or knowing that others see you as powerful helps you feel confident in group settings. At the same time, we are all familiar with the misuse of power in group settings and the relational damage it can cause. Positive or negative, power resides in the relationships among group members. Some types of power facilitate conflict among group members, and other types prevent conflict from developing. It's how power is communicated and used that determines its influence on and for group members.

Bases of Power

Power exists in relationships among group members. When a group member has power, that member has interpersonal influence over other group members because they have accepted or allowed the attempt at power to be successful. If you perceive the influence of another group member and alter your behavior because of that influence, power exists. Although power traditionally has been seen as residing primarily in group leaders, any member of the group can develop power and use it in relationships with other group members. Six power bases have been identified in research: reward, coercive, legitimate, referent, expert, and informational (French & Raven, 1968; Raven, 1993).

You are probably most familiar with **reward power**. Rewards can be relationally oriented, such as attention, friendship, or favors. They can also take on tangible forms, such as gifts or money. Group members behave and communicate in a certain way because they are rewarded when they do so. In contrast to the positive influence of rewards, threats represent negative or **coercive power**. In group settings, coercive power results from the expectation that you can or will be punished by another group member. Coercion can take the form of denying a group member the opportunity to participate or threatening to take something of importance away from a group member.

Legitimate power is the inherent influence associated with a position or role in the group. Leaders or facilitators often have legitimate power—they can call meetings and make assignments. Group members allow the member with legitimate power to do these things because the power is formal, or inherent in the role the person has within the group. This type of power exists within the role, not within the person. Without another power base, a leader relying solely on legitimate power will have little real influence in a group.

Expert power is influence based on what a group member knows or can do. Group members develop expert power when they offer their unique skills to help the group, and their behavior matches the expectations they have created. Suppose Amber says she can use computer-aided design software to design the team's new office space. Her team members will reward her with this expert power only when she demonstrates this skill and the office layout is approved by the group. Saying you can do something is not enough; your performance must match the expectations you create.

Informational power is persuasion or influence based on what information a group member possesses or the logical arguments the member presents to the group. In a mountaineering team, everyone must work together to safely complete the trek. Team members who possess a diversity of expertise can strengthen the team. For example, one member is responsible for checking the weather forecasts and briefing the others before the climb, another member is certified in first aid and CPR, and a third member has the most hours of climbing experience. Each of these members has more legitimate informational power in one area than the others. If one member is hurt, the member who is certified in first aid should have the most influence on how to treat the injury. Finally, **referent power** is influence given by you to another group member based on your desire to build a relationship with the member. In other words, you admire or want to be like another group member. Thus, you allow yourself to be influenced by this person. For instance, if Wes admires Henry and wants to be like him, Wes will allow himself to be influenced by Henry and will follow his suggestions and recommendations. Anyone in the group can possess referent power, which is often based on charisma. And members can have referent power over others without intending to do so. A group member with a pleasant or stimulating communicator style often develops referent power with others, which gives this person additional opportunities to develop power bases with these same group members.

Of these types of power, all except coercive power are essential for effective group process. Group members want someone to be in control (legitimate power); like it when others compliment them on their contributions (reward power); find it beneficial when someone is the group's motivator, cheerleader, or contact person (referent power); and expect others to contribute their skills and knowledge (expert, informational, and legitimate power).

A group member can hold little power or can develop power in many areas. But to be influential, the base of power must be essential to the functioning of the group. Position power is not powerful if the position is with another group. For example, the leader of your work team will not necessarily have power on the company basketball team.

For a group member to have power, other members must support or endorse that power (Clegg, 1989). Oftentimes this happens only after we communicate in a way that demonstrates our power. For example, if Andy does not profess his expertise in creating graphics for the group's final report, other group members cannot create this power relationship with him. Andy's power arises only if the others are aware of his knowledge and skill. Thus, power emerges through interaction. Although the group leader or facilitator typically holds more power than other group members, all members should develop and demonstrate some base of power to augment their credibility in and worth to the group. When power is distributed among group members, participation is more balanced, and cohesiveness and satisfaction are enhanced.

How important is it that you develop a power base as a group member? Very. Power used positively creates attraction from other group members. We tend to like to be associated with powerful people. In fact, power has a greater effect on other group members than status (Bradley, 1978). This is because power is developed within the group's relationships, whereas status is generally brought into the group. You may have status or prestige because of where you live, what your parents do for a living, what car you drive, and so on. But these status issues may not be salient or relevant to the group and its activity. Would it really matter to another group member that you drove an expensive car if you did not follow through with your group assignments? Would it matter that last semester you worked for a prestigious law firm if you did not share your knowledge with the group? Try the Putting It All Together feature "Group Structure and Group Size" to better understand the power bases of a group experience.

A power source that is often overlooked is the control of resources—real or imagined. As groups work on their tasks, information and materials from outside the group frequently are needed. For example, when a group member volunteers to use his or her connections to obtain permission to use the dean's conference room for the group's meetings, he or she is exerting power over needed resources. Group members are often thankful that someone in the group has access to these resources and impressed that the individual can obtain what they cannot.

However, overusing these connections can create a defensive climate in the group. Here power can be perceived as strategic manipulation. For instance, if a team member volunteers to reserve a conference room, then it is possible that she will schedule it to fit her schedule.

If power is neither inherently good nor bad, how does power relate to conflict? There are two primary ways (Sillince, 2000). First, those with power use the communication resources of a group differently than those with less power. Powerful members of a group talk more, respond to questions more, issue more challenges, and introduce more new topics into the group than do less powerful members. Using these communication strategies, a powerful member is more likely to set the agenda for the group, and that can cause conflict. Second, less powerful group members often want more power and try to find ways to increase their power base. This can cause conflict because the more powerful members may feel threatened or unappreciated.

PUTTING THE PIECES TOGETHER

Group Structure and Group Size

Think of a recent group experience in which you took on a relatively minor role in the group. How was legitimate power used by the member in charge or the leader? To what extent did the leader use other bases of power to influence group members? How did this use of power affect the structure of the group? What bases of power did other members have or develop? Was power easily shared among members?

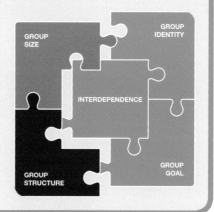

CONFLICT MANAGEMENT STRATEGIES

You may think that there is little difference between the terms *conflict resolution* and *conflict management*, but the two terms represent widely divergent views of conflict. Resolving conflict requires that you view conflict as a destructive phenomenon or as a disruption that you need to eliminate. Thus, the only kind of *good* conflict is the absence of conflict. In contrast, **conflict management**, implies that conflict is a normal and inevitable situation that groups must handle. Groups that manage their conflicts take advantage of conflict situations to solicit alternative views not previously addressed. Managing conflict results in creative and innovative solutions.

There are five general conflict management strategies: collaborating, competing, accommodating, avoiding, and compromising (see Figure 7.1). Although you probably have a primary orientation toward managing conflict, group members can learn new skills and approaches as well. Not all conflict situations are alike and the conflict management strategy you're most comfortable with may not be the best strategy for all conflicts.

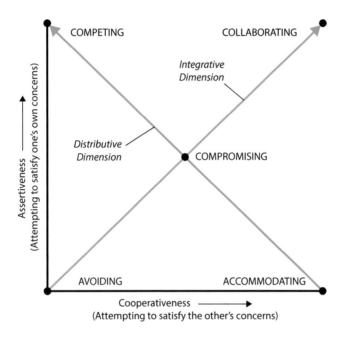

Figure 7.1 Five Approaches to Managing Conflict

Collaborating

Which is the most effective conflict management strategy? Many people would argue that using **collaboration** helps a group achieve a win-win outcome—an outcome with which everyone can agree—because information sharing and collaboration are promoted. Collaboration is an **integrative conflict management strategy** because you attempt to maximize the gains of all conflicting parties. This promotes rather than inhibits relationships among group members (Canary & Spitzberg, 1989).

In collaborating, the parties replace their incompatible goals with the superordinate goal of solving the problem even though their initial ideas for how to solve the problem differ. For example, even though conflict partners might have different ideas for resolving the problem, their common interest is in finding a solution. Thus, parties must communicate with one another to redefine the situation so that they can identify a shared or mutually acceptable interest or goal. Besides sharing the goal, the opposing parties must develop or build a common language in order to create a shared frame from which to view the problem.

Ultimately, this means that opposing parties who see each other as enemies must be able to move from that framing device to one in which the other parties are viewed as partners. To effectively work in the problem-solving mode, a new "we" must be created to include all parties involved. Framing others as adversaries must give way to a frame of allies.

Collaboration is an integrative strategy because it relies on parties communicating with one another. How can you initiate this strategy? You can ask other group members how they feel about the problem or let others know that something about the group or its task is bothering you (Jarboe & Witteman, 1996). Or you can self-disclose—a good way to get others to self-disclose and open channels of communication (Sillars & Wilmot, 1994).

As communication between parties begins, look for objective criteria by which to evaluate potential solutions. This cooperative strategy allows both parties to find and develop common ground, and diminishes the emotional and subjective aspects of the conflict. Groups that can achieve integrative conflict management produce higher-quality outcomes and generate higher group member satisfaction (Wall & Galanes, 1986; Wall et al., 1987). Because collaboration requires a good-faith effort from everyone and open communication among everyone, it is easier to initiate and sustain when group identity and task interdependence is high.

There are some difficulties with using a collaborative approach. First, it takes the most time and effort. Collaborators must question and listen to the other side in order to truly understand them. It may be difficult to use a collaborative approach in situations with a deadline or requiring efficiency. Second, collaboration works best if both sides are using the same style. It is hard to be collaborative with someone who does not reciprocate a desire to find an outcome that will leave both sides satisfied.

Although collaboration can take time and energy, it is a constructive way of managing differences, and it is the conflict management style people report using most often (Farmer & Roth, 1998). Openly discussing differences, having access to a variety of opinions, and carefully critiquing assumptions help create commitment to the group, as well as trust among and respect for group members (Thomas, 1992). Collaboration also can offset problems caused by initial differences among members or unequal participation caused by diversity within the group (Kirchmeyer & Cohen, 1992). More importantly, collaboration can produce higher-quality decisions and solutions.

Additionally, collaborating should be used when you view the issue as too important to compromise, when you have a long-term relationship with the other party and other conflicts are inevitable, when you could learn from merging your insights with the insights of others, and when you need to build a sense of community and commitment. Although the other strategies may seem effective in certain situations, they also have costs or risks associated with them.

What are the alternatives to the integrative strategy of collaboration? There are several, but none can create the same win-win outcome as collaboration. Two strategies—competing and accommodating—are **distributive conflict management strategies,** meaning that they are characterized by a win-lose orientation, or an outcome that satisfies one party at the expense of the other. Group members who use one of the distributive strategies often show anger and use sarcasm. One of these strategies may settle the conflict, but the relational aspects of the group will be damaged because of the strategy's win-lose orientation. When win-lose strategies are used, the quality of the outcome is also lower (Wall et al., 1987).

Competing

Competing as a conflict management strategy emphasizes your own triumph at the other person's expense. In a sense, you take from the conflict but give very little. In using a competing strategy and wielding power over others, you are being assertive and uncooperative. Group members who use a competing style are likely to force the issue and dominate interaction. They will also believe that they are right and the other person is wrong.

When group members compete, communication channels close down (Deutsch, 1969). In fact, you might go out of your way not to talk to other group members as part of the competition. And even when communication is taking place, you may be suspicious of the information you receive from other parties. Thus, error and misinformation abound. Competing also contributes to the view that the solution to the conflict can be of only one type—the type that is imposed by one side on the other.

Competing can be used when decisive action is vital, as in an emergency, or when you need to implement an unpopular action. Competing can be effective when the conflict is with others who would take advantage of you if you used a noncompetitive strategy or when you know you are right (just be sure you are!).

Accommodating

The other distributive conflict management strategy is **accommodating**, in which you give everything and take very little from the conflict. Here you are cooperative, yet unassertive. You focus on trying to satisfy the other's concerns rather than your own. You try to smooth over issues and relationships by being obliging and yielding. For example, each time Henry brings up a sensitive issue, Nell becomes submissive and quiet. Even when Henry tries to force Nell to talk about the problem, she lowers her head and says something like "Whatever you say, Henry. I'm sure you must be right. You've never led us down the wrong path before." In essence, Nell accommodates Henry and his viewpoint to end the conflict.

Although the accommodation style focuses on the other person, there still may be advantages for the speaker. Oftentimes when someone gets their way, there is an expectation that the next time around the other will reciprocate. In other words, accommodators may be building up credit for future interactions. Accommodators may also believe that more competing styles could potentially make the problem worst, and thus it is simpler and better in the long term for the other side to get their way.

Accommodating is especially effective if you discover that you are wrong. By accommodating, you demonstrate that you are willing to learn from others. Accommodating can also be effective when you need to satisfy others to retain their cooperation; in other words, the issue is more important to them than it is to you. And, because you value the long-term nature of the relationship, it is important to be reasonable and to demonstrate harmony in and loyalty to the relationship. Thus, accommodation can be an effective strategy for managing minor internal group disagreements while the group is resolving more significant problems.

Avoiding

Neither integrative nor distributive, the **avoiding** conflict management strategy is nonconfrontive. Group members choosing this strategy try to sidestep the conflict by changing the topic or shifting the focus to other issues. They hope that if they ignore it or do not draw attention to it, the conflict will disappear. How is this strategy used to end a conflict? Generally, people who use the avoiding conflict management strategy verbally withdraw from the conversation. They can also physically withdraw by not showing up. Members of work groups often use the avoiding strategy. One member will acknowledge a problem he has with another group member and then back off (e.g., "I get pretty ticked off sometimes, but it's not really a problem"; "That's not how I would do it"). This type of denial is to be expected, given that members are assigned to these types of task groups and often do not have a choice in group member selection. This type of forced intimacy can be characterized by nervous tension and denial; thus, one party to the conflict withdraws and the conflict ceases to exist. Although not recommended as a strategy for managing most conflicts, avoidance can be the most effective strategy when it allows group members who must work together to focus on their task (De Dreu & Van Vianen, 2001).

Avoiding is effective when the issue is trivial and you can let go of it or when other matters are more pressing. Sometimes it makes sense simply to walk away from a conflict. Avoiding can be an effective strategy when you perceive no chance of satisfying your concerns. Why fight over something you cannot have? As a teenager, you probably used avoiding with your parents to let everyone cool down and gain perspective before dealing with an important but sensitive issue again.

Compromising

A fifth strategy, compromising, also deserves attention. **Compromising** is an intermediate strategy between cooperativeness and assertiveness. Although compromising may settle the problem, it also will offer incomplete satisfaction for both parties. You have given up something, but you are still holding out for something better. Although a compromise may be easier to obtain than collaboration, it is at best a temporary fix (Putnam & Wilson, 1983; Thomas, 1977). Groups tend to manage conflict with compromise when they feel time pressures to reach an agreement. Unfortunately, giving in to a compromise may mean that not all ideas or concerns have been heard.

You have probably compromised with a roommate over who will perform household tasks, such as taking out the trash. These compromises are okay at first because they solve the immediate problem by ending the fight about who will take the trash out right now. But over the long term, compromises tend not to hold. Eventually, your roommate will forget to take out the trash when it is his turn, and you will blow up and start looking for a new living arrangement.

Compromising may be effective if you and the other party are willing to accept a temporary settlement. Also, a compromise may be the best you can achieve when both sides are adamantly fixed on opposing or mutually exclusive goals. For example, suppose members of management and union representatives are meeting as a group to discuss a potential strike. What management offers to forestall a strike is likely to be different from what the union representatives want. The only type of settlement likely to be achieved is a compromise. Generally, these two groups are fundamentally opposed to each other's view, so anything more than a compromise is unlikely. Recognize, however, that the resolution achieved through compromise is only temporary. Parties with fundamentally conflicting views are likely to reinitiate the conflict or start another one.

Which Strategy Should You Choose?

In conflict situations, you are managing three views of the situation: (a) your view of the conflict, (b) your belief of what the other person's view is, and (c) your evaluation of the relationship between you and the other person. When conflicts occur, it is typical to start with a strategy that emphasizes your view of the problem. Even if you enter the conflict with little concern about your view, that quickly changes. You would not be in the conflict

 THEORY STANDOUT

Conflict in Virtual Teams

Poole and Garner (2006) summarize the research on conflict in virtual teams. Studies that examine how face-to-face communication is different than digital communication are conducted using the instrumental perspective of conflict. This perspective is useful as researchers are attempting to identify how technology influences team members in their management of conflict. One consistent finding is that it is not easy for team members to resolve conflict when they are not face-to-face. Why is that the case? The lean channels of digital communication can hide many nonverbal cues associated with conflict. This makes it more difficult to confront conflict (Poole & Garner, 2006). If your team meets using technology, what advice or practices could you introduce to prevent conflict from being hidden?

if your own view of the problem were not important to you. And, as you might expect, your attention to the other person's view often diminishes throughout the interaction. Thus, a pattern dominates most conflict situations: People enhance their own view of the situation while minimizing the view of the other person (Nicotera, 1994).

Initially, it seems reasonable to put your view of the conflict first. Attempts to minimize the view of the other person also seem reasonable given that you don't want to lose in conflict situations. And you probably have some interest in continuing a relationship with the other person, as people generally have conflicts with others who matter to them or with members of groups that matter to them. But remember that your conflict partner has the same orientation to the conflict. Your partner views the issue as important, is attempting to minimize your view, doesn't want to lose in the conflict, and sees you or the group as matter of personal importance. Essentially, both parties have the same, but incompatible, goals.

How you manage conflicts provides others with a means for evaluating your communication competence. Your conflict messages are assessed according to their appropriateness and effectiveness. In turn, these assessments act as a filter through which evaluations of your competence are made. One conflict episode can influence how your relationship with someone develops. Certainly a pattern of conflict over time will influence your ability to maintain relationships with others. Generally, you will be perceived more negatively and as being less competent if you manage conflicts with competing, accommodating, or avoiding strategies. In contrast, group members who use collaboration to focus on the issue or content of the conflict are perceived more positively (McKinney, Kelly, & Duran, 1997).

Most conflict situations, however, are complex enough that groups change their conflict management strategies over the course of a discussion (Poole & Dobosh, 2010). What combinations of styles are effective? Generally, group members who use some combination of collaborating, competing, and compromising are judged to be effective at conflict management because they are best at creating mutually acceptable outcomes and maintaining relationships. Once a group develops a pattern for managing its conflicts, it tends to use the same strategies in subsequent conflicts. Such a pattern can have far-reaching effects. For example, groups that manage conflict collaboratively increase group efficacy, which in turn encourages members to believe that they can also handle subsequent conflicts (Alper, Tjosvold, & Law, 2000). Moreover, groups that master collaboration as a conflict management strategy incorporate it into their decision making more than groups that rely on confrontation or avoidance (Kuhn & Poole, 2000).

How you manage conflict depends both on what you say and how you say it. Which conflict management strategy is best? It depends upon you and your involvement in the conflict situation (Thomas, 1977). Because conflict creates emotional reactions, the nonverbal messages you communicate (consciously and unconsciously) and the words you choose influence other group members' responses in conflict interactions. For example, suppose you say, "That's a good point, but I disagree." Said in a polite and respectful tone, other group members might interpret this as indicating a willingness on your part to develop a collaborative solution. But if you say, "That's the dumbest idea I ever heard" as you roll your eyes, you are likely to get a very different response from other group members. Even though the content of the two messages is very similar—that you disagree—the interpretative frames through which the messages are sent and received are quite different.

To select the strategy that you believe will be most effective, it can be helpful to analyze the conflict you're experiencing according to four dimensions: (a) the level of emotionality in the conflict, (b) the importance of the conflict, (c) the degree to which there are group norms for handling conflict, and (d) the conflict's resolution potential (Jehn, 1997).

First, identify how many negative emotions are being expressed during the conflict. These emotions might include anger, rage, annoyance, frustration, resentment, or simple discomfort. In your group, yelling, crying, banging fists, or talking in an angry tone are clear signs that negative emotions exist. Second, identify the importance or centrality of the conflict to the group. In other words, is this conflict a big deal or of little importance? The importance of a conflict is often tied to the perceived consequences of being in the conflict. If the outcome of a conflict will greatly influence the identity of a group (e.g., splitting a larger team into two separate teams; some group members stop attending), the consequences can be considerable.

The next step is to identify the norms this group has about conflict, particularly the degree to which group members find conflict acceptable. Do they regularly engage in conflict? Do they perceive it as normal for conflict to occur? For groups in which conflict is not acceptable, members often try to downplay or avoid conflict. For groups in which conflict is a regular occurrence, members may view conflict as a healthy and constructive part of the group process.

Finally, assess the conflict for its resolution potential. The key question is, do group members *believe* this conflict can be resolved? What's important here is group members' perceptions, not how an outsider might assess the resolution potential of a conflict. Some group conflicts are easy to resolve by gathering additional information or by giving group members additional time to work through difficult issues. However, other conflicts, especially personal or relational conflicts, can be difficult to resolve. Issues that influence members' perceptions of resolution potential include the degree of group member interdependence, the group's history with conflict, uncertainty about the group and its activities, and status and power differences. Regardless of the outcome, one conflict episode is connected to the next one. The feelings that result from the first conflict, or conflict aftermath, influence your awareness of the subsequent conflict and your interaction in it.

SUMMARY

The word *conflict* generally conjures up negative emotions. However, in our society and in working groups, conflict is a normal part of day-to-day activities. When parties are in conflict, they have mutually exclusive goals. Because the parties are interdependent, they cannot all have things their way simultaneously. Conflict can be productive for groups by stimulating interest and providing opportunities to evaluate alternatives.

Conflict is inherent in group interactions because different skills, values, and talents of members are needed to complete complex activities and goals. These differences, although necessary, also allow conflict to occur. Effective communication can help groups manage their differences and find solutions to conflict problems.

Conflicts can be over relational issues or substantive issues, and they can be cooperative or competitive. Conflicts can occur over judgment or cognitive tasks, over the use of (or lack of) procedures, or over incompatible personalities. Conflicts can arise over differing goals or interests, and they can develop when one party evaluates another in terms of what should have been done or accomplished. Because gender and culture are primary ways in which we identify ourselves and others, differences attributed to these characteristics can be salient in conflict interactions. Despite gender stereotypes, there is little evidence that one gender communicates differently than another in groups. Still, when gender distinctiveness is relevant to the group's task, conflict can occur. Likewise differing cultural orientations can also cause conflict. In both instances, however, we should remember that gender and intercultural differences cannot explain all instances of conflict. Many conflicts are based on other affective or substantive issues.

When relationships and interdependence develop among group members, power issues are inevitable. Power is created through communication and can be based upon rewards, coercion, role or position, charisma, expertise, or information. Power is best analyzed contextually. The extent to which power develops may be based on formalized power structures and the degree to which a struggle over power occurs. Power is fluid, not static; power in relationships changes frequently. Power can also be created when a group member has control over real or imagined resources.

Conflict between groups is common in our society. We create enemies by talking about our adversaries. We belong to multiple groups and sometimes find ourselves caught in the middle. When our group is in conflict with another, intragroup cohesiveness and commitment build as we distinguish ourselves from the out-group members.

There are five types of conflict management strategies. Collaborating, or problem solving, is an integrative strategy that can produce high-quality solutions and decisions for the group. Through discussion, all parties contribute their ideas to find one solution that satisfies everyone's concerns. The distributive conflict management strategies of competing and accommodating are characterized by a win-lose orientation. In competing, you win and the other party loses. In accommodating, you allow yourself to lose to let the other party win. Avoiding is characterized by verbal or physical withdrawal from the conflict situation. Compromising is an intermediate strategy in that it may settle the problem but also offer incomplete satisfaction for both parties.

Usually, you will select a conflict management strategy that emphasizes your view over those of others. But as the discussion continues, you are likely to change your strategy. In any case, the strategy you use affects how others judge your communication competence. Although each strategy has advantages and disadvantages, most people prefer the integrative strategy of collaborating.

DISCUSSION QUESTIONS AND EXERCISES

1 Most television shows revolve around conflict—even situation comedies. As you watch television this week, make a list of the group conflicts you see. Label each conflict according to whether it is relational, task, or process, as well as competitive or cooperative and cognitive or normative. Also note how the conflicts are managed. What conflict management strategies did characters use? What conflict management strategies would have been more effective?

2 Keep a journal for one week of the groups you are involved with and the conflicts they are experiencing. In addition to classroom groups, include your family or living group and any work groups. Describe and analyze each conflict in terms of the following characteristics: Who was involved in the conflict? When did you become aware that you were involved in the conflict? How did you communicate with the other person(s)? Did your plan for managing the conflict change as you communicated with the other person(s)? How long did the conflict last? What was its outcome?

3 You probably can remember at least one group conflict that did not turn out as you expected or wished. Think back to that conflict and reflect on which members displayed what types of power. What type of power did you display? What other power options did you have that you did not use?

 NAILING IT!

Using Group Communication Skills for Group Presentations

When group members are preparing to create a group presentation, there may be many opportunities for conflict. Certain types of conflict may be more common than others. Normative conflict is one potential type that may arise as group members practice their presentation. Even though the presentation may be well planned out, the actual practicing of the presentation may reveal differences in expectations. For example, the first presenter may be asked to provide a brief overview of the presentation. But if Elissa thinks a brief overview is 10 seconds and Shawn thinks a brief overview is 2 minutes, a normative conflict may arise. This is because we often don't know what our norms or expectations are until seeing the actual behavior. Normative conflict may be a common conflict type during group presentation preparations, but it also may be very valuable. Becoming aware of violated expectations before the final presentation allows the group to adapt accordingly.

Image Credits

CHAPTER 8

LEADING GROUPS

After reading this chapter, you should be able to:

- Describe the relationship of communication to leadership

- Describe the communication behaviors associated with group members who emerge as leaders

- Explain why and how leadership can be shared

- Develop the qualities needed to be a transformational leader

- Identify when gender assumptions inhibit or facilitate who becomes a leader

- Take steps to enhance your leadership capacity

n person or online, leadership is a communicative process of influence (Fairhust, 2007). Whether appointed or elected to the formal leadership role, the person who influences other group members is the leader of the group. Leaders influence what groups do or talk about. They also influence how groups perform their activities and achieve their goals. Because leadership roles are based on influence, it's not unusual for a group to have members in both formal and informal leadership roles.

Society's conceptualization of what a leader is has changed over time. Today, leaders must be skilled in team building and in helping team members collaborate (Martin, 2007). So, it's not surprising that leadership theory has focused on the leader as a motivator—someone who can provide the group with energy. But there is one thing you should keep in mind as you read about leadership: Research on leadership has focused almost exclusively on groups that make decisions in formal, hierarchical, or task-oriented settings. Thus, some of the findings presented here may need to be adapted for groups in which initiating, developing, and maintaining relationships are primary goals.

DEFINING LEADERSHIP

We can define leadership in a number of ways. In its broadest sense, **leadership** is the process of using interpersonal influence to help a group attain a goal (Northouse, 2017). As a process, leadership is the way a person uses noncoercive influence to direct and coordinate group activities in pursuit of group goals. Leadership in groups and teams is complicated because the leader must address the individual needs of all group members as well as facilitate the processes (i.e., information sharing, decision making, and conflict management) that arise from group interaction (Shuffler, Burke, Kramer, & Salas, 2013).

A COMMUNICATION COMPETENCY APPROACH TO LEADERSHIP

This functional view of leadership focuses on how group members communicate with one another to identify who is displaying leader-relevant actions and how others are responding to those actions. Generally, the content of leadership-relevant actions can be categorized as (a) procedural, or how the task is performed; (b) relational, or how the relationships among members of the group are being managed; and (c) technical, or the substantive content of the task (Pavitt, High, Tressler, & Winslow, 2007).

Regardless of how leadership develops in the group, the member or members who take on leadership responsibilities must communicate procedural, relational, or technical competency. The **communication competency approach to leadership** (Barge & Hirokawa, 1989; Johansson, Miller, & Hamrin, 2014) is based on the principle that a leader's communication must be competent communication. Simply communicating with group members is not enough. Competence is not synonymous with quantity of communication. To be competent, a leader must be able to adapt to the differing needs of group members and the group task. Moreover, group leaders must be flexible, possessing the ability to change to or adopt other competencies when the group needs it.

Three assumptions are the foundation of this approach. First, leadership is action that helps group members overcome the barriers or obstacles they face in achieving their goals or completing their tasks. This means that a leader must take active steps to reduce ambiguity and manage the complexity faced by the group. In other words, the leader helps the group create a system for working together and accomplishing its goals. Second, leadership occurs through communication. Thus, the relationships established and maintained between leader and group members through verbal and nonverbal communication are central to defining the nature of leadership. Third, individuals use a set of skills or competencies to exercise leadership in groups (Barge, 1994; Carter, Seely, Dagosta, DeChurch, & Zacarro, 2015; Johansson, Miller, & Hamrin, 2014).

Procedural Competencies

Procedural leadership competency is displayed when one or more group members coordinate group activities and help members function as a group. Procedures often help a group achieve its goal, and group members look to others in the group for procedural aid. The person who facilitates procedures best is likely to be selected as the group's leader (Ketrow, 1991). Thus, leaders provide team coordination; that is, they (a) successfully focus the group on its goals; (b) coordinate the skills, abilities, and resources available in the group; and (c) facilitate decision making. To do that, leaders must be organized and responsible, and knowledgeable about the project (Lambertz-Berndt & Blight, 2016). Indeed, groups perform better when their interaction is explicitly directed (Pavitt, High, Tressler, & Winslow, 2007).

To help the group accomplish its tasks or activities, a leader should be able to initiate structure or establish operating procedures. That is, when a group begins its work, the leader must help the group define its mission, and set goals and expectations. In a second set of task competencies that facilitate the group's work, leaders can help group members make sense of the group's task. This requires the leader to anticipate events and the impact it may have on the team. By articulating what may happen and describing how it will affect the team, the leader helps the team adapt to a new or modified situation. Group leaders can further help the group facilitate their work by providing performance feedback, and, if needed, provide coaching or training. Of course, leaders also need the essential task-related communication skills to encourage information flow and facilitate the group's deliberations and discussions, as well as give feedback or descriptive information about how team members are working together and progressing toward their goal.

Specific to decision-making tasks, the leader should demonstrate competency in analyzing problems, generating criteria to evaluate potential solutions, identifying those criteria for solutions or actions under consideration, and selecting the best solution or activity. Some group leaders must also demonstrate competency by coordinating the activities of their groups, especially in competition or performance tasks.

Procedural leadership behaviors are those that help the group assess and evaluate its discussions or expected outcomes. Group members recognize the need for someone to display task-relevant behaviors, such as initiating topics of discussion, giving information, and summarizing, and believe that the member who displays this type of behavior is the most influential person in the group. Groups can perform better when a leader focuses other members' attention on what information is critical for understanding the task and for obtaining information that is accurate (Pavitt, High, Tressler, & Winslow, 2007).

Relational Competencies

Relational leadership competency is displayed one or more group members help other group members cooperate with and express support for one another. In this function, leaders develop and maintain relationships with group members to foster inter-personal ties, increase motivation and goal activity, build commitment and cohesiveness among members, and create perceptions of fairness within the group. Thus, a leader must be able to demonstrate a wide repertoire of communicative behaviors, including being respectful and honest, being confident or assertive, being a good listener, sharing information and being open to information provided by others, and being competent and outgoing (Lambertz-Berndt & Blight, 2016).

There are two distinct sets of **relational competencies**: those that help group members with their internal relational dynamics, and those that connect the group to those outside the group. As individuals work together to accomplish the group task or activity, it is natural that miscommunication and conflicts will surface, challenging interpersonal relationships among group members. So, in relation to internal dynamics, effective leaders provide four types of relational assistance—interaction management, expressiveness, other-orientation, and relaxation—to help group members maintain, manage, and modify relationships within the group. Effective leaders assist the group in managing its conversations by clarifying and summarizing the comments of group members. Interaction management is also visible when the leader balances participation among group members. Managing conflicts and building consensus are further examples of the types of interaction management assistance leaders can provide.

Relational assistance with expressiveness helps groups avoid ambiguity. An effective leader encourages group members to express themselves clearly by identifying undoc-umented opinions and irrelevant remarks. In providing an other-orientation, the leader displays concern for and interest in other members, which helps the group develop a climate of trust and respect. Anxiety is a natural state in a group and occurs because individuals are often hesitant to express their ideas for evaluation. An effective leader reduces the amount of social anxiety in the group by creating a relaxed atmosphere of involvement and participation.

Thus, a leader has primary responsibility for maintaining a positive social climate among team members. To be effective in facilitating positive internal dynamics, the leader must be open or approachable and trustworthy. The leader must also be a good listener.

A leader must also have relational competencies in representing or connecting the group to others. The leader is often the connecting link between groups. In that role, the leader must monitor the external environment for opportunities or threats. To do this competently, the leader must manage the relational boundaries of the group and utilize the group network effectively.

Technical Competencies

Technical leadership competency should not be overlooked. Leaders must demonstrate technical competence relative to the technical demands of the group's activity (Bass, 1981). Leaders who cannot express or share their expertise, or who are unwilling to learn new skills on behalf of other group members, will be disregarded by group members. This does not mean that the leader of, say, a softball team must be the best fielder and hitter, or that the chairperson of the budget and finance subcommittee must be a gifted accountant and a tax law expert. It does mean, however, that the leader must possess enough technical competence to help other group members and to know when outside expertise is needed. Generally, we expect leaders to be qualified or technically competent in at least one area relevant to the group's problem or activity.

Integrating Leadership Competencies

Let's see how a leader can manage procedural, relational, and technical competencies. Kia is supervisor of an engineering team, and her team members have between 1 and 3 years of experience at this organization. Her team is charged with developing all of the materials and procedures a new customer needs when they purchase the organization's computer system. As the installation team leader, Kia's team handles three to five projects simultaneously.

> KIA: Before we start on this installation, I need to explain what's unique about this project. This is our first system installation in this company. So, besides what we normally do, we must also be brand ambassadors. Management is counting on us with the hopes that this installation goes so well that the company purchases another system.

> AARON: Okay, I'll get started by getting the specifications from the manufacturing team and I'll break them up in way that seems best for us.

> KIA: Great, thanks Aaron. Let me know if you need help from me or another member of the team. [Pause.] Aaron, would it be possible for Zack to follow you on this task? [Pause.] Zack, would you like to do that?

> ZACK: Sure . . . I've learned a lot from Aaron already. It would be great to work with him again.

> AARON: Won't Zack have his own tasks?

> KIA: Yes, Zack will have his regular responsibilities of keeping the timeline and budget. [To Zack.] I believe you can do both. Right?

> ZACK: Yes.

KIA: Frankly, I'm expecting that Zack following Aaron's work will allow Zack to improve our timeline and budget tracking.

LING: I guess I do what I always do?

KIA: Right, Ling, I want you to be the installation liaison again. You're doing a good job keeping the customers happy. [*To everyone.*] Remember, if you have a problem with the customer in anyway, contact Ling first. I'll take a look at how this project will fit with our other deadlines and get back to you by the end of the work day if I see that anything needs to shift.

First, notice how Kia demonstrates task competencies. She initiates structure for the group and helps members identify their roles for the task. Since satisfying customers is a primary goal, Kia praises Ling for her ability to do this, and reminds others that Ling will help them. With respect to relational competencies, Kia identifies the tension and ambiguity she has caused when she assigns Zack to work with Aaron. At first mention of this, Aaron seems defensive, perhaps because he believes Zack is not taking on as much responsibility as other team members. Kia provides an explanation to reduce this relational tension. Third, notice Kia's technical competencies. She expresses familiarity with the installation task and the integration of this task with others.

From a communication competency view of leadership, group members do not have to view leadership as residing in one person. Rather, many group members can provide leadership. By defining leadership as a process, we make communication central to the discussion (Clifton, 2006). Leadership is a social phenomenon, as group members in the roles of leader and follower need interaction with one another for leadership to occur. Leadership vividly demonstrates the type of interdependence found in group situations. Recall that one of the defining elements for a group, given in Chapter 2, is that members must have agreement on a goal. The interdependence created by group members sharing a collective goal forces issues of leadership to surface.

What competencies will your group require? It depends on two factors: (a) the type of goal your group is working toward and (b) the situational complexity of the group's environment. When the group's goal is primarily task-oriented (such as a sales team developing a marketing plan), the leader needs more procedural competencies. When the group's goal is primarily relation-oriented (e.g., maintaining solidarity among a fraternity group or a neighborhood association), the leader will need more relational competencies. In either case, a group leader must have some degree of technical competency. It would be difficult for other group members to look up to or follow a leader who was not at least moderately skilled in or knowledgeable about the content of the group's task. The degree of situational complexity—goal complexity, group climate, and role ambiguity—also affects the degree to which the leader needs to demonstrate these two types of competencies.

Four caveats are worth mentioning here. First, you are not exhibiting leadership if others are not following. If group members do not respond to your leadership attempts, you are not the leader. Second, being appointed as head, chair, or leader does not guarantee that you will influence others. Simply, having a title does not make anyone a leader. Group members will follow the member or members who exhibit influence in a positive manner to help them achieve their group and individual goals. Thus, leadership influence is not inherent in a position. Third, leadership and power are not synonymous. Leadership may be infused with power (Hollander, 1985), but other group members also control power in the group. Finally, the leader cannot do everything (Hollander, 1985). There are limits to everyone's capacities, knowledge, skills, and motivation in performing this role. As a result, many followers perform leadership roles in groups. Thus, the distinction between leader and follower may not be as clear as you might initially believe.

Based on expectations created by societal standards and by experiences in other group situations, members have expectations about how leaders should behave (Pavitt & Sackaroff, 1990). First, group members expect the leader to encourage participation by others. Second, they expect that the leader will keep the group organized by talking about the procedures the group will use, summarizing the group's discussion, and facilitating group discussion. Third, group members expect that the leader will work to develop and maintain harmony in the group by managing group conflicts. Finally, they expect the leader to play the role of devil's advocate or critical advisor.

BECOMING A LEADER

When we enter a new group situation, often one of the first things we want to know after identifying the group's task is who is going to be the leader. Leaders come to their positions in one of three ways: (a) they are appointed, (b) they are elected, or (c) they emerge from the group's interaction.

Appointed Versus Elected Leaders

An authority outside of the group can appoint leaders, or group members can elect their own leader. How a leader is selected affects the group environment (Hollander, 1985). Each method of leader selection validates one person as leader, and each creates a different reality for testing a leader's legitimacy.

When leaders are elected by group members—usually by a simple majority vote—members have a stronger investment in and more motivation to follow the leader than when the leader is appointed by outsiders. When things are going poorly for the group, elected leaders are more likely to be rejected by group members. Thus, elected leaders may have a greater sense of responsibility and face higher expectations for leader success than appointed leaders.

For example, suppose your group elects Jason as chairperson. You expect him to take responsibility for the group, yet you will blame him if he fails. One way to interpret this is in terms of the group giving a reward to one group member in advance, with the other group members then expecting the elected leader to "pay back" the group by producing favorable outcomes (Jacobs, 1970). Now let's examine what happens if Jason is appointed leader of your group. Your evaluation of Jason as a leader depends on his performance as leader and your confidence in whoever appointed him. If he does not perform well, you may attribute the group's failure to Jason. You can also attribute the group's failure to whoever appointed him, and you will be more likely to do so if Jason is well liked in the group. Although it may be more efficient to elect or appoint a leader, these procedures do not guarantee that the leader will be an effective communicator or that group members will perceive this person as leader of the group. Generally, a leader who is elected by the group after a process of allowing leaders to emerge and be tested is in the strongest position to get things done (Hollander, 1978).

Emerging as a Leader

Some groups rely on **emergent leadership**, whereby a leader who is not appointed or elected emerges as a result of the group's interaction. That is, a group member becomes the leader because other members accept and recognize an individual as a leader in this situation and in these specific interactions (Emery, Daniloski, & Hamby, 2011). Often, other group members assess a group member's ability to be their leader by the size, as well as the quality, of their contributions (Jones & Kelly, 2007).

Emergent leadership often occurs in groups in which no leader was appointed or in groups with ineffective leadership. At the start, group members assess the trustworthiness and authoritativeness of members to see who might be leader-worthy (Baker, 1990). The group member most likely to gain influence over other group members is the one with these characteristics:

- Is not hesitant to speak and speaks frequently
- Uses nonverbal movement to communicate a sense of dynamism, alertness, involvement, and participation
- Is supportive of and concerned with the welfare of others
- Says and does the things that others in the group want to hear
- Is charismatic
- Does not control resources to demonstrate power
- Contributes procedural and task-relevant messages

Thus, those members who take an active role and have a wide repertoire of communication skills in the group are most likely to end up in the leadership role (Hill, 2013; Pavitt, 1999). As equally important, group members who perceive themselves as leaders are more likely to become leaders (Emery, Daniloski, & Hamby, 2011).

Emergent leaders are generally those group members who demonstrate interpersonal understanding and trust of others. Using open and supportive communication, emergent leaders increase members' engagement with the task (Druskat & Pescosolidio, 2006). When one group member possesses this type of social and task awareness, other group members are likely to look to this person as the natural leader of the group. Leadership emergence can occur in two different ways. Let's use Ava as an example. Group members may willingly support the emergence of Ava as leader and encourage her to take on the leadership role. Or they may allow Ava to emerge as leader because they are passive and do not want to assume any of the group's leadership functions. In either case, a leader can only emerge through the sanctioning behavior of other group members. Thus, Ava emerges as a leader when other group members perceive her as leader and act as if she is leading them, and when her attempts to initiate action or structure the group's interaction are successful.

How you communicate within a group is important because other group members are evaluating your potential for leadership by assessing your communication skills (Schultz, 1986). In particular, your ability to communicate clear goals, give directions, and summarize will either identify you as a potential leader or eliminate you from consideration. If several members are competing for the leadership role, the degree to which you communicate in a self-assured manner contributes to your selection as leader. The member most likely to emerge as the group's leader is the one who can identify sources of differences or conflicts within the group and then develop and present a compelling rhetorical vision that can transcend those differences (Sharf, 1978).

Let's see how these principles are revealed in the following group:

NANCY: I'm glad I'm in your group. This should be fun.

QUINN: Me, too. It'll give me a chance to get to know Andrea better.

JOEL: Yeah.

ANDREA: Uh . . . what's your name, again?

NANCY: I'm Nancy, and that's Quinn and Joel.

QUINN: Can we get started? I've got another meeting in an hour.

NANCY: Sure. Where should we start?

ANDREA: I'm not sure I know enough at this point to really help out.

JOEL: Me either.

QUINN: Let's try getting started by identifying what each of us knows about the registration problem.

NANCY: Good idea, Quinn. For me, my enrollment time slot is when I'm in class. It just doesn't make sense to me. The university's enrollment system knows I'm registered for classes this semester. Why am I assigned an enrollment time that conflicts with my schedule?

QUINN: Joel, what do you think the problem is?

JOEL: I, uh, . . . don't really know. I just know it doesn't work.

QUINN: Andrea?

ANDREA: Well, it seems that . . . maybe I shouldn't say since this is my first semester.

QUINN: Okay. This is my fourth time to register this way. I agree with you, Joel, that it doesn't work. One thing I've noticed is that the registration form my advisor signs doesn't follow the registration prompts on the computer.

NANCY: Right. That sure makes it confusing.

QUINN: And I've had trouble trying to give another option when my first course selection is closed out. Well, it sounds like we've had different problems, but it also seems that we believe a different system for registering could be developed. Do you agree?

Who do you believe will emerge as leader of this group? Nancy and Quinn are certainly more assertive, and both are contributing ideas for the group to consider. Joel is both vague and tentative. Andrea bases her hesitancy to help the group on her limited experience at the university. But does that mean she could not be a good leader? If the conversation continues in a similar way, we can expect that Nancy or Quinn will emerge as leader.

SHARED LEADERSHIP

Most frequently, when we think of leadership, we think about one person in the leader role. However, given the complexity of group tasks and the distribution of group members across geography and time, it may be more effective for leadership to be shared. **Shared leadership**—sometimes called collective or distributive leadership—is the notion that there may be more than one leader or that leadership rotates among members across their work on their task (Contractor, DeChurch, Carson, Carter, & Keegan, 2012).

One principle of shared leadership is that leadership should be enacted by individuals at many or all levels. This is very different than traditional leadership models in which the leader has more formal power or status. A second principle is that leadership is located in a network of members-as-leaders who are interdependent. Third, shared leadership emerges from social interactions that are fluid and multidirectional. Thus, shared leadership focuses on collective achievement, mutual learning, and shared responsibility making it a valid alternative for team leadership (Fletcher & Kaufer, 2003).

Let's look at an example that demonstrates why shared leadership of both types is necessary. The town of Cary, North Carolina, in the United States, embarked on a multiyear process of creating a community plan as a guide for the town's growth. Across time, the town engaged in collecting data from citizens about existing conditions, generating and testing ideas for potential implementation, drafting policies, and getting feedback from the community. Across these processes, the town's council and town employees worked with a consulting firm. Citizens were invited to sessions at which they provided feedback in focus groups. Later, citizens were invited to evaluate the draft plan using online surveys.

Although a consulting group provided leadership for the entirety of the project, citizens were also invited to join self-managed groups that had the responsibilities of publicizing the process, speaking to community groups about the process, conducting focus group research, and talking about the process and the draft plan with their neighbors. Each type of group needed leadership, and there needed to be coordination across groups. Thus, leadership requirements changed across time as the project unfolded. Consulting group members were the official leaders of the project, but would have less influence than community members. Thus, citizens were invited to apply for the leadership positions that required direct contact in the community. The groups they led required specific, but different, sets of task expertise (i.e., public relations skills, public speaking skills, focus group moderator skills, knowledge of the town's history) in addition to the relational skills that foster citizen motivation and engagement.

PUTTING THE PIECES TOGETHER

Group Goal, Group Structure, and Interdependence

After reading this chapter, you should have developed some idea of your leadership effectiveness. Think about one of your group leadership experiences. How would you describe or characterize your leadership? Specifically, what communication strategies did you use? To what extent did these strategies help the group achieve its goal? In what ways did your leadership enhance or inhibit interdependence among group members? Did other group members find it easier or more difficult to work together? How did your leadership affect or alter the group's structure or its use of decision procedures? Were you the only leader? Were additional leaders required? Did additional leaders emerge? If so, why were other leaders needed? To what extent did each group member exhibit leadership to help the group?

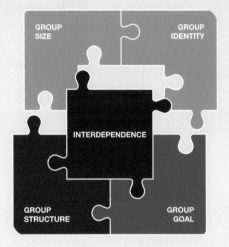

Unfortunately, for these groups the leader was always changing. Sometimes all members of the consulting group were present; at other times, only one of the consultants was in town. Likewise, citizens had work and family responsibilities that prevented them from being at all events. Despite the changing memberships, each group required leadership. This meant that a community member had to step in to provide coordination or directions for completing a task if others were not available. In this multiyear process, it would be unreasonable to expect one person, or even one set of people, to lead every aspect of the project. The leadership skills also needed to change as the project developed across time from exploration to data gathering to presentation of ideas.

This example illustrates several principles (Kramer, 2006). First, shared leadership is an ongoing process of balancing leadership roles over time. Different parts of the project required different skills from leaders and members. Second, the inconsistent availability of group members demonstrates that shared leadership must be a fluid process. Third, sharing leadership may be temporary. In this case, sharing leadership was effective and appropriate, as there was (a) a compelling vision that provided direction, (b) enough shared or easily available information among group members to complete required tasks, and (c) coordination among various groups loosely coordinated by the consulting group. Particularly in this example of community volunteers, participating in shared leadership boosted their confidence, satisfaction, and ownership—which ultimately benefited the overall project (Solansky, 2008).

Shared leadership can be a strength for a group or team, especially at the beginning of a new task. Shared leadership helps a group as members orient themselves to one another and the task. However, when a group reaches its midpoint, shared leadership may become an ineffective model of leadership for a group or team to use (Wang, Han, Fisher, & Pan, 2017). Why? Research has demonstrated that when a group nears the midpoint, group members have greater task familiarity, as the group has established behaviors and procedures for accomplishing its task. At this point, continuing with shared leadership may not be necessary, and could even be harmful.

A DISCURSIVE APPROACH TO LEADERSHIP

Discursive leadership considers that leadership develops through talk and is managed through conversation. This approach to leadership asks how a conversation functions, how leadership is evidenced in a particular conversation, and what kind of leadership emerges (Fairhurst, 2007). From the discursive leadership approach, decision-making talk both frames and defines future action of a group that needs be resolved. In the conversation among group members, influence is negotiated and those with the most influence emerge as leaders.

 THEORY STANDOUT

Discursive Leadership Perspective

Examining interaction among group members from a discursive leadership perspective illustrates how leadership occurs (Aritz & Walker, 2014). Comparing transcripts of leaders using three different styles of communication also illuminates how messages delivered by leaders facilitate or hinder cross-cultural communication.

Aritz and Walker collected interaction data from multicultural groups whose members were from East Asian and American cultures, and another set of data from homogenous groups of American participants. All groups participated in the Subarctic Survival in which group members are placed in the role of airplane crash survivors who must discuss and agree on the ranking of items to be salvaged from the aircraft.

In Case 1, the group comprised one male English speaker (Speaker 1), two male Asian speakers (Speaker 2 and Speaker 5), and two female English speakers (Speakers 3 and Speaker 4). Speaker 1 communicates with a directive style of leadership by speaking first and identifying his item to be salvaged. Then Speaker 1 uses questioning to direct others to select his preferred option.

S1: I figure you can use fire, otherwise you're screwed.

S4: Okay, so let's—

S3: But if you, but if you just have matches, what are you going to do with them?

S4: Yeah.

S1: Well, at least you can start a fire though, don't you think? I mean it could be one or two, it doesn't matter.

This directive style of leaders was the one most commonly observed when groups comprised American and Asian participants. Member contributions were not balanced. This style of leadership was likely responsible for Asian participants reporting lower satisfaction with respect to feeling included, valued, or supported within their groups.

Case 2 illustrates how a leader emerges in group interaction by demonstrating a cooperative and inclusive leadership style. This group comprised one female English speaker (Speaker 1), two female Asian speakers (Speaker 2 and Speaker 3), 1 male English speaker (Speaker 4), and two male Asian speakers (Speakers 5 and Speaker 6). Although Speaker 1 does not begin as the leader, she emerges as the leader by using yes/no questions and open-ended questions to solicit information.

Speaker 1 does this by asking questions of the two Asian females who had not spoken, thus giving them a chance to join the group (i.e., "What did you guys put as the number one?" Later, Speaker 1 recaps the group discussion by summarizing and listing the items in order, which elicits an affirmative confirmation by other speakers. This case illustrates a more cooperative and inclusive leadership style which results in greater balance among member contributions. Unfortunately, this type of leadership occurred only a few times in these intercultural groups consisting of East Asian and U.S. participants.

In Case 3, a collaborative style of leadership develops among the five American participants who begin the discussion by using questions to establish the collaborative nature of interaction in the group. The first questions used by several members in the group frame the type of discussion that will follow. The leadership style is collaborative because all the group members are actively engaged in co-constructing the rules and the process for discussion. For example:

S2: Do we wanna go around and just give, like, our top five?

S1: What's the best, what's the least.

S5: Sure.

This type of distributed leadership among group members is more likely to occur when all group members communicate with a more aggressive and direct style that may not be appropriate in all cultures.

From this perspective, we wouldn't ask *who* is the leader. Rather, we'd ask *how* is leadership being negotiated and talked out in this particular conversation. "Consequently, leadership is not necessarily the property of any one person; it can be distributed and it is open to challenge" (Clifton, 2012, p. 150). And, as you would expect, group members who emerge as leaders are those who have powerful discursive resources. Thus, in leaderless groups, and even groups with a formal leader, leadership is negotiated as group members work on their task. Moreover, leadership may be distributed among many members, it is often performed collaboratively, and it is always contested in the group's conversation.

Because a discursive approach to leadership focuses on the interaction among group members, we must remember that how leadership is discursively created in one team can be different in another team (Baxter, 2015). We should also be sensitive to how difficult it can be for minority members of a group to use discursive practices this way (Walker & Aritz, 2015).

TRANSFORMATIONAL LEADERSHIP

A **transformational leader** is an exceptionally expressive person who communicates in such a way as to persuade, influence, and mobilize others. According to this theory, acting as a role model, the transformational leader sets an example for group members to follow. This type of leader uses rhetorical skills to build a vision with which members can identify. That vision creates a sense of connection with group members and motivates them toward goal completion (Bass, 1985, 1990). Although transformational leaders are perceived by group members to be powerful, they do not rely on their position of power or the use of organizational rewards. Rather, they communicate a sense of urgency and utility—a group vision—that members find appealing.

This type of leader creates power through the use of dramatic and inspirational messages. Thus, you can find transformational leaders in all levels of organizations and in group settings in which motivating people and providing services are more important than monetary rewards. For instance, your soccer coach might be a transformational leader, and your church group may be empowered by a transformational leader. Many civic and community groups, particularly grass roots organizations, are led by transformational leaders. As you might guess, transformational leaders are successful at recruiting group members and helping them achieve high-quality performance.

Transformational leadership occurs when leaders broaden and elevate the interests of group members, when they generate awareness and acceptance of the group's purpose and mission, and when they encourage group members to look beyond their own self-interests and work for the good of the group. Thus, group members are encouraged to take on more challenges and greater responsibility. In doing so, a transformational leader can help a group that has considerable diversity develop an integrative social identity, which in turn can help a group minimize group differences, especially those based on demographics (Kunze & Bruch, 2010; Wu, Tsui, & Kinicki, 2010).

Transformational leaders have charisma. This means that they have confidence in their communication competence and conviction in their beliefs and ideals. Such a spirit generates feelings of faith, trust, and respect from other group members. But, more importantly, transformational leaders inspire others by communicating high expectations. These leaders are animated, which arouses others and heightens their motivation. Transformational leaders are intellectually stimulating, helping group members to be more aware of problems and to pay more attention to problem solving. Most importantly, and the key reason for their success, transformational leaders give special attention to each group member, treating members as individuals. Thus, each group member is treated differently according to the members' needs and capabilities.

As you can see, the way in which a transformational leader interacts with group members can be very powerful. Other studies have demonstrated that when a leader uses a transformational style, group members are better at problem solving and use fewer counterproductive messages, such as going off topic, criticizing, or complaining.

Transformational leaders are particularly good at getting group members to perform the extra work that is often necessary to achieve performance goals (Avolio, Waldman, & Einstein, 1988; Gardner & Avolio, 1998). How is this accomplished? Transformational leaders inspire their followers. Together, leader and followers create a larger collective with which members identify. As identification with the leader increases, so does commitment. Despite time and energy pressures that threaten to keep group members from contributing to group activities, transformational leaders are able to persuade group members to do whatever it takes to achieve group goals. The confidence and inspirational qualities of transformational leaders are the motivating factors for group members. Let's see how Deanna uses transformational leadership:

> I know you don't need one more thing to relearn, but there needs to be a change in pharmacy procedure. When I heard about this, I suggested that our team create the new protocol. Why? Because we're trend setters, and I know we can perform this task effectively and efficiently! Here are the details about handling patient medication. I think this new procedure has lots of merit. [*Deanna hands out the information sheet.*] As you work with patients today, please consider what recommendations you would make about handling patient medications. After the shift tonight, let's take 10 minutes to discuss your ideas. I'm sure that collectively we can produce a draft to be considered.

How can you become a transformational leader? First, you must assess the working climate and task of the group. You might rearrange or restructure work on group tasks to provide more stimulating activities. By knowing the current state of affairs in your group, you can then address what you would like the group climate to be like. Ultimately, these assessments will lead you to strategies that can help group members recognize their individuality and creativity, and their responsibility to the group. What you will find as a transformational leader is that you are valuing group members differently. Together your group will have been transformed from "what is" to "what is desirable" and "what ought to be" (Rosenthal & Buchholz, 1995).

Second, transformational leadership is based in communication ability (Levine, Muenchen, & Brooks, 2010). If you can answer yes to the following questions, you may have the communication skills necessary to be a transformational leader:

1 Does your communication act as a role model for group members?

2 Can you define and articulate a vision for the group?

3 Do you earn the trust and respect of others in the group?

4 Can you influence and inspire other group members to excel?

5 Can you stimulate group members to think in new ways?

6 Do you avoid criticizing group members in their attempts to try new things?

7 Do you consider and recognize each group member as an individual?

8 Are you willing to listen to and empathize with others?

9 Can you coach or mentor group members?

If you consistently answered yes, you likely possess the four traits necessary to be a transformational leader. First, a transformational leader demonstrates idealized influence by acting as a role model and articulating a vision and goal for the group. Second, a transformational leader creates inspirational motivation by communicating high expectations. Third, a transformational leader creates intellectual stimulation by challenging members to think creatively. Finally, a transformational leader practices individualized consideration by providing a supportive climate that helps each group member develop and reach the member's full potential.

GENDER ASSUMPTIONS ABOUT LEADERSHIP

Our gender assumptions about leadership are firmly embedded in society (Ridgeway, 2001), and are frequently reproduced in groups and teams. One reason for this may be the way in which the male leadership assumption is entrenched in our language, which makes it difficult for us to examine our gender stereotypes about leadership (Walker & Aritz, 2015). For example, recent research demonstrates that group members continue to view male and female leadership differently in terms of the gender stereotypes leaders display, as well as the gender stereotypes group members hold (Wolfram & Gratton, 2014). One way we may reinforce this is through the language we use. When talking about leadership in general, it is common for someone to use masculine pronouns.

It can be difficult to avoid assuming that males are more likely linked to leadership roles when group members use gender-specific language, such as in "the person we elect as leader, well, he should be forceful, strong, and willing to work as hard as we do" or "the chairman will decide when the report will be due." You can avoid this assumption and encourage both men and women to consider the leadership role in your group by using gender-neutral language (for example, chairperson, not chairman) when talking about group roles.

As our societies and workplaces become more internationalized, we need to be mindful that not all cultures had such gendered views of leadership. For example, groups in Turkey, a country with more feminine and collectivist characteristics, neither sex or gender role predicted who would emerge as group leaders (Türetgen, Unsal, & Erdem, 2008). Further, research has also demonstrated that when group leaders hold strong and positive beliefs about diversity, groups have higher levels of cohesion and are less likely to create subgroups based on gender differences.

 ## MESSAGE AND MEANING

Sung (2011) published a journal article that examined the gendered nature of leadership as displayed on the television reality show *The Apprentice*. In this show, competitors form teams; each week someone from each team is "fired." In the following excerpt from the show, Sung identifies Omarosa's performance of leadership as a mixed masculine and feminine, yet predominantly masculine discourse style. This conversation (Sung, 2011., p. 99) was held in a cab. Heidi is in the cab with Omarosa when she receives a phone call from two other team members, Jessie and Kwame, requesting that Omarosa get the phone number of the foundation they are going to work with. As Sung describes, her rejection is made in a masculine style.

Omarosa: [*Answering the call from Jessie.*] Hello?

Jessie: Hey, Omarosa, can I get the number for Katie Card, plus your contact for the foundation?

Omarosa: Okay. Why, why are we calling her?

[*Pause.*]

Omarosa: Hey, let me speak to Kwame.

Kwame: Yeah, give me the number for Katie.

Omarosa: I wanna talk with her as well cos I haven't had an opportunity to talk with her just yet.

Kwame: Right now we need the number quickly.

Omarosa:	[*Talking to Heidi.*] Are we here?

(we are here)

Kwame:	Okay, what's the number?
Omarosa:	Let's talk when we get together.
Kwame:	Would you please give it to me?

[*Omarosa hangs up her cell phone.*]

Kwame:	Hello?
Omarosa:	[*Talking to Heidi.*] I'm sorry I had to bang it on them. They're not listening to me.

What meanings to you extract from this conversation? What arguments would you make to support Omarosa's leadership style as feminine? Masculine? How does her gendered leadership style influence her effectiveness as leader?

There is evidence that women and men prefer different styles of leadership (Berdahl & Anderson, 2005). When all group members are women, decentralized leadership is preferred. When all group members are men, or there are more men than women, centralized leadership is preferred. Interestingly, groups in which the number of men and women are the same, or in groups in which there are more women than men, centralized leadership is used at the beginning of a group. Over time, however, leadership becomes decentralized.

LEADERSHIP IN VIRTUAL GROUPS

Especially in organizational settings, leaders will use both face-to-face and online communication with members of their teams. If the team is communicating on video and audio platforms, we would expect that most of what is known about group and team leadership would be salient there as well. However, some teams use textual online communication, such as chat, which significantly reduces auditory and visual cues. In face-to-face settings, leaders rely on these cues to understand how team members are working together, and how they feel about the work and each other. In an online textual environment, it's easy to quickly compose a message and send it without thinking how the message will be received. As a result, leaders of teams in online environments are likely to have fewer cues by which to measure uncertainty (Gilstrap & Hendershot, 2015). This may cause leaders to over-communicate with their team members.

Research has shown, however, that communicating online frequently with team members who have not met face-to-face may not be beneficial to group performance. In other words, more online communication may not increase trust among team members or with the team leader (Chen, Wu, Ma, & Knight, 2011). A better strategy, when possible, is for team leaders to use both face-to-face and online communication, and to move to face-to-face interaction when uncertainty is high.

ENHANCING YOUR LEADERSHIP ABILITY

Effective team leadership is critical to a group's success (Hirokawa & Keyton, 1995; Larson & LaFasto, 1989). To be an effective leader, you must be in control of three factors: knowledge, performance, and impression. Together, these three factors form the basis of how group members evaluate your communication competence and leadership ability.

First, are you knowledgeable about leadership issues? Do you understand a variety of leadership styles, and can you explain why different types of leadership may be needed? Do you know if your group has a greater need for relational support or for task guidance? Can you identify the decision procedure that is most needed by your group? However, being knowledgeable about leadership isn't sufficient to make you a competent group leader. Other group members can't benefit from your knowledge unless you demonstrate your knowledge through your leadership performance.

Second, can you perform a variety of leadership behaviors and functions? Or are you stuck, having to rely on one type of leadership behavior? Is your leadership situationally appropriate? Being flexible and able to adapt to the needs and expectations of other group members is a hallmark of effective leadership (Nye, 2002). Still, there are some leadership behaviors that are effective in nearly all group situations: establishing and communicating the goal or intention of the group, keeping the group focused on its primary activities, taking steps to establish a positive group climate, monitoring or facilitating interactions among team members, and modeling competent group communication skills (Galanes, 2003). These are common leadership expectations across a variety of groups. The leadership performance you communicate to and with other group members is what other group members evaluate.

Third, what kind of impression do you make as a leader? A group leader who is generous with his or her time and energy, is willing to do favors or make sacrifices for others, shows personal interest in others, and praises others' ideas and actions will create a favorable impression with group members (Rozell & Gundersen, 2003).

In many group situations, leadership may be better expressed as facilitating group member interactions leading to goal realization. Too frequently, leadership is conceptualized as an overly directive style, with the leader arguing for a particular position, refuting information that challenges it, and advocating for a decision that supports this position.

While this style may satisfy the leader's needs, it is unlikely to satisfy other group members. Moreover, this style of leadership can have detrimental effects on a group. By imposing leader preferences, the flow of information from and among other group members is stifled (Cruz, Henningsen, & Smith, 1999).

Leadership is like walking a tightrope. You must balance task and relational concerns throughout the group process (Barge, 1996). The effectiveness of a leadership style will change as the group matures and moves from a beginning to an ending point. You must be able to anticipate and deal with unexpected problems and to regain control if the situation warrants it. Your flexibility as a leader will dictate your balance, sense of control, and confidence—and hence your success as a group leader. Try the "Putting the Pieces Together: Group Goal, Group Structure, and Interdependence" feature to assess your leadership effectiveness.

SUMMARY

Leadership is a process of influence that occurs when group members interact. According to the functionalist view of leadership, it is important for leaders to have the ability to manage several types of group situations. Procedural, task, and maintenance behaviors are all important as group leaders navigate the complex social dynamics of group interaction.

Leaders may be appointed, elected, or emerge from the group interaction. Elected leaders generally have a greater sense of responsibility and a higher level of accountability than appointed leaders. Emergent leaders are usually group members who are active and dominant in the group's conversation, are trustworthy and authoritative, and can monitor the group situation to meet the task and relational needs of members. Additionally, as a group juggles a variety of challenges and goals, shared leadership may be necessary. In this type of leadership, members use the interdependent nature of task and group interaction to allow multiple members the ability to influence the process. Shared leadership allows a group to be more flexible and adapt according to members who have skills appropriate for a given task.

The communication competency approach to leadership is based upon a leader's competence in both task and relational skills. A third competency, technical skills, enhances these other areas. A leader helps organize and manage a group's environment, facilitates members' understanding of obstacles they face, and helps members plan and select the most effective actions. The more complex the group activity, the more complex the leader's communication needs to be.

Transformational leadership theory explains why some leaders are more effective than others. A transformational leader communicates a sense of urgency and utility, which motivates group members. Group members report that transformational leaders are charismatic, inspiring, and intellectually stimulating, and that they treat each group member as an individual. Thus, this type of leader can empower group members to accomplish more than they originally thought possible.

Society holds stereotypes about leadership and gender. Sometimes these stereotypes are reinforced when masculine language is used to describe leadership approaches. Research has shown there to be differences in how females and males lead; however, both can be effective leaders.

Effective team leadership is critical to a group's success. You must be knowledgeable on leadership issues and be able to perform a variety of leadership behaviors and functions, and you should leave a favorable impression as a leader. Together, these three factors form the basis for how others evaluate your communication competence as a leader.

DISCUSSION QUESTIONS AND EXERCISES

1 Select at least two people you know who lead or direct groups, and ask them to participate in informal interviews on their views of leadership. You might select someone who (a) chairs a task force or project team in a for-profit organizational setting, (b) leads a not-for-profit group of volunteers, (c) chairs a committee for an educational or government organization, or (d) leads a religious study or self-help group. If possible, find someone who leads an online team. Develop at least five questions to guide your interaction with your two leaders. For example, how do they view their role as leader? What leadership functions do they perform for the group? How did they come to be in that particular leadership role? How do they believe other members of the group perceive them and evaluate their leadership? If there is one thing they might do to improve their leadership, what is it?

2 Think of a community, regional, or national leader who is a transformational leader. What evidence do you have to support that claim? Do others agree with your assessment? Is your evidence based on the leader's communication behavior, the communication behavior of the leader's followers, or the outcomes achieved by the group? Which of these do you believe is the best direct evidence that transformational leadership is an effective method for creating and sustaining positive leader-member relationships?

3 Identify the leadership task, relational, and technical competencies that you feel comfortable using in groups. Are there leadership competencies that you should develop further? What leadership competencies do you lack? What could you do to develop those behaviors you identified?

4 Set a timer for 3 minutes. In that time, think of as many labels as you can for "leader." In addition to your own experiences, also think about what leaders

may have been called at different points in history, in organizations, in families, in friendship groups, in community and civic groups, and so on. Compare your list with other students' lists. How did your lists differ? What labels did you overlook? How do different labels imply different approaches to group or team leadership?

 NAILING IT!

Using Group Communication Skills for Group Presentations

When delivering a group presentation, it may be important to have a specific individual provide leadership or guidance. This person may be a coordinator, synthesizer, facilitator, or present a particular important part of the presentation, based on the leadership needs of the group. For example, a coordinator may introduce the members of the group and the topic of the presentation, and may also help with transitions during the presentation. A synthesizer may present the last part of the presentation, bringing all previous presenters' messages together for a final meaningful summary. A facilitator may help engage the audience with the group presentation in a meaningful way. Of course, a leader may play several of these roles at once. Importantly, a leader should ensure a clear structure to the presentation. Additionally, the leader is likely the person group members will turn to if any difficulties arise.

Image Credits

CHAPTER 9

FACILITATING GROUP MEETINGS

After reading this chapter, you should be able to:

- Create a draft of a group charter to present to your group or team

- Carry out the pre-meeting responsibilities as a leader or member of a group

- Design and lead an effective group meeting

- Select and prepare appropriate visuals to help the group record what is happening

- Take effective minutes for your group meeting

- Carry out the post-meeting responsibilities as a leader or member of a group

- Assist your group in overcoming typical meeting obstacles

Most group interaction depends to some degree on meetings. Indeed, interaction among group members within a meeting is necessary for groups to be effective (Somech & Drach-Zahavy, 2007). For some groups, meetings will be the only opportunities for all group members to meet and interact. Even for groups that perform physical tasks (e.g., a fire fighting team, a cheerleading squad), a group meeting may be held before or after the task. Meetings may be held to create ideas, exchange opinions, solve problems, make decisions, negotiate agreement, or develop policy or procedures. Regardless, meetings are events at which group members make sense of themselves, their task, the group, and the environment (Schwartzman, 1989).

Essentially, group meetings are the core of group interaction. Some meetings are private, other times nonmembers are invited to attend. Other group meetings are open to the public. For some public meetings, the public serves as an audience at the meeting; in some of these meetings, members of the public can participate in the meeting. Finally, some group's meetings are recorded in detail (e.g., written notes or minutes, or digitally recorded), whereas others groups meet without documenting what happened. Regardless, group meetings are opportunities for relationships to develop among people, tasks, resources, roles, and responsibilities (Baran, Shanock, Rogelberg, & Scott, 2012; Mirivel & Tracy, 2005).

Meeting interaction is never neutral or benign. Research has demonstrated that what is said in meetings is interpreted strategically by other group members—even in meetings that are routine and follow a standardized agenda. While tasks are the focus of most meetings, group members infer relational intent or relational strategies from others' meeting interaction. Thus, meetings are also events where relationships are defined between and among group members (Beck & Keyton, 2009).

Since meetings can vary dramatically in their private or public nature, level of formality, number of attendees, and scope of activities, most people who attend meetings develop their own criteria for determining a meeting's effectiveness (Beck, Littlefield, & Weber, 2012; McComas, 2001). Thus, what you may believe is effective interaction at a meeting may be evaluated as ineffective by others.

There are, however, generally accepted principles of meeting management. This chapter explores methods of managing group interactions during meetings and describes the responsibilities of both leaders and group members. Too frequently, meetings become sites of information transmission and fail to make use of group members' knowledge and skills (Myrsiades, 2000). Thus, it is the responsibility of all group members to manage meetings to facilitate group productivity.

Traditionally, group or team leaders take on the responsibility for much of the planning associated with meetings. But members also have obligations. **Meeting citizenship behaviors** are those actions that members can take to maintain a positive social and communication climate. To support the goals of the meeting, members can be prepared to speak up when input is requested, volunteer helpful information, make suggestions to the agenda, and encourage other members to participate by asking questions. By taking on these responsibilities, members help to more effectively facilitate the meeting (Baran et al., 2012).

 MESSAGE AND MEANING

Meeting agendas provide structure to group discussion. Not only do agendas list meeting topics for all members to see, but leaders can also designate amounts of time for each item. Members may gain insight into how complex or important meeting items are based on the length of time given to the respective issue. It is also common for leaders to describe the agenda as tentative, in case adjustments need to be made as new topics develop just before or during the meeting, or if one topic requires the entire meeting time. These adjustments may allow leaders to keep the meeting discussion focused on the topic at hand, as in this case during a team meeting of special education instructors at an elementary school:

JILL (leader): So, the first item on the agenda is whether we should increase the number of students we work with.

PAM: I think we should. If we don't do it, the district [of education] may force us to anyway. If we increase it, at least we will have a say in the matter.

CALVIN: I agree. The writing is on the wall—let's just go ahead and do it.

TERESA: I'm not so sure. We are already pretty busy.

AIDEN: We should also increase the number of teachers we have. I'm afraid the next budget hasn't allotted enough for new teacher hires.

JILL: I appreciate your point Aiden, which you have brought up a few times. To make sure we discuss that issue, I'm going to add it as agenda item number 4. Teresa, could you elaborate a bit more on your concerns about increasing the number of students?

TERESA: Sure. My first concern is that we all have different workloads currently based on …

Note that during the meeting Jill added an item to the agenda in order to discuss Aiden's point. Do you believe Jill was justified in handling Aiden's comment in this way? How does this adjustment benefit or harm the discussion? How does adding the agenda item address Aiden's concern?

One final caveat: Most of the research on meetings has been conducted on work teams or public meetings. As you know, group interaction spans a wide variety of contexts. For example, athletes on sports team have meetings before games. Some meetings in health care settings are attended by social workers, therapists, parents, and children (for examples, see Davis, 2008; Wittenberg-Lyles et al., 2013). The team meets to discuss and assess progress and to develop new goals. In this case, the health of the child is the focus, and the role of the team is to ensure that goals are met. While this type of team differs from those meetings for which members have a formal hierarchical structure and tasks assigned by outsiders, some of the principles and procedures described in this chapter can be modified and used effectively.

DEVELOPING A GROUP CHARTER

If yours is a group that will meet over an extended period, developing a charter can help your group develop cohesiveness and find unity of purpose. A **group charter** or mission statement describes the goals or mission of the group, and describes behaviors that are appropriate in this particular group. Developing a charter early in the group's history is recommended, as doing so gives team members the opportunity to discuss and agree on expectations related to member contributions, how meetings will be managed, and how work will be distributed and, perhaps, evaluated. Talking through these issues and affirming them in writing will help the group move effectively toward its goal.

To develop a group charter, the group must discuss and agree upon what members view as important and what they hope to accomplish in this group experience. Group goals are generally the primary component of a charter or mission statement (Mathieu & Rapp, 2009). Each goal should be listed individually, and both task and relational goals should be included. What individual members can expect to learn or obtain from the group can also be listed. Figure 9.1 provides an example of a group charter. As you can see, the charter is specific and clear, and provides direction for the group. However, it does not dictate how the group will meet its objectives.

Check your charter by answering the following questions:

- Is the statement understandable to all group members?
- Is it brief enough that team members can remember it and keep it in mind?
- Does it clearly specify the activities of the team?
- Does it reflect realistic goals?
- Is it in line with members' values and beliefs?
- Is it inspiring or motivating to members?

Not only does a charter or mission statement help a group define and solidify its purpose, this document can be used to stimulate group discussion at a later meeting (Heath & Sias,

---

Group Charter

Group's Mission Statement: To work interdependently as team members to identify relevant issues, resolve problems, learn new skills, and have fun.

Our group will develop a strategic plan for our organization for the next five years. The plan must: (a) be accepted by the executive committee to which this group reports, (b) be implemented by the rest of the organization, and (c) meet a set of conditions given to us by the executive committee.

In working on the strategic plan, each group member should develop skills in group facilitation, organizational forecasting, and team member effectiveness.

Our goal is to complete the first objective in 6 months from our start date.

Figure 9.1 A Sample Group Charter

1999). Posting the charter or mission and asking "Are we on track?" or "What are we doing to implement our mission?" or "Has our mission changed?" helps group members assess their progress toward their purpose and goals. Does having a team charter really make a difference? Yes, teams that do develop a group charter report greater member satisfaction and group cohesiveness, more effective communication, and greater effort by team members (Aaron, McDowell, & Herdman, 2014).

DEVELOPING A CODE OF CONDUCT

Additionally, some groups and teams also create a **code of conduct**. The purpose of this document is to help group members identify behaviors that are expected from team members and avoid behaviors that are not (Hill & Rapp, 2014). A code of conduct lists those behaviors that members feel are appropriate and will help them be effective in the group. Figure 9.2 provides an example.

Too frequently, group members do not discuss what they expect from one another in terms of behavior. Left undiscussed, members are unsure of what is appropriate or inappropriate behavior. Thus, they use behavioral norms from past group experiences to guide their behavior. Of course, norms from previous groups are not always transferrable to other group situations. Attendance and preparedness are examples of individual behavior to be included in the code of conduct. Group-level behaviors—those related to role sharing within the group, decision-making rules, meeting attendance, election procedures, and group structure—can also be described and included. Specifying both individual and group behaviors ensures that all members are aware of what is expected of them in this group.

A code of conduct provides a set of guidelines—much as rules establish the guidelines by which you participate in any sport. Guidelines provided by the code of conduct create equity in the group process because all group members share in their creation. By developing a group charter and a code of conduct, members are more likely to share perceptions about what constitutes effective group membership. Developing these documents also helps a group crystallize its identity and culture.

IMPORTANCE OF MEETING MANAGEMENT PROCEDURES

Meetings can be valuable in helping group members reach their goal, as the two most common functions of meetings are to generate and share information. But they can also

Code of Conduct
created and agreed to by all group members,
August 14, 2017

As a team, we expect all members of the team to support the team's charter. Our communication, actions, and decisions should emphasize teamwork, not individual accomplishment. Each group member is responsible for being involved in the day-to-day business of the team. Each group member expects to receive information and influence from all other group members.

As a group, we will elect a leader for each month we are together as a team. By rotating the leadership role, we will help to develop each member's leader and follower skills. The leader is to provide overall direction and support for the team. Followers are to carry through their assigned responsibilities and inform the leader if they encounter any obstacles.

We expect to make decisions as a team using the majority vote rule. In cases where a minority vote member is so uncomfortable with the decision outcome that he or she cannot support the group's decision, he or she may ask the group to reconsider the issue.

Group members are expected to attend all meetings. When a member cannot attend, other members will expect his or her assignments to be completed and handed in to the leader before the next meeting. In the event any member finds that he or she cannot fulfill the responsibilities of being a member of this team, he or she may ask the group for a reduction in, or termination of, group responsibilities.

Figure 9.2 A Sample Code of Conduct

waste valuable time. Whether meetings are positive or negative really depends on how prepared you are for the meetings' activities and what meeting facilitation skills you can contribute to the group. Even though some organizations are replacing meetings with more frequent use of technology that allows employees to meet across divisions in time and geography, there is no technology that can fully replace face-to-face meetings.

Whether face-to-face or online, you need to be skilled in basic meeting management procedures. Even simple agendas can provide structure for groups and keep meetings running smoothly. Procedures help group members coordinate their thinking and provide a set of objective rules all members can follow. You have probably been a member of a group that did not accomplish what it intended because another topic was introduced into the discussion. As a result, the group spent most of its time on this new topic, forcing you and other group members to make important decisions in the last 10 minutes without adequate discussion.

Meeting management procedures and facilitation strategies benefit groups by balancing members' participation. When all group members share their input, higher-quality decisions result and members are more supportive of the group's output. There are many other advantages to using meeting management and facilitation strategies. These techniques help to uncover and then manage conflicts that can steal valuable resources and time from the group. They provide structure that can be revisited if a group takes a temporary detour, and they encourage group members to reflect on their meeting process and progress.

Meeting management procedures and facilitation strategies help teams develop more effectively and overcome obstacles. Being able to help your group manage its meetings and providing it with facilitation expertise are responsibilities that go along with group membership. Fulfilling each of these responsibilities allows you to participate in the group to the best of your abilities. At the same time, you are helping your group's interaction become more effective and efficient. You might think that the leader should bear these responsibilities. But when group members participate in helping the group's interaction develop effectively, the group's process is smoother and members are more likely to feel satisfied on both task and relational dimensions (Kauffeld & Lehmann-Willenbrock, 2012).

Let us first explore meeting planning. You have probably used some of these procedures in the past, but just because your group has developed an agenda does not necessarily mean that it effectively manages its time together. There is more to formal meeting planning than simply listing items of business.

MEETING PLANNING

Meetings should not just happen, but many do. When a meeting is called, most of us jot down the time and date, and then show up. But that is really not enough.

Pre-Meeting Planning and Preparation

The group's leader or facilitator should do pre-meeting planning, and every group member should do some pre-meeting preparation as well. If you need some motivation to do this extra work before your next group meeting, think about this: A typical group meeting generates somewhere between 100 and 600 speaking turns or opportunities for individuals to talk (Scheerhon, Geist, & Teboul, 1994). Can you imagine trying to make sense out of so much information without some prior knowledge beforehand?

Leader Pre-Meeting Responsibilities

Before calling any meeting, the leader should first decide if there is enough business to hold a meeting, and if so, what the meeting's purpose should be. If there is not enough business, or if a clear purpose does not emerge, do not hold a meeting. One way to make these decisions is to list the specific business items you want the group to consider or accomplish during its next meeting. Now look at the items. Can they be organized in some fashion that will make sense and move the group forward? If not, are these issues really ones that the entire group needs to discuss? Could talking individually with some group members take care of these issues?

It may seem obvious to consider the overall purpose of the meeting, but answering these questions can force you to consider why you need a meeting in the first place. Perhaps you are going to call a meeting because your boss requested the vacation schedule for your department. Is a meeting the best way to collect and coordinate this information? If you cannot identify a purpose for the meeting, do not have one!

Now consider the participants. You need to sort out who should be invited to the meeting and who should be informed about it. The two lists are not always the same. If a key person cannot attend, should the meeting be cancelled or rescheduled? Or should the meeting go on regardless of who shows up? Answering these questions can help you determine the importance of those attending the meeting, as well as the importance of the meeting itself.

Once you have decided that there is a valid reason for the group to meet, you need to consider how long the meeting should be. Everyone identifies a start time, but few groups know when they can expect to be finished. Identifying a stop time is important because it can help a group focus on its work. Knowing that time is limited is a motivator that can keep group members from delaying action or making a decision. Group members appreciate knowing when a meeting should be finished. This actually increases attendance because it allows group members to schedule around the meeting and avoid time conflicts. This is important because group members are likely to hold membership in other groups, and time devoted to meetings must be integrated with their other responsibilities.

 SKILL BUILDER

Developing a Meeting Agenda

For the next meeting you will participate in (for this class, at work, in your community), develop an agenda. If the group typically uses an agenda, try not to rely on a past agenda for form or substance. As you develop the agenda, use the principles described in the chapter to identify the meeting's activities, and provide enough information for the agenda to be useful to members before and during the meeting. What would you say to group members to encourage them to use an agenda to help structure group meetings? What specific advantages can your group expect from implementing this meeting procedure?

Time limitations make an agenda that much more important. An agenda lists what the group needs to consider in detail and what the order of consideration will be. Group members should receive a copy of the agenda before the group meets and not simply at the beginning of the meeting. This way, they can plan what they want to say and collect data or information to support their point of view. When group members have an agenda before the group meets, they are better prepared to contribute effectively and efficiently. Figure 9.3 shows a sample agenda.

The **agenda** should list the meeting's start and stop times, the location of the meeting, the expected attendees, and the overall goal of the meeting, as well as the specific goal of each agenda item (e.g., to share information, to discuss a proposal, or to make a decision). Additionally, the agenda should identify or describe any preparations that group members should make, such as "Come to the meeting with ideas on how to help our

---

Agenda
Project Development Work Group
Thursday, January 29, 1:00 to 2:00 p.m. Conference Room A

Participants: Cynthia, Dan, Lu, Marquita, Tyron
Purpose: Project Update Tracking

Welcome

Introduce any guests

Preview agenda; ask for additional agenda items

Information sharing

     Review developments since January 15th meeting

     Dan, report on final numbers for December's project activity

     Cynthia, tell group about presentation to Federal Railways

Discussion items

     Progress on planning of telephone service cut-over

     Evaluation of new project tracking board

Decision item

     Need decision on feasibility of upgrading digital networks

     (bring cost estimates)

Suggestions for next meeting's agenda

Set next meeting date/time

Adjourn

Figure 9.3 A Sample Agenda

department pass its safety assessment." Notice how the agenda starts with items that are easy for the group to manage and that give group members the opportunity to contribute. Welcoming members, asking for additional agenda items, and sharing information are activities that do not take much time but that can help the group establish a positive or supportive climate. Now that the group has warmed up, it's time to take on more difficult tasks. Unless decisions are interdependent and need to be made in a particular sequence, it's best to make easy decisions first and work your way up to the more difficult ones. Wrapping up the meeting by discussing the agenda and date for the next meeting gives members an opportunity to regain their composure if the decision making was contentious. Ending on a positive note with respectful and positive messages completes the meeting cycle (Tropman, 2003). Try "Skill Builder: Developing a Meeting Agenda" to test your skills in this area.

Is creating an agenda worth the effort? Yes! Research has demonstrated that an agenda helps "guide attendees through the meeting, regulate activities, facilitate discussion, and minimize the need to backtrack" (Odermatt, Konig, & Kleinmann, 2015, p. 55). As important, when a written agenda is distributed before the meeting and used during the meeting, meeting effectiveness is improved (Leach, Rogelberg, Warr, & Burnfield, 2009). Once an agenda is complete and distributed to all group members, the group leader still has preparation work to do:

- Given the items on the agenda, what leadership style should you use?
- What decision procedures will be most appropriate?
- Will the group meeting require any equipment?
- Have space and equipment been reserved?
- Are there enough seats?
- Can the participants fit comfortably around the table?
- Does the table and the configuration of the room enable all participants to see and speak to one another easily?
- Is the room available when you need it?
- Do you need to make a reservation?
- Will you need refreshments?
- What level of documentation is needed?
- What agendas, minutes, or reports will the meeting require?
- How many copies will be needed and who will make them?
- Will it be necessary to have overheads, flip charts, chalkboards, or technology during the meeting?
- Do you have to make an equipment reservation?

After this needs assessment, you are ready to plan the meeting and invite those you identified as necessary participants and inform others who simply need to know about the meeting. Make sure to give adequate lead time and send along the agenda and any other documentation they will need prior to the meeting. If you want participants to prepare in some special way for the meeting (e.g., to bring budget requests; to prepare a work schedule), make sure to tell them that. The more completely you prepare for the meeting, the more quickly the group will be able to work on its business and complete its activities.

Physical Environment and Material Resources

Usually, it is the leader who arranges for or secures the physical environment in which a group will meet. It is important to find a quiet meeting place where the group can have privacy. This type of setting promotes relational development because group members feel more comfortable negotiating differences of opinion in private. To the extent possible, seating arrangements should emphasize equality. Circular tables are more likely to provide this perception because conversational distance between all members is about the same. Circular settings also promote an open network of communication in which each group member can easily talk to every other member or to the entire group at once. When chairs are arranged in a lecture format (all chairs facing forward toward the leader or facilitator), it encourages one-way communication and reliance on the leader. A group member who is part of the audience has to gain formal acknowledgment that it is okay and appropriate to speak. And other group members may not be able to see the speaker. These physical conditions inhibit free-flowing interaction and limit the opportunities to develop relationships with other group members.

Stand-up meetings are becoming more popular, especially for group tasks that can be addressed within 10 to 20 minutes (Odermatt et al. 2015). These types of meetings are not less effective than meetings in which members sit at a table. But, stand up meetings encourage team members to keep the meeting short!

The greater the level of connectivity and embeddedness among group members, the more difficult it is for a group to find a time to meet. As our organizations become more team-oriented, meeting time and meeting preparation time become even more serious considerations. Groups that meet formally might also require time and space to meet informally in between regularly scheduled meetings. Informal interaction further anchors group member relationships and gives members an opportunity to test ideas with others before presenting them to the entire group. You may think time is only a problem for organizational groups, but this is not so. Given the variety of demands on your schedule, your family, personal, and recreational groups may be even more pressed for adequate time.

Group Member Pre-Meeting Responsibilities

You have just put your next work group meeting on your calendar. Now what? To be an effective contributor, you should review the agenda (or ask for one if it is not provided) to determine if you need to prepare anything before the meeting. For instance, in looking at the agenda, Dan sees that his group is going to begin considering alternative work schedules at its next meeting. He has not been asked to prepare anything, but he knows that these discussions will be emotional. Even though his group members complain frequently about the schedule they work, changing the work schedule will also cause problems. First, Dan reviews the overtime records to see how much overtime each member has worked. Then he reviews the project record to see if there is any pattern to how projects flow into the department. He notices that only a few projects come in the first week of the month but that the pace picks up steadily each week until many projects must be worked on simultaneously and completed by month's end. This gives him an idea: Why not propose that everyone work flextime the first 2 weeks of the month and take some additional time off? This would balance out the overtime needed during the final 2 weeks of the month. Now, Dan has an alternative based on data to present to the group for consideration.

Preparing for a meeting may require talking with other group members. For example, after reviewing her agenda, Marta believes that she should talk with Dan about the scheduling issues. As a single mother who depends on child care, she has a special interest in changes in schedules. She must get to the child care center by 6 p.m. or face a late penalty and an anxious child. Marta talks first with other parents in the group to see how they manage their child care arrangements. Cynthia tells her about one child care center that is open until 8 p.m. and Karen tells her that the company is scheduled to open an on-site child care center within a few months. At the meeting, Marta suggests that the work team lobby the company's executive board about the importance of an on-site child care center. With that benefit, employees like Marta will be willing to work unusual schedules. Although the child care center issue is not on the agenda, child care considerations affect the group's discussion of work schedules. Without talking beforehand to Cynthia or Karen, Marta would not know of any alternative child care arrangements or of the company's plans for an on-site child care center. Without this knowledge, Marta could easily steer the group off its primary topic to more emotional issues.

CONDUCTING THE MEETING

The group's leader or facilitator should arrive at the meeting site early to make sure everything is ready. When it is time for the meeting to start, the leader can call the meeting to order, preview the agenda with the group, and ask if other topics need to be added to it. By presenting the agenda as tentative rather than firm, the leader gains group members' support when together they agree that the agenda includes all important items (Schwarz, 1994). Posting the agenda so everyone can see it will help keep the meeting moving along. Before starting the meeting, the group should agree on the ground rules (e.g., when the meeting will end, what will happen if there is a tie vote). Finally, the group should review developments since the previous meeting. These should be brief reports to bring group members up to date.

Now the group is ready to move ahead with new business. As leader, taking each agenda item in order, you can announce the item and then ask what process might be most appropriate for this item of business. You can make suggestions but should be open to the ideas of other group members. With the item of business described and the process decided upon, you proceed with the discussion or action item. Generally, the leader's role is to initiate and structure discussion, not to control the discussion content. It is normal, if not always desirable, for group members to look to the leader for approval. One way to break this pattern and encourage input from everyone is to ask one member to respond to what another member says. This keeps the group discussion from developing into a pattern in which the leader says something each time a group member speaks.

Sometimes members complain, taking up valuable group time unnecessarily. For complaining members, your job as leader is to listen carefully to the complaints for their relevance to the agenda item. If a complaint is really about another topic, ask other group members to respond so you can gauge the extent to which this is a group rather than an individual concern. If it is a group concern, suggest that this issue be made another agenda item for later in the meeting (if there is time) or for a future meeting. If it is an individual issue, let the complaining group member know that you will speak with the member about it after the meeting. Besides controlling complaining speakers, you may also have to encourage less talkative members to contribute. You can do this by asking open-ended questions, such as "David, you've worked at other companies with rotating schedules. What can you tell us about your experiences?"

When different ideas are presented, summarize these in a compare-and-contrast format. Ask group members if your summaries are complete and accurate. If group members are quiet, do not assume their apparent consensus. Ask questions until you believe that group members really do agree on the substance of the issue. When an argument or conflict begins, do not take sides. Rather, ask group members to clarify their comments and probe for alternative viewpoints. You should reveal your own viewpoint only if it differs from those already expressed. To help clarify what the conflict is really about, ask group members to write down their response to the statement "I believe our conflict is about. . . ." This technique allows all group members to identify their perceptions of the conflict. Then ask group members to read their statements to the group. You may find that there is disagreement over what the conflict actually is about. Once the conflict is identified and agreed upon by all group members, encourage joint problem solving through discussion. When it is time for the group to make a decision, consider the advantages of each of the decision-making procedures described in Chapter 5. Be sure to let group members know if the decision they are making is a binding one or if a vote is simply an opportunity to see how group members are currently thinking about an issue.

Taking Minutes

Groups need a record, or **minutes**, of what they did at each meeting. Minutes should report on who attended the meeting, what was discussed, what was decided, who agreed to take on what responsibilities, and what the group plans to do next. Generally, the group's secretary or recorder takes the minutes, finalizes them, and presents them to the group at the next meeting. Many groups prefer that the minutes be prepared and distributed prior to the next group meeting. This gives members ample opportunity to review the record for accuracy. At the next group meeting, the minutes should be reviewed and corrected, if needed, before being accepted by the group as its formal record of activity. Figure 9.4 shows the minutes that resulted from the meeting conducted with the agenda displayed in Figure 9.3.

Besides providing a review of the meeting, the most important part of the minutes is to list member assignments for the next meeting. A main reason group meetings become

---

Minutes

Project Development Work Group

Thursday, January 29, 1:00 to 1:40 p.m. Conference Room A

Participants: Cynthia, Dan, Lu, Marquita, Tyron

Guest: Jensen

Purpose: Project Update Tracking

Lu called the meeting to order at 1:00; all members of the work group were present. Jensen Clark attended the meeting at Lu's invitation.

Lu reported on three items that occurred since the January 15 meeting: (a) promotion of competing software, (b) manufacturing status of our software, and (c) results from software demonstrations. Competing software has entered the market but has received unfavorable reviews. Our software is still on target for a March 1 release date, and feedback from the demonstrations has been positive. *Decision*: The group decided that additional demonstrations were not warranted. *Action*: Dan will check manufacturing status every Friday and email an update to each member of the group. *Action*: Lu will ask the marketing department to watch consumer reaction of competing software.

Dan reported that December project activity was slightly off due to higher than anticipated vacation days. January numbers appear to be in line with estimates.

Cynthia reported that her presentation to Federal Railways…

page 1 of 2

Figure 9.4 Sample Meeting Minutes

dysfunctional is a lack of follow-up on assignments. Without a reminder, group members may forget their assignment from one meeting to the next. Meetings become pointless and frustrating if group members are not ready with their assignments. Meeting minutes are one way to combat this problem.

Managing Relational Issues

Besides conducting the meeting and helping the group accomplish what is on the agenda, the leader or facilitator is also responsible for developing and maintaining a supportive group climate. Greeting group members as they arrive and engaging them in small talk can help establish a friendly meeting environment. If group members do not know one another well, brief self-introductions, name badges, and table tents can help them learn names more quickly.

If the meeting is long, suggest taking a break. This not only gives people time to take care of personal needs or get a snack but also relieves the tensions that can develop in groups. Another way to help group members feel more comfortable is to ask for volunteers for assignments. When someone volunteers, ask other members who know and like this person to work with the volunteer.

As the leader, you also have primary responsibility for establishing and setting group norms. Group members will follow your lead. As the meeting progresses, analyze norms for their effectiveness. Just because your group has always done it a certain way does not mean that it is effective. When you speak, try to use "we" and "our team" rather than "I" language. These subtle cues help create a team atmosphere other members can accept and adopt.

Because conflict is a natural outgrowth of group discussions, watch for cues from group members that conflicting positions or hidden agendas are developing. Conflict cues include rising voices as the conversation goes back and forth between group members and the use of more dominant nonverbal behaviors, such as a visible tightening of arms and faces, forceful gestures, and averted bodies. Some group members become silent and withdraw from a group's conversation when conflict arises.

A hidden agenda may be developing when one group member dominates the conversation while dismissing input from others. A **hidden agenda** exists when a group member has an ulterior motive. Group members ask the question or raise the issue for personal gain or personal satisfaction, not to help the group. Loaded questions ("So, you don't think I would be a good chairperson?") are often associated with hidden agendas, causing other group members either to retreat or to respond with the answer the person is looking for merely to keep peace in the group. When you see cues that conflict or hidden agendas developing, deal with them. The longer you wait, the more entrenched they become, making them more difficult for the group to manage and making the group less effective. (See Chapter 7 for strategies for managing conflicts.)

Using Space

Four principles should guide the selection and use of meeting space (Schwarz, 1994). First, all group members should be able to see and hear one another. Many different room configurations can accommodate this goal, but round or rectangular tables generally are best for groups of less than 10. A U-shaped table configuration can work well for groups of 20 or so. But, members should only be seated on the outside of the U so they can easily see one another. Second, the seating arrangement should allow each member to easily view the flip chart, the white board, or the screen. Third, if nonparticipants are invited to the meeting to provide information or simply to observe, they should not sit with the group members who will discuss or vote on issues before the group. Nonparticipants can easily contribute when called upon if they sit outside or just beyond the participants. This seating arrangement keeps nonparticipants from invading the psychological or relational space of group members. As a final consideration, the space for the group meeting should fit the needs of the group but not be so large as to allow for empty seats among participants. Group members may need space for writing, and they should not feel crowded. But allowing for too much extra space between members may increase the psychological distance among them and impede group progress.

Using Visuals

Even the best meetings and the best groups can profit from keeping visual records of what is happening in the group. Although a secretary or recorder may be taking minutes, these generally reflect group outcomes or the final decisions made by group members. Graphics or visuals can be used to keep track of the group's process and progress. By keeping and posting a running record of the group's key ideas and central themes, several positive things occur. First, group members know immediately if others are accurately hearing them. As a group posts its ideas on a flip chart or white board, it is easy to determine whether another group member accurately summarized someone's 4-minute statement and to correct misperceptions as needed. Second, writing what people say makes members feel acknowledged and part of the group process. When this type of validation occurs, group members are more likely to continue to contribute to the group discussion, which increases levels of participation, cooperation, and involvement. Third, visualizing or graphing what is going on in a group helps to spark the creativity of group members. Providing a visualization of the interaction helps group members both analyze and synthesize ideas before the group. Finally, visualizing the group's interaction provides a graphic record for the group, helping to reinforce group decisions. In this case, seeing is believing. The visuals can also be used for making minutes more detailed. The graphic record can be referred to in future meetings when the group needs to revisit something it has already addressed.

What does it take to visualize a group meeting? Markers and flip chart pads or white boards are the best tools. Making visuals does not require artistic talent, but it does require that you be interested in what is happening in the group and be able to follow the interaction. Most group members can visualize or graph a group's interaction with just a little practice.

Here is how the process works. Any group member can visually track the group's interaction. The role of this person is to capture what people say, not to evaluate ideas. Record everything, as accurately as you can, in group members' words. Your job is to provide some structure or organization to what people say. You might want to use different colors—say, green for positive attributes, red for negative attributes, and purple for questions that still need to be explored. Periodically stop and ask other group members if you have captured everything accurately and clearly. Use asterisks (*), boxes and circles, and underlining to highlight important items or to indicate what has been decided upon. Use forms (stick people, smiling faces, dollar signs, check marks, question marks—anything you feel comfortable drawing) to help structure or organize the record.

Other visual techniques that can assist your group include mapping, clustering, and flow charts. In the clustering technique, you place comments together within circles as themes start to emerge in a group's discussion. Starting with just a few spread-out circles helps you cluster items together. And you can draw lines out to other ideas to connect circles (themes). The clustering technique helps groups separate and integrate ideas. The mapping technique is similar to clustering in that it separates and integrates ideas, but it adds elements to reflect the flow of the group's discussion. The group member developing the visual reflects the decisions made during the discussion by noting the questions members ask and the answers the group develops. In mapping, it's a good idea to start on the left side with general ideas and questions and to work toward the right as the group develops the answers. Arrows can be drawn to connect answers to questions and to indicate the sequence of the discussion. Look at the map of a group meeting in Figure 9.5. Can you tell what this group discussed?

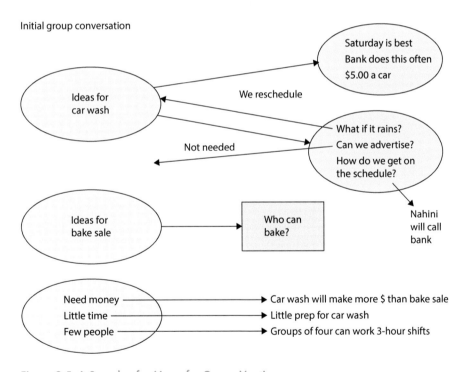

Figure 9.5 A Sample of a Map of a Group Meeting

Whatever visualizing or graphing techniques your group uses, do not throw them away. The group's secretary or recorder can use them to write more detailed minutes. Group members might want to refer back to them between meetings to see if an idea was discussed. And because the visualizations are a pictorial record of the group's process, they can even be used to settle disputes.

Making Assignments

Most group meetings reach a point at which additional information is needed. The leader may assign individual members these responsibilities, or group members may volunteer. In either case, you need to develop action statements and get agreement about what is to be completed.

For example, it becomes obvious to Terry that his group needs more information on how to use the company's videoconferencing system before this group will agree to adopt its use. Being comfortable with technology, Terry offers to find information about training for the group. Sounds good, right? But what exactly is Terry going to do? Will he find out when the training is scheduled? Will he explore what is covered in the training? Will he see if there is a training manual that can be placed near their computers? When should he report back to the group? And how? By email? By specifying what should be accomplished, Terry's expectations will parallel those of others. When assignments are made or accepted in meetings, this action should immediately be noted for inclusion on the next meeting's agenda. It helps create continuity in the group when group members report back on what they have accomplished, and it keeps all group members informed of progress toward group goals.

Ending the Meeting

At the end of the meeting, the group should do two things. First, members should review decisions and plans for action. Taking this step helps everyone understand precisely what decisions were made and who is responsible for following through for the group. Second, if the group does not have a regular meeting time, members should schedule the next meeting and discuss a tentative agenda. This step helps group members view the meetings as having continuity, rather than each meeting being an independent activity.

Meeting Virtually

Meeting virtually has many of same challenges as meeting face-to-face. These six guidelines are offered as action items in preparing for an online meeting (Allison, Shuffler, & Wallace, 2015).

1   Select a facilitator. The person in this role does not have to be the team's leader, but should have expertise in the technology being used for the meeting.

2   Select the communication technology. Choice of technology should match team members' communication preferences and meet the purpose of the meeting. (See Messersmith, 2015, for a review of group meeting technologies.)

3 Set norms for the meeting. Virtual meetings require a more formal structure and it may be necessary to determine how members will signal they want to talk.

4 Set and reinforce team roles. Clarify team goals and responsibilities at the beginning of the meeting.

5 Acknowledge both time zone and cultural differences. Rotate meetings so everyone can share in the inconvenience of a bad meeting time. If language barriers are present, add email, teleconferencing, or videoconferencing.

6 Follow up with action items. Use appropriate technology (often email) to follow up with members.

POST-MEETING FOLLOW-UP

Most leaders consider their job done when the group concludes its meeting. However, to make meetings more effective, a few follow-up steps should be performed. First, the leader should review the minutes with the person who took them and distribute them to each group member. This should be done as soon after the meeting as possible. This enables other group members to review the minutes for completeness and accuracy so that corrections can be made as soon as possible and the minutes be redistributed. Because the minutes include action statements for which group members agreed to be responsible, this reminds them of their commitment to the group. Second, if a group's actions will affect other groups or individuals, the leader should share the group's decisions with those parties. And third, when reviewing the actions to be taken from this agenda, the leader should begin preparing the initial framework for the group's next agenda.

The leader has another responsibility toward the group. After each meeting, the leader should analyze what went well and what did not work. To a great extent, the leader is responsible for making sure the group realized its goals during the meeting. Did that occur, and if not, why not? The leader should also think back over the meeting's interaction to assess whether individual group members' goals appear to be in alignment with the group's goals. If not, what could the leader do to encourage or motivate group members?

After important group business is conducted, the leader should also analyze to what extent inequality was an issue in the group. Some inequalities may stem from the leader's influence attempts. Some leaders are too assertive or dominant in their communicator style, which effectively shuts down members' contributions. In a sense, this influence pattern diminishes the need for a meeting, in that the leader is the only group member talking, giving input, and making decisions. Another type of negative influence occurs when a leader always looks to and speaks to the same group members. By consistently relying on only certain group members to answer questions and take on responsibilities for the group, the leader is implicitly saying to the others "You don't count" or "I don't trust you to do this for us." In either case, the leader's influence creates subgroups—the dominant subgroup that performs most of the group's work and a subordinate subgroup whose members are expected to follow along meekly. A leader can avoid these problems by making eye contact periodically with all group members, encouraging more silent group members to give their opinions, deferring the input of more dominant group members, and using decision-making procedures to help equalize any undue influence in the group.

Group members also have post-meeting responsibilities. If you were assigned or took on a responsibility to the group, be sure to fulfill it. If you believe the group forgot to cover something important, ask the leader to make sure it is part of the next meeting's agenda.

OVERCOMING MEETING OBSTACLES

Despite your best efforts in planning for and conducting meetings, problems can still arise. You have probably encountered one or several of six general obstacles to effective group meetings: (a) long meetings, (b) unequal member involvement and commitment, (c) the formation of cliques, (d) different levels of communication skills, (e) different communicator styles, and (f) personal conflicts (Gastil, 1993). Let's examine each obstacle and consider how you can help your group overcome each one.

PUTTING THE PIECES TOGETHER

Group Identity, Interdependence, and Group Structure

Reflect on a meeting in which your group experienced one or more obstacles, like those described in this chapter. First, identify the obstacles that arose. Now, assess each obstacle for its impact on group member identity. For example, did the length of the meeting cause members to resent being in the group? Did the formation of cliques cause negative feelings and emotions and threaten the identity of the group? To what degree did the obstacles that arose affect interdependence among group members? How could you determine that interdependence was adversely affected? Finally, what structural elements of the group—group roles, norms, and communication network—contributed to these problems? Using the principles of meeting management, what suggestions to group structure would you make to prevent these obstacles from occurring in the future?

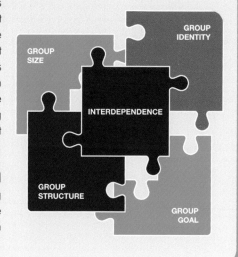

Long Meetings

No one likes long meetings, but a lack of preparation by group members actually contributes to this dilemma. Review what happened at the last meeting and what the group wants to accomplish at this meeting. At the meeting, speak in a clear but concise manner. Do not ramble, and do not let other group members do so either. If a group member gets off track, ask them to clarify their points. If your group has several long-winded talkers, you might want to consider asking group members to establish a time limit for individuals to contribute to the discussion. This can quicken the pace of the meeting. Keep side conversations to a minimum because one side conversation tends to escalate into several more. Having definite starting and stopping times for your meetings can help. And if you cannot cover all of the agenda items in your meeting, ask members for their commitment to continuing the meeting or schedule a follow-up.

Unequal Member Involvement and Commitment

You cannot be directly responsible for another member's level of involvement. However, there are ways to encourage equal participation. Asking questions to all members may help, as well as linking the interests of each member to the goal or activity of the group. Pointing out individual member benefits can help them identify with the group more strongly. Generally, when members identify with the group, they become more committed. Another strategy for increasing involvement and commitment is to allow the group to create and develop its own goals. When members help direct the activities of the group, their involvement and commitment follow. These strategies can help a group overcome social loafing, or the failure of group members to perform to their potential (Comer, 1995). When group member participation is unequal, less talkative group members may become detached from the group because they feel as if their contributions do not matter.

Formation of Cliques

Cliques, or subgroups, develop when there is a reason or need to communicate outside the group setting. When cliques develop, not all group members will have access to needed information. You probably cannot entirely avoid the formation of cliques, but you can reduce the impact of cliques on the group by having an alternative means of communicating with all group members. You can post the group's minutes, activities, or agenda online or on a bulletin board. If it is going to be a long time until the next group meeting and group members do not have access to a common area, send crucial information to all members. Ask group members to communicate important developments that occur between group meetings to all other members before the start of the next meeting. Finally, be sure to recognize personally each group member early in the group's discussion.

Using their names and asking them questions that personally involve them in the group's discussion increases each member's involvement in the full group.

Different Levels of Communication Skill

You may think there is not much you can do to enhance another group member's lack of communication skill, but there is. You might begin a group session by asking all group members to report on what they accomplished while away from the group or to reflect on what happened in the previous group meeting. The important thing here is to give each group member an opportunity to speak freely. You can help other members improve their skills by asking them questions that you know they can answer easily but that still contribute to the group. For example, you know that Marianne did a great deal of work checking out three sites for the festival. But you also know that she has some difficulty in giving detailed descriptions. Here is how you can help: Ask Marianne to tell the group about the three sites. When she pauses, ask her which site she prefers. What did she particularly like about that site? What criteria did she use in selecting sites? By asking Marianne follow up questions you know she can answer, you are helping her overcome her anxiety, as well as providing details for other group members so that they can appreciate the work Marianne did.

Different Communicator Styles

People differ in their personalities and their communicator styles. What can you do to decrease differences among communicator styles in your group? The key is to remain flexible and to accept other styles. If everyone had the same communicator style, the group's interaction could be boring and less productive. Think about maximizing the opportunities that differences offer to the group rather than negating others who communicate differently.

Personal Conflicts

Personal conflicts and personality conflicts are especially likely to happen if the group is feeling other pressures (such as time, resource, or deadline pressures). Rather than panic when these conflicts occur, use them as opportunities to learn more about other group members. Having an expectation that some conflict may occur will prevent you from being caught off guard when such situations arise. Another way to avoid personal conflicts is to create a supportive climate in which members can express their feelings in the group. Sometimes conflicts occur simply because we think someone said something other than what they did. When a conflict does arise, help members work through it by having each side express its views clearly. Finally, if an intense conflict develops, direct the group's attention to the primary conflict issue before continuing with other group activities or business. Failing to deal with the conflict when it arises will likely escalate the conflict later. The "Putting the Pieces Together: Group Identity, Interdependence, and Group Structure" feature will give you further insight into conflict and other meeting obstacles.

 THEORY STANDOUT

Strategic Meeting Interaction

Beck and Keyton's theory of strategic meeting interaction assumes that all types of interactions, whether verbal or nonverbal, are strategic (Beck & Keyton, 2009; Beck, Paskewitz, & Keyton, 2015). The theory makes three assumptions. First, team members adapt their messages to the relational and task aspects of group context. Second, strategic meeting interaction allows the examination of both messages produced and messages received by all group members in the interaction setting. Third, strategic meeting interaction provides a basis to examine the potentially different meanings that are produced from the same interactions. Their study of a regular end-of-work-week meeting revealed that, in some meeting interactions, members had similar interpretations of what had happened. At other times, members have considerably different view of what was going on. Why? When members described the strategic intent of others, they identified the *relational* intent of the messages. But when members described the strategic intent of their own messages, they identified the *task* intent of the messages. This suggests that team members are less aware of their relational strategies and, perhaps, even their relational intentions. Unfortunately, then, members may base their subsequent messages in the meeting on a foundation that other members do not share.

SUMMARY

Meeting management procedures and facilitation strategies are designed to capitalize on the strengths of group members and group processes. Meeting planning includes pre-meeting planning and preparation by group members and by the group leader. An agenda, identifying both start and stop times and all items the group will consider, should be prepared and distributed before any group meeting. Remember: If you cannot identify a specific purpose and goals for a meeting, do not have one.

The group's leader conducts the meeting according to the agenda. However, the leader's role is to initiate and structure discussion, not to control discussion content. Besides helping the group move through its business issues, the leader is also responsible for developing and maintaining a supportive group climate. Introducing members, establishing norms, and managing conflict are some of these responsibilities.

One way to help your group is to develop a group charter or mission statement and a code of conduct. A group charter describes the goals or mission of the group; a code of conduct describes behaviors that are appropriate for this particular group. Both can provide direction and clarity for group members.

A secretary or recorder should take minutes at each meeting. Minutes should include what was discussed or decided, who agreed to take on what responsibilities, and what the group plans to do next. Minutes should be distributed, and revisions made, as soon as possible.

The space in which a group meets is important. All group members should be able to see and hear one another easily. The size of the space for the meeting should fit the needs and size of the group. Members should feel neither too crowded nor too distant from others in the group. Using visuals and graphics can help a group record what is happening in the group. Listing topics of conversation, drawing a diagram of the group's conversation, clustering ideas together, creating data tables, and drawing organizational charts are just a few types of visualization that help a group capture a pictorial memory of its interaction.

In most meetings, group members volunteer for or are given assignments to be completed before the next meeting. These actions should be noted both in the minutes and on the next meeting's agenda. At the end of a meeting, the group should review decisions and plans for actions, schedule the next meeting time, and discuss future agenda items.

Most groups experience some obstacles. Long meetings, unequal member involvement and commitment, the formation of cliques, differing levels of communication skills, different communicator styles, and personal conflicts are common obstacles groups must overcome. Any group member can help a group surmount these barriers.

DISCUSSION QUESTIONS AND EXERCISES

1 Think of your most recent group experience—one in which the group will meet again. Write a three- to five-page paper analyzing your group by answering these questions:

a. What did your group accomplish? How does that compare to what it should have accomplished?

b. What is one aspect of the group process or procedure that was effective, and one aspect that was ineffective?

c. Which meeting management strategies would have helped your group? How? Be specific.

d. What did you learn about yourself as a group member that you can carry forward to the next group experience? What did you learn about the group that you can apply in the next group session?

2 Gather the agendas of several different meetings. Compare and analyze them for their effectiveness. If the agendas are from meetings you attended, consider the usefulness of the agenda to the structure and purpose of the meeting. If the agendas are from meetings of other individuals, ask them to what degree the agendas helped them prepare for the meeting (if they got the agenda ahead of time) and to what degree the agenda reflected the meeting's activities.

3 Interview at least three people who have been members of organizational groups or teams, or community or civic groups. Ask each person to describe how the group or team accomplished its work at meetings. If these are not mentioned, ask each person about the group's use of agendas, graphics, and minutes.

 NAILING IT!

Using Group Communication Skills for Group Presentations

Your group is ready to make its presentation. The few hours before the presentation can be hectic. How can you use meeting management techniques to help calm everyone down, smooth out the remaining issues, and deliver a great presentation? Return to your group charter, and let your group members know that together they've met the group goal. Make a written list on a notecard of the last few things that need attention. Use this list as a way to check in with every group member. Before the presentation, take a few minutes for a group huddle. Thank members for the time, skills, and energy they put into developing the presentation. Be sure to encourage them to do their best during the presentation. After the presentation, check in with them again. Point out what they did in the presentation (or in developing the presentation) that was especially effective and the audience enjoyed. Finally, if your group borrowed equipment or supplies, make sure those are returned. Although the group presentation is not a meeting, many of the same techniques apply.

Image Credits

CREATING AND DELIVERING TEAM PRESENTATIONS

Y ou've been assigned a team presentation. Now what do you do? Whether you are a first-time or experienced presenter, presenting as a group can create some new challenges! This appendix is divided into three sections focusing on developing, preparing for, and making the presentation, respectively.

DEVELOPING YOUR PRESENTATION

Thinking About Your Presentation

- Ask yourself, what is the purpose of the presentation? To persuade? Inspire? Inform? Teach? Instruct? Entertain?

- As a group, outline or map your presentation. Decide who will be responsible for each part of the presentation and for transitions between the parts. Even though individual members might specialize in various parts of the presentation, every group member is responsible for all of the material in the presentation.

- Consider the unique talents of your team members.

- All team members should have a part in the presentation.

- Consider your audience in developing the presentation material.

- Watch the local news for examples of how to make transitions between parts of the presentation.

- If you have been given 25 minutes for the presentation, plan on filling 20 of it. Presentations seldom start on time—perhaps because latecomers are accommodated, the previous class let out late, or a few announcements are made. It's better to finish early and have time for questions than to shove 25 minutes of material into 20 minutes or to run overtime.

- Develop your material with three specific main points you want the audience to learn from your presentation. Outline or map these points before you begin, deliver the three points, and summarize these points.

- Organize your points in one of these ways: (a) from simple to complex, (b) in chronological order, (c) from general to specific, or (d) from problem to solution.

PREPARING FOR THE PRESENTATION

Setting Up the Room

- Ask your instructor if you can rearrange the room for your presentation. Changing how the room is set up creates interest and signals that something different is about to happen. If you do so, it should be done before any class members arrive.
- Try some of these shapes: a U-shape, angled tables or chairs, amphitheater style, a circle with a large opening. Or turn all of the chairs in a different direction, making another wall the temporary *front* of the classroom.
- Don't use the lectern just because one is there. If you're not going to use it, remove it. A lectern can create an unnecessary barrier between you and your audience.

Using Visual Aids

- Make a commitment to using visual aids in your presentation. They add value to your presentation and increase your effectiveness.
- Use visual aids to serve as your notes, help maintain audience interest, underscore your points, and keep you focused.
- For every visual aid you use, ask whether it is worth it and what objective it serves. You and your group members are the presentation. The visual aids are just helpers.
- Don't use too many visual aids—no more than one per minute.
- Don't turn the lights out even when projecting visuals. This will only put your audience to sleep!
- Use visuals as reminders to yourself, but don't read them word for word—the audience can do that!
- If you have a list of concepts on a slide, use the transition feature to reveal each item as you talk about it. Otherwise, your audience will read the list while you are reporting on the first item. Revealing concepts item by item also helps you control your thinking and your rate of speaking.
- Simplify. Use the simplest visual aid that gets your point across, easily and clearly.
- Think horizontally. People are used to viewing television.
- Use color and contrast; it makes a greater impact.
- Include no more than four colors per visual.
- Use dark print on a light background or light print on a dark background.
- Maintain the same background color throughout your presentation.
- Don't use red for text. Use it to highlight with bullets, arrows, and so on.

- Avoid red/green contrasts; some people are color blind.
- In planning a color scheme, use darker colors on the bottom, medium colors in the middle, and lighter colors on top.
- Use short titles.
- Use plenty of white space. Don't crowd the slide or chart.
- Use graphics, charts, pictures, audio, or video to help communicate complex ideas.
- Use pie charts to show the distribution of a whole into its component parts (e.g., budgets or times).
- Use bar charts to represent quantity by the length or height of the bar. Use color coding to help audience members interpret the bars (e.g., blue for this year and yellow for last year).
- Make sure the visual aids use a consistent form, color scheme, and type style so the result is a *group* presentation.
- Have all group members proofread all visual aids regardless of who designed or made them.
- Rehearse with the visual aids.

Preparing and Using Flip Charts

- Recognize that flip charts are one of the cheapest and most effective presentation aids (i.e., they can't break down and they allow the lights to be at their brightest). They can be prepared ahead of time or used spontaneously during the presentation.
- Don't use a flip chart if there are more than 30 audience members—not all members will be able to see it.
- Leave a blank page at the beginning of your flip chart pad.
- Staple a blank sheet behind each flip chart page you are going to use. This way writing won't bleed through, and it makes the pages easier to turn.
- Don't think you have to be an artist to use a flip chart. Well-spaced, large letters, and simple figures and diagrams work well on flip charts.
- Use very light blue lines—which you can see but the audience can't—to help you keep your lettering straight and all the same height (two-inch height is recommended).
- As a rule of thumb, include no more than six lines per flip chart. Begin each item with a bullet so audience members can tell where to stop and start.
- Use two flip charts. One can be prepared ahead of time, and the other can be used spontaneously during the presentation.
- Place flip charts to the side of the presentation space. The presenter is more important than the flip chart.

Using PowerPoint Presentations

- Ensure that your memory stick works with the computer you will be using. Also email yourself a copy of the presentation; that way you can download the file if necessary.
- Ensure that the version of PowerPoint in which you created the presentation is the version installed on the computer. Not all versions are compatible.
- Have a *welcome* slide with the title of your presentation up when the audience comes in.
- The last slide should be a prompt for questions or provide contact information for the speakers.
- Use a wireless device to advance the slides. That way, the speaker is not trapped behind equipment.
- Incorporate charts, graphics, pictures, animation, and video to help make your point. Don't, however, let these features overshadow what you have to say.
- If your presentation is more textual than graphic, try using circles, squares, or triangles to group text together for more impact.
- For text, use the 6 x 6 rule: no more than six words per line, and no more than six lines per slide.
- Use uppercase and lowercase text.
- Put a paper copy of each slide on the floor. If you can read it while standing up, the type is probably large enough. If not, the type is too small.
- As you show a new slide, allow a second or two for the visual impact to sink in. Then give the explanation.

Using Video

- Use no more than 2 to 3 minutes of video at a time.
- Know where the pause and stop buttons are on the screen.
- Test the video out on others before you show it to your audience. Is it as funny or moving or dramatic as you think?
- Check the volume before the presentation.

Using Handouts

- Check for accuracy (grammar, punctuation, spelling).
- Don't reproduce your visual aids and distribute them at the beginning of the presentation. You'll be sure to lose your audience!

- If you must use a handout because of complexity or detail, distribute it when you come to that part of the presentation.

- If you want audience members to have a complete set of handouts, tell them they'll be available after your presentation, and hand them out as they go out the door.

Using Numbers and Statistics

- Round off numbers so the audience can remember them. Which would you remember better: nearly $5 million or $4,789,187?

- Use the most recent statistics you can find. Don't present 2000 figures in 2018. What were you doing in 2000?

Preparing Your Notes

- Put your notes on 5 x 7 note cards. They are easy to hold, and they don't make noise.

- Alternatively, try putting your notes on the four sides of an empty manila file folder. You can keep your handouts or overheads in it before and after the presentation.

Working as a Team

- Act like a team. A group presentation isn't a series of individual presentations.

- Agree on who will handle questions from the audience. Generally, those who presented the material should respond to the question.

- Work out transitions between sections. Use the next speaker's name in handing off—for example, "That covers decision-making groups. Now Andrew will cover families as groups."

- Assign one member to keep track of the time during the presentation. Have preplanned cues for signaling information about time.

- Focus on the audience. Make the presentation to the audience, not your group.

- When you're not speaking, look at the person who is speaking.

- Be sure to tell the audience the agenda for your presentation. When multiple people speak, the audience needs a road map.

- Rehearse as a team.

Rehearsing Your Presentation

- Do not play it by ear. Your audience deserves a rehearsed presentation.

- Recognize that writing out the presentation is not the same as rehearsing it.

- Keep in mind that rehearsals tend to run shorter than the actual presentation. A 20-minute rehearsal usually means a 25- to 30-minute presentation.

- Rehearse using all of the visual aids and equipment you plan to include in the presentation. There is no substitute for a dress rehearsal.

- Have all members do their parts as planned. Filling in for someone at rehearsal increases the likelihood that you'll fill in for that person at the presentation. Again, there is no substitute for a dress rehearsal.

- Review all visual aids for spelling, grammar, and punctuation.

- Check the voice levels of all presenters. Ask a couple of friends (but not anyone who will be part of the audience) to help you by playing the role of audience members during your rehearsals. They can give you valuable feedback.

- If you can, rehearse in the room in which you'll give your presentation.

- Talk about what you'll wear for the presentation. You won't look like a group if four of you show up in dress clothes and one of you wears jeans. Clothing should be coordinated, but it doesn't have to match.

- Know that the best rehearsal is a video rehearsal. Get a friend to record your presentation, or set up a camera with a wide-angle shot. Video is the most powerful tool for identifying flaws. If you don't have access to video, at least audiorecord the rehearsal. You'll be amazed at what you'll hear.

DELIVERING THE PRESENTATION

Introduction

- Introduce all members of the group.

- Be sure to tell audience members why your topic is important. Give them at least three reasons they should pay attention to what you have to say.

- Capture the audience's attention by answering the question "What's in it for me?"

Communicating Verbally

- Do not start with humor or a joke.

- Do not apologize or make excuses for anything or anyone.

- Use specific language—for example, "We can increase membership by 60 percent" rather than "We can increase membership a lot."
- Use vivid language, paint word pictures, and use metaphors.
- Use action words.
- Use short, simple words.
- Eliminate clichés or overused phrases.
- Think of your presentation as a conversation with audience members.
- Anchor new information in something familiar to the audience.
- Use transitions:

  "That brings us to our next point."

  "Now that we've discussed X, let's talk about Y."

  "So far we've covered decision making and leadership. Now let's take a look at conflict."

  "In addition to consensus building, we need to address conflict."

  "To begin, let's take a look at …"

  "The next important factor is …"

  "That's the first reason to be flexible as a leader. The next reason is …"

  "Finally, let's consider …"

  "In conclusion, …"

  "To summarize, …"

  "We'd like to leave you with this thought."

Communicating Nonverbally

- Move around when you talk.
- Use hand movements and arm gestures.
- Vary the quality of your voice. It's easy to do this if you avoid the straight presentation of information. It's easier to be expressive when you use analogies, tell stories, give demonstrations, and ask questions.
- Make eye contact with your audience.
- Manage your nonverbal adaptors.
- If you're using visual aids, turn and look at the aid to get the point securely in your mind. Then turn to the audience and address the point to them. Keep looking at the audience until you are finished and are ready to address the next point on the visual aid.

Handling the Question-and-Answer Session

- While you're developing the presentation, make a list of questions you believe audience members will ask. Prepare an answer for each one.

- Be aware that you're likely to be met with silence if you ask, "Are there any questions?" Rather, ask, "Are there any questions about how leaders should be flexible?" or "Are there any questions about the difference between task and relational messages?"

- If you ask the audience a question, pause for a moment to give members time to think of one.

- If there are no questions, continue by saying "One question we had when we started our research was …" or "One of the most frequent questions asked about [the topic] is …"

- When an audience member asks you a question, start your response by restating the question so all audience members can hear it. Many times, others in the audience haven't heard the question, which means you're responding to something that doesn't make any sense to them.

- Assuming the Q & A session happens at the end of the presentation, after the last question thank the audience for the questions and then summarize and close out the presentation.

Handling Interruptions From the Audience

- If you are interrupted by a question that will be answered later as part of your planned presentation, say, "Dale, I'm coming to that in about 2 minutes" or "The answer is yes, and I'll explain it fully in just a few minutes."

- If you are interrupted by a question that will not be part of your planned presentation, say, "Dale, that's a good question. I'd like to answer it at the end of the presentation."

- If you are interrupted by a question or comment that you prefer not to answer publicly, say, "Dale, that's interesting (or "I hadn't thought of that"). Let's talk about it after the presentation."

SUGGESTED READING

Brennan, M. (2016, Nov. 29). To persuade people, trade PowerPoint for papier-mâché. *Harvard Business Review Digital Articles*, 2–5.

Duarte, N. (2008). *Slideology: The art and science of creating great presentations.* Sebastopol, CA: O'Reilly Media.

Duarte, N., & Sanchez, P. (2016). *Illuminate: Ignite change through speeches, stories, ceremonies, and symbols.* New York, NY: Portfolio/Penguin.

Glonek, K. L., & King, P. E. (2014). Listening to narratives: An experimental examination of storytelling in the classroom. *International Journal of Listening, 28*, 32–46. doi:10.1080/10904018.2014.861302

Hertz, B., van Woerkum, C., & Kerkhof, P. (2015). Why do scholars use PowerPoint the way they do? *Business and Professional Communication Quarterly, 78*, 273–291. doi:10.1177/2329490615589171

Hertz, B., Kerkhof, P., & van Woerkum, C. (2016). PowerPoint slides as speaking notes: The influence of speaking anxiety on the use of text on slides. *Business and Professional Communication Quarterly, 79*, 348–359. doi:10.1177/2329490615620416

Kernbach, S., Bresciani, S., & Eppler, M. J. (2015). Slip-sliding-away: A review of the literature on the constraining qualities of PowerPoint. *Business and Professional Communication Quarterly, 78*, 292–313. doi:10.1177/2329490615595499

Pruim, D. E. (2016). Disaster day! Integrating speech skills though impromptu group research and presentation. *Communication Teacher, 30*, 62–66. doi:10.1080/17404622.2016.1139148

Reynolds, G. (2014). *Presentation Zen: A simple visual approach to presenting in today's world* (2nd ed.). San Francisco, CA: New Riders.

Worley, R., & Dyrud, M. (Eds.). (2004). Presentation and the PowerPoint problem. *Business Communication Quarterly, 67*, 78–94.

Worley, R., & Dyrud, M. (Eds.). (2004). Presentation and the PowerPoint problem—Part II. *Business Communication Quarterly, 67*, 214–231.

GLOSSARY

accommodating A win-lose conflict management strategy exemplified by trying to satisfy the other's concerns.

affective ties In a communication network, relationships built on the liking or trusting of another group member.

affective trust A type of trust among group members based on the interpersonal concern group members show for one another outside of the group task.

agenda A list of activities or topics to be considered at a group meeting; should also include starting and stopping times, the location of the meeting, the attendees, and the overall goal of the meeting, as well as the specific goal of each agenda item and any preparations that group members should make.

avoiding conflict management strategy A nonconfrontive strategy for managing conflict, based on verbal, physical, or psychological withdrawal.

bona fide group perspective A theoretical frame that illuminates the relationship of the group to its context or environment by recognizing a group's permeable and fluid boundaries and the time and space characteristics of its interactions.

brainstorming A group procedure designed to help groups generate creative ideas.

centralized communication network Communication network that imposes restrictions on who can talk to whom and for which one or two group members control those restrictions.

certainty An attribute of a negative communication climate, group members communicate as if they possess all the answers or believe they can predict what another group member is going to say or do.

coalition formation Phenomenon that occurs when one member takes sides with another against yet another member of the group; creates an imbalance of power; can only occur with at least three group members.

code of conduct A group document that describes behaviors appropriate for the group.

coercive power A type of power resulting from the expectation that one group member can be punished by another.

cognitive conflict A type of conflict involving disagreement over interpretations or analyses of information or data; also known as *judgment conflict*.

cognitive ties In a communication network, describe who knows whom.

cognitive trust Based on group members' assessments about the reliability, dependability, and competence of other group members.

cohesiveness The degree to which members desire to remain in the group.

collaboration A conflict management strategy based on parties sharing a superordinate goal of solving the problem even though their initial ideas for how to solve it differ.

communication The process of symbol production, reception, and usage; conveyance and reception of messages; and meanings that develop from those messages; all communication is strategic in that people communicate to accomplish a specific purpose.

communication climate The atmosphere that results from group members' use of verbal and nonverbal communication and listening skills; can be defensive or supportive.

communication competency approach to leadership A model for leadership based on three principles: (1) leadership is action that helps a group overcome barriers or obstacles, (2) leadership occurs through interaction, and (3) there is a set of skills or competencies that individuals use to exercise leadership in groups.

communication network The interaction pattern or flow of messages between and among group members; creates structure for the group based on patterns of who talks to whom.

communication overload Communication that is too extensive or complex and that comes from too many sources; causes stress and confusion among group members.

communication underload Communication that is infrequent and simple; causes group members to feel disconnected from the group.

competing A distributive conflict management strategy exemplified by forcing; emphasizes one party winning at the other party's expense.

competitive conflict Polarizations; one side winning with the other side losing.

compromising A conflict management style; an intermediate strategy between cooperativeness and assertiveness; compromising may settle the problem but will also offer incomplete satisfaction for both parties.

concurrency A dimension of time; group members completing tasks simultaneously or one at a time.

conflict Situation in which at least two interdependent parties capable of invoking sanctions on each other oppose each other; based on real or perceived power; occurs because parties have mutually desired but mutually unobtainable objectives.

conflict aftermath The feelings that group members have developed as a result of a conflict episode; the legacy of the conflict interaction.

conflict management The relational skill of keeping group members focused on task-related ideas rather than personal differences.

connectivity The degree to which several groups share overlapping tasks or goals.

consensus A decision procedure in which each group member agrees with the decision or in which group members' individual positions are close enough that they can support the group's decision.

controlling behavior A dimension of defensive communication climate in which the sender assumes to know what is best for others.

cooperative conflict A type of disagreement that helps move the group along with its task or activities.

cooperative information sharing paradigm A model of how group members share information when trying to make a decision. See *hidden profile*.

copresence Group member's behavior and messages are shaped by others in the group; a sense of being with other group members even if they are not physically present.

decentralized communication network Communication network that allows each group member to talk to every other group member.

defensive climate A communication climate based on negative or threatening group interaction.

delay The manner in which group members resist setting deadlines or time to work.

description A dimension of a supportive communication climate that occurs when a group member responds to the idea instead of evaluating the group member who offered the idea.

developmental perspective on conflict Perspective that views conflict as a natural part of the group's development; can be productive if conflict emergence and resolution helps the group move forward; can be destructive if a group does not allow conflict to emerge.

distributive conflict management strategy A win-lose conflict management strategy exemplified by competitiveness or accommodation; yields an outcome that satisfies one party at the expense of the others.

embeddedness The degree to which the group is central to its larger organizational structure.

emergent leadership A type of leadership in which a group member is not appointed or elected to the leadership role; rather, leadership develops over time as a result of the group's interaction.

empathy A dimension of supportive communication climate that expresses genuine concern for other group members; conveys respect for and reassurance of the receiver.

equality A dimension of supportive communication climate in which trust and respect for all group members is expressed.

evaluation A dimension of a defensive communication climate in which a group member uses language to criticize other group members.

expert power A type of influence based on what a group member knows or can do.

false consensus A belief among group members that they all agree when they do not; agreeing to a decision only in order to be done with the task.

faultlines Demographic characteristics or other attributes salient for a particular group and its task; members are likely to communicate with similar others, which can divide a group into subgroups.

flexibility A dimension of time; how rigidly or flexibly time and deadlines are structured.

formal ties Who reports to whom or any other power-laden relationship in a communication network.

functional theory of group decision making Comprised of a set of critical functions group members should engage in for effective decision-making and problem-solving activities: (a) thoroughly discuss the problem, (b) examine the criteria of an acceptable solution before discussing specific solutions, (c) propose a set of realistic alternative solutions, (d) assess the positive aspects of each proposed solution, and (e) assess the negative aspects of each proposed solution.

group Three or more members who identify themselves as a group and who can identify the interdependent activity or goal of the group.

group charter A group document that describes the goals or mission of the group.

group goal An agreed-upon task or activity that the group is to complete or accomplish.

group identity The result when members identify themselves with other group members and the group goal.

groupings People identified as a group when they have little or no expectation that interaction will occur with one another; often based on demographic characteristics.

group polarization Tendency for groups to make decisions or choose solutions more extreme than any member would prefer individually.

group roles Interactive positions within a group; the micro components of a group's structure.

group size The number of members in the group; the minimum number of members is three; the maximum number depends primarily on the complexity of the task or activity.

group structure The patterns of behavior that group members come to rely on; develops with or emerges from group rules and norms.

groupthink A type of faulty decision making based on the tendency of highly cohesive groups to adopt faulty solutions because members failed to critically examine and analyze options while under pressure from the external environment.

heterogeneity The expressed differences in cultural values that influence group members' interactions.

hidden agenda A group member has an ulterior motive; uses the group for personal gain or personal satisfaction.

hidden communication Interaction among only some members of the group; often used to build alliances.

hidden profile In decision making, information is distributed among group members such that some information is shared by all members and other information is held by only one member.

informational power Persuasion or influence based on what information or knowledge a group member possesses or presents as arguments to group.

instrumental perspective on conflict A productive conflict, which helps group members figure out what the goals are, and how to accomplish its tasks; or destructive, which impedes the group from reaching their goals.

integrative conflict management strategy A win-win conflict management strategy based on problem solving or collaboration; produces an outcome with which all parties can agree.

interdependence Phenomenon whereby both group and individual outcomes are influenced by what other individuals in the group do; group members must rely upon and cooperate with one another to complete the group activity.

law of inherent conflict The premise that no matter the issue or group, there will be significant conflict stemming from different perceptions of relative factors.

leadership As a process, how a person uses positive influence to direct and coordinate the activities of group members toward goal.

legitimate power A type of power based on the inherent influence associated with a position or role in the group.

linearity The manner in which group members create times for some events over others; putting group tasks in some order.

material ties In a communication network describe the relationship among two members who give resources to one another.

meaning The understanding that is extracted from the way messages follow one another in interaction.

meeting citizenship behaviors Actions taken by group members to maintain a positive social and communication climate.

minutes A record of what the group did or accomplished at a meeting; should reflect who attended the meeting, what content was discussed, what was decided, who agreed to take on what responsibilities, and what the group plans to do next; usually taken by the group's secretary.

motivated information sharing paradigm An explanation for why groups are ineffective at sharing necessary information (i.e., groups do not know if they have all the information necessary to make a decision.

neutrality A dimension of defensive communication climate expressed when a group member reacts in a detached or unemotional way; a lack of warmth or caring for other members, making them feel as if they are not important.

nominal group technique (NGT) A decision-making procedure in which the group temporarily suspends interaction to take advantage of independent thinking and reflection before coming together as a group to discuss the ideas generated.

norm An expectation about behavior; an informal rule adopted by a group to regulate group members' behaviors.

normative conflict A type of conflict that occurs when one party has expectations about and evaluates another party's behavior.

pace The tempo or rate activity of group interaction.

performative act Messages exchanged that do something; for example, group interaction that introduces group members to one another.

persuasive arguments theory Posits that cognitive processes of individual group members prior to meetings lead to interaction outcornes.

political perspective on conflict Struggle for power is the source of conflict; if alternative points of view surface, conflict can be productive; if a conflict reaffirms or strengthens dominant members, conflict can be destructive.

power The influence of one person over another; the ability to get things done or to find needed resources; power bases are reward, coercion, legitimacy, expertise, information, and referent.

problem orientation A dimension of a supportive communication climate that strives for answers and solutions to benefit all group members and to satisfy the group's objective.

procedural leadership competency Behavior exhibited when group members coordinate group activities; helps members function as a group and achieve their goal.

process conflict Disagreements about coordination of group member duties, the group's time management, and/or access to resources.

provisionalism A dimension of a supportive communication climate that is committed to solving the group's problems by hearing all of the ideas; encourages the experimentation and exploration of ideas in the group.

proximity ties In a communication network describe group members who are spatially close or electronically linked to one another.

punctuality The manner in which group members set deadlines or respond to one another promptly.

ranking A decision procedure in which members assign a numerical value to each available position; rankings are then ordered.

referent power A type of influence given by a group member to another member based on a desire to build a relationship with that member.

relational competencies Skills individuals use to help manage relationships among group members and to create and maintain connections with those outside the group.

relational conflict Conflict based interpersonal relationships, emotions, or personalities.

relational dimension Group interaction that provides social and emotional support, as well as a mechanism for developing and maintaining role identities within a group.

relational groups Groups with membership based on personal or social relationships; examples include support groups, fraternities/sororities, and friendship groups.

relational leadership competency Displayed when group members cooperate with and express support for one another.

reward power A type of positive influence, relationally oriented and based on such things as attention, friendship, or favors, or materially oriented and based on tangible influence such as gifts or money.

satisfaction The degree to which a group member feels fulfilled or gratified based upon experiences in the group.

scarcity The degree to which resources are available to the group.

separation A dimension of time; how group members isolate their meetings from other interactions.

shared leadership Enacted by all or many group members; also called collective or distributive leadership; leadership rotates among members.

socialization The reciprocal process of social influence and change between new and established group members.

social loafing The idea that individual efforts decrease as the size of the group increases; a detachment from the group that occurs when group members feel as if they are not needed to produce the group's outcome or as if their individual efforts are not recognized by other members.

sociogram A visual representation of the group members' communication network or relationships; reveals the number and pattern of network ties among group members.

spontaneity A dimension of a supportive communication climate exemplified by a group member who is open and honest with other group members; creates immediacy with other group members.

strategic A dimension of a defensive communication in which senders manipulate others by placing themselves above the group or its task; or how speakers adapt their messages so that they will accomplish their goals.

superiority A dimension of a defensive communication climate exemplified when group members continually reinforce their strength or position over others.

superordinate goal A task or goal so difficult, time-consuming, and burdensome that it is beyond the capacity of one person.

supportive climate A communication climate based on positive group interaction.

task conflict Conflict based on issues or ideas, or disagreement about the group's task.

task dimension A group's interaction that focuses on its task, activity, or goal.

task-oriented team Also labeled *work groups* and *decision-making teams*; their purpose is to accomplish work tasks; it is generally assumed that group interaction should be geared toward planning, debating, or implementing group decisions.

team cognition The level of knowledge or commonly shared information (about one another or the task) among group members.

technical leadership competency Demonstrated when group members display the task or technical competencies required by the group's activity.

theory of effective intercultural workgroup communication An explanation of how group members' cultural differences their group interactions.

time perspective Group members completing their tasks with a focus on the past, present, or future.

transformational leader A type of leadership based on the premise that the leader sets an example for group members to follow; uses rhetorical skills to build a vision that members can identify with and use as a guiding force toward goal completion.

trust A group member's positive expectation of another group member; reliance on another group member in a risky situation.

urgency Group members approach their tasks as if there were a crisis or pressing deadline.

voting A decision procedure in which group members cast a written or verbal ballot in support of or against a specific proposal; generally, a majority or two-thirds vote is needed to support a proposition.

REFERENCES

Aaron, J. R., McDowell, W. C., & Herdman, A. O. (2014). The effects of a team charter on student team behaviors. *Journal of Education for Business, 89,* 90–97. doi:10.1080/08832323.2013.763753

Allison, B. B., Shuffler, M. L., & Wallace, A. M. (2015). In J. A. Allen, N. Lehmann-Willenbrock, & S. G. Rogelberg (Eds.), *The Cambridge handbook of meeting science* (pp. 680–705). New York, NY: Cambridge University Press.

Alper, S., Tjosvold, D., & Law, K. S. (2000). Conflict management, efficacy, and performance in organizational teams. *Personnel Psychology, 53,* 625–642. doi:10.1111/j.1744-6570.2000.tb00216.x

Anderson, C. M., Riddle, B. L., & Martin, M. M. (1999). Socialization processes in groups. In L. R. Frey, D. S. Gouran, & M. S. Poole (Eds.), *The handbook of group communication theory & research* (pp. 139–163). Thousand Oaks, CA: SAGE.

Aritz, J., & Walker, R. C. (2014). Leadership styles in multicultural groups: Americans and East Asians working together. *Journal of Business Communication, 51,* 72–92. doi:10.1177/2329488413516211

Arrow, H., & McGrath, J. E. (1993). Membership matters: How member change and continuity affect small group structure, process, and performance. *Small Group Research, 24,* 334–361. doi:10.1177/1046496493243004

Avolio, B. J., Waldman, D. A., & Einstein, W. O. (1988). Transformational leadership in a management game simulation. *Group and Organization Studies, 13,* 59–80. doi:10.1177/105960118801300109

Baker, D. C. (1990). A qualitative and quantitative analysis of verbal style and the elimination of potential leaders in small groups. *Communication Quarterly, 38,* 13–26. doi:10.1080/01463379009369738

Bakar, H. A., & Sheer, V. C. (2013). The mediating role of perceived cooperative communication in the relationship between interpersonal exchange relationships and perceived group cohesion. *Management Communication Quarterly, 27,* 443–465. doi:10.1177/0893318913492564

Bales, R. F. (1950). *Interaction process analysis: A method for the study of small groups.* Cambridge, MA: Addison-Wesley.

Bales, R. F., & Cohen, S. P. (1979). *SYMLOG: A system for the multiple level observation of group.* New York, NY; Free Press.

Ballard, D. I., & Seibold, D. R. (2000). Time orientation and temporal variation across work groups: Implications for group and organizational communication. *Western Journal of Communication, 64,* 218–242. doi:10.1080/10570310009374672

Ballard, D. I., & Seibold, D. R. (2004). Communication-related organizational structures and work group temporal experiences: The effects of coordination method, technology type, and feedback cycle on members' construals and enactments of time. *Communication Monographs, 71,* 1–27. doi:10.1080/03634520410001691474

Baran, B. E., Shanock, L. R., Rogelberg, S. G., & Scott, C. W. (2012). Leading group meetings: Supervisors' actions, employee behaviors, and upward perceptions. *Small Group Research, 43,* 330–355. doi:10.1177/1046496411418252

Barge, J. K. (1994). *Leadership: Communication skills for organizations and groups.* New York, NY: St. Martin's.

Barge, J. K. (1996). Leadership skills and the dialectics of leadership in group decision making. In R. Y. Hirokawa & M. S. Poole (Eds.), *Communication and group decision making* (2nd ed., pp. 301–342). Thousand Oaks, CA: SAGE.

Barge, J. K., & Hirokawa, R. Y. (1989). Toward a communication competency model of group leadership. *Small Group Behavior, 20,* 167–189. doi:10.1177/104649648902000203

Barki, H., & Pinsonneault, A. (2001). Small group brainstorming and idea quality: Is electronic brainstorming the most effective approach? *Small Group Research, 32,* 158–205. doi:10.1177/104649640103200203

Baron, N. S. (2010). Discourse structures in instant messages: The case of utterance breaks. *Language@Internet, 7.* Retrieved from http://nbn-resolving.de/urn:nbn:de:0009-7-26514

Baruah, J., & Paulus, P. B. (2008). Effects of training on idea generation in groups. *Small Group Research*, *39*, 523–541. doi:10.1177/1046496408320049

Bass, B. M. (1981). *Stogdill's handbook of leadership. A survey of theory and research.* New York, NY: Free Press.

Bass, B. M. (1985). *Leadership and performance beyond expectations.* New York, NY: Free Press.

Bass, B. M. (1990). From transactional to transformational leadership: Learning to share the vision. *Organizational Dynamics*, *18*(3), 19–31.

Baxter, J. (2015). Who wants to be the leader? The linguistic construction of emerging leadership in differently gendered teams. *International Journal of Business Communication*, *52*, 427–451. doi:10.1177/2329488414525460

Bazarova, N. N., Walther, J. B., & McLeod, P. L. (2012). Minority Influence in virtual groups: A comparison of four theories of minority influence. *Communication Research Communication Research*, *39*, 295–316. doi:10.1177/0093650211399752

Beck, S. J., & Keyton, J. (2009). Perceiving strategic meeting interaction. *Small Group Research*, *40*, 223–246. doi:10.1177/1046496408330084

Beck, S. J., & Keyton, J. (2012). Team cognition, communication, and message interdependence. In E. Salas, S. F. Fiore, & M. Letsky (Eds.), *Theories of team cognition: Cross-disciplinary perspectives* (pp. 471–494). New York, NY: Routledge.

Beck, S. J., Littlefield, R. S., & Weber, A. (2012). Public meeting facilitation: A naïve theory analysis of crisis meeting interaction. *Small Group Research*, *43*, 211–235. doi:10.1177/1046496411430531

Beck, S. J., Paskewitz, E. A., & Keyton, J. (2015). Toward a theory of strategic meeting interaction. In J. A. Allen, N. Lehmann-Willenbrock, & S. G. Rogelberg (Eds.), *The Cambridge handbook of meeting science* (pp. 305–324). New York, NY: Cambridge University Press.

Behfar, K. J., Friedman, R., & Oh, S. H. (2016). Impact of team (dis)satisfaction and psychological safety on performance evaluation biases. *Small Group Research*, *47*, 77–107. doi:10.1177/1046496415616865

Behfar, K. J., Mannix, E. A., Peterson, R. A., & Trochim, W. M. (2011). Conflict in small groups: The meaning and consequences of process conflict. *Small Group Research*, *42*, 127–176. doi:10.1177/1046496410389194

Bell, B. S., & Kozlowski, S. W. J. (2002). A typology of virtual teams: Implications for effective leadership. *Group & Organization Management*, *27*, 14–49. doi:10.1177/1059601102027001003

Bell, M. A. (1983). A research note: The relationship of conflict and linguistic diversity in small groups. *Central States Speech Journal*, *34*, 128–133. doi:10.1080/10510978309368131

Berdahl, J. L., & Anderson, C. (2005). Men, women, and leadership centralization in groups over time. *Group Dynamics*, *9*, 45–57. doi:10.1037/1089-2699.9.1.45

Berry, G. R. (2011). Enhancing effectiveness on virtual teams: Understanding why traditional team skills are insufficient. *Journal of Business Communication*, *48*, 186–206. doi: 10.1177/0021943610397270

Bettenhausen, K. L. (1991). Five years of groups research: What we have learned and what needs to be addressed. *Journal of Management*, *17*, 345–381. doi:10.1177/014920639101700205

Bonito, J. A. (2002). The analysis of participation in small groups: Methodological and conceptual issues related to interdependence. *Small Group Research*, *33*, 412–438. doi:10.1177/104649640203300402

Bradley, P. H. (1978). Power, status, and upward communication in small decision-making groups. *Communication Monographs*, *45*, 33–43.

Brown, T. M., & Miller, C. E. (2000). Communication networks in task-performing groups: Effects of task complexity, time pressure, and interpersonal dominance. *Small Group Research*, *31*, 131–157. doi:10.1177/104649640003100201

Burgoon, J. K., & Dunbar, N. E (2006). Nonverbal expressions of dominance and power in human relationships. In V. Manusov & M. L. Patterson (Eds.), *The SAGE handbook of nonverbal communication* (pp. 279–297). Thousand Oaks, CA: SAGE.

Byrd, J. T., & Luthy, M. R. (2010). Improving group dynamics: Creating a *Academy of Educational Leadership Journal*, *14*, 13–26.

Canary, D. J., & Spitzberg, B. H. (1989). A model of the perceived competence of conflict strategies. *Human Communication Research, 15,* 630–649. doi:10.1111/j.1468-2958.1989.tb00202.x

Carron, A. V., Brawley, L. R., Bray, S. R., Eys, M. A., Dorsch, K. D., … Terry, P. C. (2004). Using consensus as a criterion for groupness: Implications for the cohesion-group success relationship. *Small Group Research, 35,* 466-491. doi:10.1177/1046496404263923

Carter, D. R., Seely, P. Q., Dagosta, J., DeChurch, L. A., & Zaccaro, S. J. (2015). Leading for global virtual teams: Facilitating teamwork processes. In J. L. Wildman & R. L. Griffith (Eds.), *Leading global teams: Translating multidisciplinary science to practice* (pp. 225-252). New York, NY; Springer.

Cartwright, D. (1968). The nature of group cohesiveness. In D. Cartwright & A. Zander (Eds.), *Group dynamics: Research and theory* (3rd ed., pp. 91–109). New York, NY: Harper & Row.

Chen, C. C., Wu, J., Ma, M., & Knight, M. B. (2011). Enhancing virtual learning team performance: A leadership perspective. *Human Systems Management, 30,* 215–228. doi: 10.3233/HSM-2011-0750

Clegg, S. (1989). *Frameworks of power.* Newbury Park, CA: SAGE.

Clifton, J. (2006). A conversation analytical approach to business communication. *Journal of Business Communication, 43,* 202–219. doi:10.1177/0021943606288190

Clifton, J. (2012). A discursive approach to leadership: Doing assessments and managing organizational meanings. *Journal of Business Communication, 49,* 148–168. doi:10.1177/0021943612437762

Cohen, S. G. (1990). Hilltop Hospital top management group. In J. R. Hackman (Exl.), *Groups that work (and those that don't): Creating conditions for effective teamwork* (pp. 56–77). San Francisco, CA: Jossey-Bass.

Cohen, S. G., & Bailey, D. E. (1997). What makes teams work: Group effectiveness research from the shop floor to the executive suite. *Journal of Management, 23,* 239–290. doi:10.1177/014920639702300303

Comer, D. R. (1995). A model of social loafing in real work groups. *Human Relations, 48,* 647–667. doi:10.1177/001872679504800603

Contractor, N. S., DeChurch, L. A., Carson, J., Carter, D. R., & Keegan, B. (2012). The topology of collective leadership. *Leadership Quarterly, 23,* 994–1011. doi:10.1016/j.leaqua.2012.10.010

Cruz, M. G., Henningsen, D. D., & Smith, B. A. (1999). The impact of directive leadership on group information sampling, decisions, and perceptions of the leader. *Communication Research, 26,* 349–369. doi:10.1177/009365099026003004

Darics, E. (2014). The blurring boundaries between synchronicity and asynchronicity: New communicative situations in work-related instant message. *International Journal of Business Communication, 5,* 337–358. doi:10.1177/2329488414525440

Davis, C. S. (2008). Dueling narratives: How peer leaders use narrative to frame meaning in community mental health care teams. *Small Group Research, 39,* 706–727. doi:10.1177/1046496408323068

De Dreu, C. K., & Van Vianen, A. E. (2001). Managing relationship conflict and the effectiveness of organizational teams. *Journal of Organizational Behavior, 22,* 300–328. doi:10.1002/job.71

Delbecq, A. L., Van de Ven, A. H., & Gustafson, D. H. (1975). *Group techniques for program planning: A guide to nominal group and delphi processes.* Glenview, IL: Scott, Foresman.

DeStephen, R. S., & Hirokawa, R. Y. (1988). Small group consensus: Stability of group support of the decision, task process, and group relationships. *Small Group Behavior, 19,* 227–239. doi:10.1177/104649648801900204

De Dreu, C. K. W., & Weingart, L. R. (2003). Task versus relationship conflict, team performance, and team member satisfaction: A meta-analysis. *Journal of Applied Psychology, 88,* 741–749. doi:10.1037/0021-9010.88.4.741

de Vries, R. E., Van den Hooff, B., & de Ridder, J. A. (2006). Explaining knowledge sharing: The role of team communication styles, job satisfaction, and performance beliefs. *Communication Research, 33,* 115–135. doi:10.1177/0093650205285366

Druskat, V. U., & Pescosolido, A. T. (2006). The impact of emergent leader's emotionally competent behavior on team trust, communication, engagement, and effectiveness. In N. Ashkanasy, W. J. Zerbe, & C. Hartel (Eds.), *Research on emotion in organizations* (Vol. 2, pp. 27–58). Oxford, England: Elsevier.

Du-Babcock, B., & Tamaka, H. (2013). A comparison of the communication behaviors of Hong Kong Chinese and Japanese business professionals in intracultural and intercultural decision-making meetings. *Journal of Business and Technical Communication, 43,* 21–42. doi:10.1177/1050651913479918

Ellingson, L. L. (2003). Interdisciplinary health care teamwork in the clinic backstage. *Journal of Applied Communication Research, 31,* 93–117. doi:10.1080/0090988032000064579

Emery, C., Daniloski, K., & Hamby, A. (2011). The reciprocal effects of self-view as a leader and leader emergence. *Small Group Research, 42,* 199–224. doi:10.1177/1046496410389494

Fairhurst, G. T. (2007). *Discursive leadership.* Los Angeles, CA: SAGE.

Farmer, S. M., & Roth, J. (1998). Conflict-handling behavior in work groups: Effects of group structure, decision processes, and time. *Small Group Research, 29,* 669–713. doi:10.1177/1046496498296002

Firestien, R. L. (1990). Effects of creative problem solving training on communication behavior in small groups. *Small Group Research, 21,* 507–521. doi:10.1177/1046496490214005

Fisher, B. A. (1971). Communication research and the task-oriented group. *Journal of Communication, 21,* 136–149. doi:10.1111/j.1460-2466.1971.tb00911.x

Fletcher, J. K., & Kaufer, K. (2003). Shared leadership: Paradox and possibility. In C. L. Pearce & J. A. Conger (Eds.), *Shared leadership: Reframing the hows and whys of leadership* (pp. 21–47). Thousand Oaks, CA: SAGE

French, J. R. P., & Raven, B. (1968). The bases of social power. In D. Cartwright & A. Zander (Eds.), *Group dynamics: Research and theory* (pp. 259–269). New York, NY: Harper & Row.

Frey, L., & SunWolf. (2005). The symbolic-interpretive perspective of group life. In M. S. Poole & A. B. Hollingshead (Eds.), *Theories of small groups: Interdisciplinary perspectives* (pp. 185–239). Thousand Oaks, CA: SAGE.

Galanes, G. J. (2003). In their own words: An exploratory study of bona fide group leaders. *Small Group Research, 34,* 741–770. doi:10.1177/1046496403257649

Gardner, W. L., & Avolio, B. J. (1998). The charismatic relationship: A dramaturgical perspective. *Academy of Management Review, 23,* 32–58. doi: 10.5465/AMR.1998.192958

Gastil, J. (1993). Identifying obstacles to small group democracy. *Small Group Research, 24,* 5–27. doi:10.1177/1046496493241002

Gastil, J. (2010). *The group in society.* Los Angeles, CA: SAGE.

Gersick, C. J. G., & Hackman, J. R. (1990). Habitual routines in task-performing groups. *Organizational Behavior and Human Decision Processes, 41,* 65–97. doi:10.1016/0749-5978(90)90047-D

Gibb, J. R. (1961). Defensive communication. *Journal of Communication, 11,* 141–148. doi:10.1016/0749-5978(90)90047-D

Gilstrap, C., & Hendershot, B. (2015). E-leaders and uncertainty management: A computer-supported qualitative investigation. *Qualitative Research Reports in Communication, 18,* 86–96. doi:10.1080/17459435.2015.1086424

Golembiewski, R. T. (1962). *Making decisions in groups.* Glenview, IL: Scott, Foresman.

Gonzales, A. L., Hancock, J. T., & Pennebaker, J. W. (2010). Language style matching as a predictor of social dynamics in small groups. Communication *Research, 37,* 3–19. doi:10.1177/0093650209351468

Gouran, D. S., & Hirokawa, R. Y. (1983). The role of communication in decision making groups: A functional perspective. In M. S. Mander (Ed.), *Communications in transition* (pp. 168–185). New York, NY: Praeger.

Gouran, D. S., Hirokawa, R. Y., Julian, K. M., & Leatham, G. B. (1993). The evolution and current status of the functional perspective on communication in decision-making and problem-solving groups. In S. A. Deetz (Ed.), *Communication yearbook 16* (pp. 573–600). Newbury Park, CA: SAGE.

Graham, E. E., Papa, M. J., & McPherson, M. B. (1997). An applied test of the functional communication perspective of small group decision-making. *Southern Communication Journal, 62,* 269–279. doi:10.1080/10417949709373064

Green, S. G., & Taber, T. D. (1980). The effects of three social decision schemes on decision group process. *Organizational Behavior and Human Performance, 25,* 97–106. doi:10.1016/0030-5073(80)90027-6

Green, T. B. (1975). An empirical analysis of nominal and interacting groups. *Academy of Management Journal, 18,* 63–73. doi:10.2307/255625

Greene, C. N. (1989). Cohesion and productivity in work groups. *Small Group Behavior, 20,* 70–86. doi:10.1177/104649648902000106

Grice, H. P. (1999). Logic and conversation. In A. Jaworski & N. Coupland (Eds.), *The discourse reader* (pp. 76–88). London, England: Routledge.

Guenter, H., van Emmerik, H., Schreurs, B., Kuypers, T., van Iterson, A., & Notelaers, G. (2016). When task conflict becomes personal: The impact of perceived team performance. *Small Group Research, 47,* 569–604. doi:10.1177/1046496416667816

Guetzkow, H., & Gyr, J. (1954). An analysis of conflict in decision-making groups. *Human Relations, 1,* 367–382. doi:10.1177/001872675400700307

Gully, S. M., Devine, D. J., & Whitney, D. J. (1995). A meta-analysis of cohesion and performance: Effects of level of analysis and task interdependence. *Small Group Research, 26,* 497–520. doi:10.1177/1046496412468069

Hackman, J. R. (1992). Group influences on individuals in organizations. In M. D. Dunnet & L. M. Hough (Eds.), *Handbook of industrial and organizational psychology* (Vol. 3, pp. 199–267). Palo Alto, CA: Consulting Psychologists Press.

Hardy, J., Eys, M. A., & Carron, A. V. (2005). Exploring the potential disadvantages of high cohesion in sports teams. *Small Group Research, 36,* 166–187. doi:10.1177/1046496404266715

Harrison, D. A., Price, K. H., & Bell, M. P. (1998). Beyond relational demography: Time and the effects of surface- and deep-level diversity on work group cohesion. *Academy of Management Journal, 41,* 96–107. doi:10.2307/256901

Heath, R. G., & Sias, P. M. (1999). Communicating spirit in a collaborative alliance. *Journal of Applied Communication Research, 21,* 356–376. doi:10.1080/00909889909365545

Henningsen, D. D., & Henningsen, M. L. (2004). The effect of individual difference variables on information sharing in decision-making groups. *Human Communication Research, 30,* 540–555. doi:10.1111/j.1468-2958.2004.tb00744.x

Henry, K. B., Arrow, H., & Carini, B. (1999). A tripartite model of group identification: Theory and measurement. *Small Group Research, 30,* 558–581. doi:10.1177/104649649903000504

Hill, R. P., & Rapp, J. M. (2014). Codes of ethical conduct: A bottom-up approach. *Journal of Business Ethics, 123,* 621–630. doi:10.1007/s10551-013-2013-7

Hill, S. E. K. (2013). Team leadership. In P. G. Northouse (Ed.), *Leadership: Theory and practice* (6th ed., pp. 287–318). Los Angeles, CA: SAGE.

Hirokawa, R. Y. (1982). Group communication and problem-solving effectiveness I: A critical review of inconsistent findings. *Communication Quarterly, 30,* 134–141. doi:10.1080/01463378209369440

Hirokawa, R. Y. (1983). Group communication and problem-solving effectiveness: An investigation of group phases. *Human Communication Research, 9,* 291–305. doi:10.1111/j.1468-2958.1983.tb00700.x

Hirokawa, R. Y. (1988). Group communication and decision-making performance: A continued test of the functional perspective. *Human Communication Research, 14,* 487–515. doi:10.1111/j.1468-2958.1988.tb00165.x

Hirokawa, R. Y., & Johnston, D. D. (1989) Toward a general theory of group decision-making: Development of an integrated model. *Small Group Behavior, 20,* 500-523. doi:10.1177/104649648902000408

Hirokawa, R. Y., Erbert, L., & Hurst, A. (1996). Communication and group decision-making effectiveness. In R. Y. Hirokawa & M. S. Poole (Eds.), *Communication and group decision making* (pp. 269–300) Thousand Oaks, CA: SAGE.

Hirokawa, R. Y., & Johnston, D. D. (1989). Toward a general theory of group decision making: Development of an integrated model. *Small Group Behavior, 20,* 500–523. doi:10.1177/104649648902000408

Hirokawa, R. Y., & Keyton, J. (1995). Perceived facilitators and inhibitors of effectiveness in organizational work teams. *Management Communication Quarterly, 8,* 424–446. doi:10.1177/0893318995008004002

Hoffman, L. R., & Kleinman, G. B. (1994). Individual and group in problem solving: The valence model redressed. *Human Communication Research, 21,* 36–59. doi:10.1111/j.1468-2958.1994.tb00338.x

Hollander, E. P. (1978). *Leadership dynamics A practical guide to effective relationships.* New York, NY: Macmillan.

Hollander, E. P. (1985). Leadership and power. In G. Lindzey & E. Aronson (Eds.), *The handbook of social psychology* (Vol. 2, pp. 485–537). New York, NY: Random House.

Hollingshead, A. B. (1996). The rank-order effect in group decision making. *Organizational Behavior and Human Decision Processes, 68,* 181–193. doi:10.1006/obhd.1996.0098

Hollingshead, A. B., Jacobsohn, G. C., & Beck, S. J. (2007). Motives and goals in context: A strategic analysis of information-sharing groups. In K. Fiedler (Ed.), *Social communication* (pp. 257–280). New York, NY: Psychology Press.

Jacobs, T. O. (1970). *Leadership and exchange informal organizations.* Alexandria, VA: Human Resources Research Organization.

Jackson, J. W. (2008). Reactions to social dilemmas as a function of group identity: Rational calculations, and social context. *Small Group Research, 39,* 673–705. doi:10.1177/1046496408322761

Janssens, M., & Brett, J. (2006). Cultural intelligence in global teams: A fusion model of collaboration. *Group & Organization Management, 31,* 124–153. doi:10.1177/1059601105275268

Jarboe, S. (1996). Procedures for enhancing group decision making. In R. Y. Hirokawa & M. S. Poole (Eds.), *Communication and group decision making* (pp. 345–383). Thousand Oaks, CA: SAGE.

Jarboe, S. C., & Witteman, H. R. (1996). Intragroup conflict management in task-oriented groups: The influence of problem sources and problem analyses. *Small Group Research, 27,* 316–338. doi:10.1177/1046496496272007

Jehn, K. (1995). A multimethod examination of the benefits and detriments of intragroup conflict. *Administrative Science Quarterly, 40,* 256–282. doi:10.2307/2393638

Jehn, K. A. (1997). A qualitative analysis of conflict types and dimensions in organizational groups. *Administrative Science Quarterly, 42,* 530–557. doi:10.2307/2393737

Jehn, K. A., & Mannix, E. A. (2001). The dynamic nature of conflict: A longitudinal study of intragroup conflict and group performance. *Academy of Management Journal, 44,* 238–251. doi:10.13189/ujm.2016.040204

Johansson, C., Miller, V. C., & Hamrin, S. (2014). Conceptualizing communicative leadership: A framework for analysing and developing leaders' communication competence. *Corporate Communications: An International Journal, 10,* 147–165. doi:10.1108/CCIJ-02-2013-0007

Jones, T. S. (2000). Emotional communication in conflict: Essence and impact. In W.F. Eadie & P.E. Nelson (Eds.), *The language of conflict and resolution* (pp. 81–104). Thousand Oaks, CA: SAGE.

Jones, E. E., & Kelly, J. R. (2007). Contributions to a group discussion and perceptions of leadership: Does quantity always count more than quality? *Group Dynamics: Theory, Research, and Practice, 11,* 15–30. doi:10.1037/1089-2699.11.1.15

Katz, N., Lazer, D., Arrow, H., & Contractor, N. (2005). The network perspective on small group: Theory and research. In M. S. Poole & A. B. Hollingshead (Eds.), *Theories of small groups: Interdisciplinary perspectives* (pp. 277–312). Thousand Oaks, CA: SAGE.

Katzenbach, J. R., & Smith, D. K. (1993). *The wisdom of teams: Creating the high-performance organization.* New York, NY: HarperBusiness.

Kauffeld, S., & Lehmann-Willenbrock, N. (2012). Meetings matter: Effects of team meetings on team and organizational success. *Small Group Research, 43,* 130–158. doi:10.1177/1046496411429599

Kellermann, K. (1992). Communication: Inherently strategic and primarily automatic. *Communication Monographs, 59,* 288–300. doi:10.1080/03637759209376270

Ketrow, S. M. (1991). Communication role specializations and perceptions of leadership. *Small Group Research, 22,* 492–514. doi:10.1177/1046496491224005

Keyton, J. (1991). Evaluating individual group member satisfaction as a situational variable. *Small Group Research, 22,* 200–219. doi:10.1177/1046496491222004

Keyton, J. (1999). Relational communication in groups. In L. R. Frey, D. S. Gouran, & M. S. Poole (Eds.), *The handbook of group communication theory and research* (pp. 192–222). Thousand Oaks, CA: SAGE.

Keyton, J., & Beck, S. J. (2010). Examining emotional communication: Laughter in jury deliberations. *Small Group Research, 41,* 386–407. doi:10.1177/1046496410366311

Keyton, J., Beck, S. J., & Asbury, M. B. (2010). Macrocognition: A communication perspective. *Theoretical Issues in Ergonomics Science, 11,* 272–286. doi:10.1080/14639221003729136

Kiesler, S., & Cummings, J. N. (2002). What do we know about proximity and distance in work groups? A legacy of research. In P. J. Hinds & S. Kiesler (Eds.), *Distributed work* (pp. 57–80). Cambridge, MA: MIT Press.

Kirchmeyer, C., & Cohen, A. (1992). Multicultural groups: Their performance and reactions with constructive conflict. *Group and Organization Management, 17,* 153–170. doi:10.1177/1059601192172004

Kirschbaum, K. A., Rask, J. P., Fortner, S. A., Kulesher, R., Nelson, M. T., Yen, T., & Brennan, M. (2014). Physician communication in the operating room. *Health Communication, 30,* 317-327. doi:10.1080/10410236.2013.856741

Knutson, T. J., & Kowitz, A. C. (1977). Effects of information type and level of orientation on consensus-achievement in substantive and affective small group conflict. *Central States Speech Journal, 28,* 54–63. doi:10.1080/10510977709367919

Kramer, M. W. (2005). Communication and social exchange processes in community theater groups. *Journal of Applied Communication, 33,* 159–182. doi:10.1080/00909880500045049

Kramer, M. W. (2006). Shared leadership in a community theater group: Filling the leadership role. *Journal of Applied Communication Research, 34,* 141–162. doi:10.1080/00909880600574039

Kramer, M. W. (2011). Toward a communication model for the socialization of voluntary members. *Communication Monographs, 78,* 233–255. doi:10.1080/03637751.2011.564640

Kramer, M. W., Kuo, C. L., & Dailey, J. C. (1997). The impact of brainstorming techniques on subsequent group processes: Beyond generating ideas. *Small Group Research, 28,* 218–242. doi:10.1177/1046496497282003

Kramer, T. J., Fleming, G. P., & Mannis, S. M. (2001). Improving face-to-face brainstorming through modeling and facilitation. *Small Group Research, 32,* 533–557. doi:10.1177/104649640103200502

Krauss, R. M., & Morsella, E. (2000). Communication and conflict. In M. Deutsch & P. T. Coleman (Eds.), *The handbook of conflict resolution: Theory and practice* (pp. 131–143). San Francisco, CA: Jossey-Bass.

Kuhn, T., & Poole, M. S. (2000). Do conflict management styles affect group decision making? Evidence from a longitudinal field study. *Human Communication Research, 26,* 558–590. doi:10.1111/j.1468-2958.2000.tb00769.x

Kunze, F., & Bruch, H. (2010). Age-based faultlines and perceived productive energy: The moderation of transformational leadership. *Small Group Research, 41,* 593–620. doi:10.1177/1046496410366307

Lafond, D., Jobidon, M-E., Aube, C., & Tremblay, S. (2011). Evidence of structure-specific teamwork requirements and implications for team design. *Small Group Research, 42,* 507–535. doi:10.1177/1046496410397617

Lam, C. (2013). The efficacy of text message to improve social connectedness and team attitude in student technical communication projects: An experimental study. *Journal of Business and Technical Communication, 27,* 180–208. doi:10.1177/1050651912468888

Lam, C. (2015). The role of communication and cohesion in reducing social loafing in group projects. *Business and Professional Communication Quarterly, 78*, 454–475. doi:10.1177/2329490615596417

Lambertz-Berndt, M., M., & Blight, M. G. (2016). "You don't have to like me, but you have to respect me": The impacts of assertiveness, cooperativeness, and group satisfaction in collaborative assignments. *Business and Professional Communication Quarterly, 79*, 180–199. doi:10.1177/2329490615604749

Lammers, J. C., & Krikorian, D. H. (1997). Theoretical extension and operationalization of the bona fide group construct with an application to surgical teams. *Journal of Applied Communication Research, 25*, 17–38. doi:org/ 10.1080/00909889709365463

Larkey, L. K. (1996). Toward a theory of communicative interactions in culturally diverse workgroups. *Academy of Management Review, 21*, 463–491. doi:10.5465/AMR.1996.9605060219

Larson, C. E., & LaFasto, F. M. J. (1989). *TeamWork. What must go right/what can go wrong.* Newbury Park, CA: SAGE.

Lau, D., & Murnighan, J. K. (1998). Demographic diversity and faultlines: The compositional dynamics of organizational groups. *Academy of Management Review, 23*, 325–340. doi:10.5465/AMR.1998.533229

Leach, D. J., Rogelberg, S. G., Warr, P. B., & Burnfield, J. L. (2009). Perceived meeting effectiveness: The role of design characteristics. *Journal of Business and Psychology, 24*, 65–76. doi:10.1007/s10869-009-9092-6

Levine, K. J., Muenchen, R. A., & Brooks, A. (2010). Measuring transformational and charismatic leadership: Why isn't charisma measured? *Communication Monographs, 77*, 576–591. doi:10.1080/03637751.2010.499 368

Lewicki, R. J., McAllister, D. J., & Bies, D. J. (1998). Trust and distrust: New relationships and realities. *Academy of Management Review, 23*, 438–458. doi:10.2307/259288

Lia, J., & Robertson, T. (2011). Physical space and information space: Studies of collaboration in distributed multi-disciplinary medical team meetings. *Behaviour & Information Technology, 30*, 443–454. doi:10.1080/ 0144929X.2011.577194

Lira, E. M., Ripoll, P., Piero, J. M., & Zornoza, A. M. (2008). The role of information and communication technologies in the relationship between group effectiveness and group potency: A longitudinal study. *Small Group Research, 39*, 728–745. doi:10.1177/1046496408323481

Liu, X.-Y., Hartel, C. E. J., & Sun, J. J-M. (2014). The workgroup emotional climate scale. *Group & Organization Management, 39*, 626–663. doi:10.1177/1059601114554453

Lovaglia, M., Mannix, E. A., Samuelson, C. D., Sell, J., & Wilson, R. K. (2005). Conflict, power, and status in groups. In M. S. Poole & A. B. Hollingshead (Eds.), *Theories of small groups: Interdisciplinary perspectives* (pp. 139–184). Thousand Oaks, CA: SAGE.

Martin, A. (2007). *What's next? The 2007 changing nature of leadership survey.* Greensboro, NC: Center for Creative Leadership. Retrieved from http://www.ccl.org/wp-content/uploads/2015/04/WhatsNext.pdf

Mathieu, J. E., & Rapp, T. L. (2009). Laying the foundation for successful team performance trajectories: The roles of team charters and performance strategies. *Journal of Applied Psychology, 94*, 90–103. doi:10.1037/ a0013257

McComas, K. A. (2003). Citizen satisfaction with public meetings used for risk communication. *Journal of Applied Communication Research, 31*, 164-184. doi: 0.1080/0090988032000064605

McDowell, W. C., Herdman, A. O., & Aaron, J. (2011). Charting the course: The effects of team charters on emergent behavioral norms. *Organization Development Journal, 29*, 79–88.

McGrath, J. E. (1984). *Groups: Interaction and performance.* Englewood Cliffs, NJ: Prentice-Hall.

McGrath, J. E., Berdahl, J. L., & Arrow, H. (1995). Traits, expectations, culture, and clout: The dynamics of diversity in work groups. In S. E. Jackson & M. N. Ruderman (Eds.), *Diversity in work teams: Research paradigms for a changing workplace* (pp. 17–45). Washington, DC: American Psychological Association.

McKinney, B. C., Kelly, L., & Duran, R. L. (1997). The relationship between conflict message styles and dimensions of communication competence. *Communication Reports, 10,* 185–196. doi:10.1080/08934219709367674

Meng, J., Fulk, J., & Yuan, Y. C. (2015). The roles and interplay of intragroup conflict and team emotion management of information seeking behaviors in team contexts. *Communication Research, 42,* 675–700. doi:10.1177/0093650213476294

Merolla, A. J. (2010). Relational maintenance and noncopresence reconsidered: Conceptualizing geographic separation in close relationships. Communication *Theory, 20,* 169–193. doi:10.1111/j.1468-2885.2010.01359.x

Messersmith, A. S. (2015). Preparing students for 21st century teamwork: Effective collaboration in the online group communication course. *Communication Teacher, 29,* 219-226. doi:10.1080/17404622.2015.1046188.

Meyers, R. A. (1989). Persuasive arguments theory A test of assumptions. *Human Communication Research, 15,* 357–381. doi:10.1111/j.1468-2958.1989.tb00189.x

Meyers, R. A., Brashers, D. E., & Hanner, J. (2000). Majority-minority influences: Identifying argumentative patterns and predicting argument-outcome links. *Journal of Communication, 50*(4), 3–30. doi:10.1111/j.1460-2466.2000.tb02861.x

Mirivel, J. C., & Tracy, K. (2005). Premeeting talk: An organizationally crucial form of talk. *Research on Language and Social Interaction, 38,* 1-34. doi:10.1207/s15327973rlsi3801

Moscovici, S. (1976). *Social influence and social change.* London, England: Academic Press.

Moye, N. E., & Langfred, D. W. (2004). Information sharing and group conflict: Going beyond decision making to understand the effects of information sharing on group performance. *International Journal of Conflict Management, 15,* 381–410.

Mullen, B., Anthony, T., Salas, E., & Driskell, J. E. (1994). Group cohesiveness and quality of decision making: An integration of tests of the groupthink hypothesis. *Small Group Research, 25,* 189–204. doi:10.1177/1046496494252003

Mullen, B., Johnson, C., & Salas, E. (1991). Productivity loss in brainstorming groups: A meta-analytical integration. *Basic and Applied Social Psychology, 12,* 3–23. doi:10.1207/s15324834basp1201_1

Myers, S. A., Shimotsu, S., Byrnes, K., Frisby, B. N., Durbin, J., & Loy, B. N. (2010). Assessing the role of peer relationships in the small group communication course. *Communication Teacher, 24,* 43–57. doi:10.1080/17404620903468214

Myrsiades, L. (2000). Meeting sabotage: Met and conquered. *Journal of Management Development, 19,* 879–884. doi:org/10.1108/02621710010379182

Nemeth, C. J. (1986). Differential contributions of majority and minority influence. *Psychological Review, 93,* 23-32. doi:10.1037/0033-295x.93.1.23

Nemeth, C., Swedlund, M., & Kanki, B. (1974). Patterning of the minority's responses and their influence on the majority. *European Journal of Social Psychology, 4,* 437-439. doi:10.1002/ejsp.2420040104

Nicotera, A. M. (1994). The use of multiple approaches to conflict: A study of sequences. *Human Communication Research, 20,* 592–621. doi:10.1111/j.1468-2958.1994.tb00336.x

Northouse, P. G. (2017). *Leadership: Theory and practice* (7th ed.). Los Angeles, CA: SAGE.

Nye, J. L. (2002). The eye of the follower: Information processing effects on attributions regarding leaders of small groups. *Small Group Research, 33,* 337–360. doi:10.1177/10496402033003003

Odermatt, I., Konig, C. J., & Kleinmann, J. (2015). Meeting preparation and design characteristics. In J. A. Allen, N. Lehmann-Willenbrock, & S. G. Rogelberg (Eds.), *The Cambridge handbook of meeting science* (pp. 49–68). New York, NY: Cambridge University Press.

Oetzel, J. G. (2002). The effects of culture and cultural diversity on communication in work groups. In L. R. Frey (Ed.), *New directions in group communication* (pp. 121–137). Thousand Oaks, CA: SAGE.

Oetzel, J. G. (2005). Effective intercultural workgroup communication theory. In W. B. Gudykunst (Ed.), *Theorizing about intercultural communication* (pp. 351–371). Thousand Oaks, CA: SAGE.

Oetzel, J. G., Burns, T. B , Sanchez, M. I., & Perez, F. G. (2001). Investigating the role of communication in culturally diverse work groups: A review and synthesis. In W. B. Gudykunst (Ed.), *Communication yearbook* 25 (pp. 237–269). Mahwah, NJ: Erlbaum.

Oetzel, J. G., McDermott, V. M., Torres, A., & Sanchez, C. (2012). The impact of individual differences and group diversity on group interaction climate and satisfaction: A test of the effective intercultural workgroup communication theory. *Journal of International & Intercultural Communication, 5,* 144–167. doi:10.1080/17513057 .2011.640754

Orlitzky, M., & Hirokawa, R. Y. (2001). To err is human, to correct for it divine: A meta-analysis of research testing the functional theory of group decision-making effectiveness. *Small Group Research, 32,* 313–341. doi:10.1177/104649640103200303

Osborn, A. F. (1963). *Applied imagination* (3rd ed.). New York, NY: Scribner.

Pace, R. C. (1990). Personalized and depersonalized conflict in small group discussions: An examination of differentiation. *Small Group Research, 21,* 79–96. doi:10.1177/1046496490211006

Paulus, P. B., Nakui, T., Putman, V. L., & Brown, V. R. (2006). Effects of task instructions and brief breaks on brainstorming. *Group Dynamics: Theory, Research, and Practice, 10,* 206–219. doi:10.1037/1089-2699.10.3.206

Pavitt, C. (1993). What (little) we know about formal group discussion procedures: A review of relevant research. *Small Group Research, 24,* 217–235. doi:10.1177/1046496493242004

Pavitt, C. (1999). Theorizing about the group communication-leadership relationship: Input-process-output and functional models. In L. R. Frey, D. S. Gouran, & M. S. Poole (Eds.), *The handbook of group communication theory and research* (pp. 313–334). Thousand Oaks, CA: SAGE.

Pavitt, C., High, S. C., Tressler, K. E., & Winslow, J. K. (2007). Leadership communication during group resource dilemmas. *Small Group Research, 38,* 509–531. doi:10.1177/1046496407304333

Pavitt, C., & Sackaroff, P. (1990). Implicit theories of leadership and judgments of leadership among group members. *Small Group Research, 21,* 374–392. doi:10.1177/1046496490213006

Pescolido, A. T. (2003). Group efficacy and group effectiveness: The effects of group efficacy over time on group performance and development. *Small Group Research, 34,* 20–42. doi:10.1177/1046496402239576

Pescosolido, A. T., & Saavedra, R. (2012). Cohesion and sports teams: A review. *Small Group Research, 43,* 744–758. doi:10.1177/1046496412465020

Poncini, G. (2002). Investigating discourse at business meetings with multicultural participation. *International Review of Applied Linguistics in Language Teaching, 40,* 345–373. doi:10.1515/iral.2002.017

Pondy, L. R. (1967). Organizational conflict: Concepts and models. *Administrative Science Quarterly, 12,* 296–320. doi:10.1002/job.4030130304

Poole, M. S. (1991). Procedures for managing meetings: Social and technological innovation. In R. A. Swanson & B. O. Knapp (Eds.), *Innovative meeting management* (pp. 53–110). Austin, TX: 3M Meeting Management Institute.

Poole, M. S., & Garner, J. T. (2006). Perspectives on workgroup conflict and communication. In J. G. Oetzel & S. Ting-Toomey (Eds.), *The SAGE handbook of conflict communication: Integrating theory, research, and practice* (pp. 267–292). Thousand Oaks, CA: SAGE.

Poole, M. S., & Dobosh, M. (2010). Exploring conflict management processes in jury deliberation through interaction analysis. *Small Group Research, 41,* 408–426. doi:10.1177/1046496410366310

Poole, M. S., & Zhang, H. (2005). Virtual teams. In S. A. Wheelan (Ed.), *The handbook of group research and practice* (pp. 363–384). Thousand Oaks, CA: SAGE.

Prapavessis, H., & Carron, A. V (1997). Cohesion and work output. *Small Group Research, 28,* 294–301. doi:10.1177/1046496497282006

Putnam, L. L. (2006). Definitions and approaches to conflict and communication. In J. G. Oetzel & S. Ting-Toomey (Eds.), *The SAGE handbook of conflict communication: Integrating theory, research, and practice* (pp. 1–32). Thousand Oaks, CA: SAGE.

Putnam, L. L., & Stohl, C. (1990). Bona fide groups: A reconceptualization of groups in context. *Communication Studies, 41*, 248–265.

Putnam, L. L., & Stohl, C. (1996). Bona fide groups: An alternative perspective for communication and small group decision making. In R. Y. Hirokawa & M. S. Poole (Eds.), *Communication and group decision making* (2nd ed., pp. 147–178). Thousand Oaks, CA: SAGE.

Putnam, L. L., & Wilson, C. E. (1983). Communicative strategies in organizational conflicts: Reliability and validity of a measurement scale. In M. Burgoon (Ed.), *Communication yearbook 6* (pp. 629–652). Beverly Hills, CA: SAGE.

Raven, B. H. (1993). The bases of power: Origins and recent developments. *Journal of Social Issues, 49*, 227-251. doi:10.1111/j.1540-4560.1993.tb01191.x

Reid, F. J. M., & Reid, D. J. (2010). The expressive and conversational affordances of mobile messaging. *Behavior & Information Technology, 29*, 3–22. doi:10.1080/01449290701497079

Reimer, T., Reimer, A., & Czienskowski, U. (2010). Decision-making groups attenuate the discussion bias in favor of shared information: A meta-analysis. *Communication Monographs, 77*, 121–142. doi:10.1080/03637750903514318

Reimer, T., Reimer, A., & Hinsz, V. (2010). Naïve groups can solve the hidden-profile problem. *Human Communication Research, 36*, 443–467. doi:10.1111/j.1468-2958.2010.01383.x

Renz, M. A. (2006). The meaning of consensus and blocking for cohousing groups. *Small Group Research, 37*, 351–376. doi:10.1177/1046496406291184

Riddle, B. L., Anderson, C. M., & Martin, M. M. (2000). Small group socialization scale: Development and validity. *Small Group Research, 31*, 554–572. doi:10.1177/104649640003100503

Ridgeway, C. L. (2001). Gender, status, and leadership. *Journal of Social Issues, 57*, 637–655. doi:10.1111/0022–4537.00233

Rosenthal, S. B., & Buchholz, R. A. (1995). Leadership: Toward new philosophical foundations. *Business and Professional Ethics Journal, 14*, 25–41. doi:10.5840/bpej199514315

Rozell, E. J., & Gundersen, D. E. (2003). The effects of leader impression management on group perceptions of cohesion, consensus, and communication. *Small Group Research, 34*, 197–222. doi:10.1177/1046496402250431

Ruback, R. B., Dabbs, J. M., & Hopper, C. H. (1984). The process of brainstorming: An analysis with individual and group vocal parameters. *Journal of Personality and Social Psychology, 47*, 558–567. doi:10.1037/0022-3514.47.3.558

Sargent, L. D., & Sue-Chan, C. (2001). Does diversity affect group efficacy? The intervening role of cohesion and task interdependence. *Small Group Research, 32*, 426–450. doi:10.1177/104649640103200403

Scheerhorn, D., Geist, P., & Teboul, J. C. B. (1994). Beyond decision making in decision-making groups: Implications for the study of group communication. In L. R. Frey (Ed.), *Group communication in context: Studies of natural groups* (pp. 247–262). Hillsdale, NJ: Erlbaum.

Schultz, B. (1986). Communication correlates of perceived leaders in the small group. *Small Group Research, 17*. 51-65. doi:10.1177/104649648601700105

Schwarz, R. M. (1994). *The skilled facilitator: Practical wisdom for developing effective groups*. San Francisco, CA: Jossey-Bass.

Schwartzman, H. B. (1989). *The meeting: Gatherings in organizations and communities*. New York, NY: Plenum Press.

Schweiger, D. M., & Leana, C. R. (1986). Participation in decision making. In E. A. Locke (Ed.), *Generalizing from laboratory to field settings: Research findings from industrial-organizational psychology, organizational behavior, and human resource management* (pp. 147–166). Lexington, MA: Lexington Books.

Sharf, B. F. (1978). A rhetorical analysis of leadership emergence in small groups. *Communication Monographs, 45,* 156–172. doi:10.1080/03637757809375960

Shaw, M. E. (1981). *Group dynamics: The psychology of small group behavior.* New York, NY: McGraw-Hill.

Shin, Y. (2014). Positive group affect and team creativity: Mediation of team reflexivity and promotion focus. *Small Group Research, 45,* 337–364. doi:10.1177/1046496414533618

Shuffler, M. L., Burke, C. S., Kramer, W. S., & Salas, E. (2013). Leading teams: Past, present, and future perspectives. In M. G. Rumsey (Ed.), *The Oxford handbook of leadership* (pp. 144–166). Oxford, England: Oxford University Press.

Sillars, A. L., & Wilmot, W. W. (1994). Communication strategies in conflict and mediation. In J. A. Daly & J. M. Wiemann (Eds.), *Strategic interpersonal communication* (pp. 163–190). Hillsdale, NJ: Erlbaum.

Sillince, J. A. A. (2000). Rhetorical power, accountability and conflict in committees: An argumentation approach. *Journal of Management Studies, 37,* 1125–1156. doi:10.1111/1467-6486.00219

Smith, K. K., & Berg, D. N. (1987). *Paradoxes of group life.* San Francisco, CA: Jossey-Bass.

Socha, T. J. (1999). Communication in family units: Studying the first group. In L. Frey (Ed.), *The handbook of group communication theory and research* (pp. 475–492). Thousand Oaks, CA: SAGE.

Solansky, S. T. (2008). Leadership style and team processes in self-managed teams. *Journal of Leadership & Organizational Studies, 14,* 4332–341. doi:10.1177/1548051808315549

Somech, A., & Drach-Zahavy, A. (2007). Schools as team-based organizations: A structure-process-outcomes approach. *Group Dynamics: Theory, Research, and Practice, 11,* 305–320. doi:10.1037/1089-2699.11.4.305

Spink, K. S., & Carron, A. V. (1994). Group cohesion effects in exercise classes. *Small Group Research, 25,* 26–42. doi:10.1177/1046496494251003

Stasser, G., & Titus, W. (1985). Pooling of unshared information in group decision making: Biased information sampling during discussion. *Journal of Personality and Social Psychology, 48,* 1467–1478. doi:org/10.1037/0022-3514.48.6.1467

Stasser, G., & Titus, W. (1987). Effects of information load and percentage of shared information on the dissemination of unshared information during group discussion. *Journal of Personality and Social Psychology, 53,* 81–92. doi:org/10.1037/0022-3514.53.1.81

Stohl, C., & Putnam, L. L. (2003). Communication in bona fide groups: A retrospective and prospective account. In L. R. Frey (Ed.), *Group communication tn context: Studies of bona fide groups* (pp. 399–414). Mahwah, NJ: Erlbaum.

Sung, C. C. M. (2011). Doing gender and leadership: A discursive analysis of media representations in a reality TV show. *English Text Construction, 4,* 85–111. doi:10.1075/etc.4.1.05sun

SunWolf. (2008). *Peer groups: Expanding our study of small group communication.* Los Angeles, CA: SAGE.

SunWolf. (2010). Investigating jury deliberation in a capital murder case. *Small Group Research, 41,* 380–385. doi:10.1177/1046496410366484

SunWolf, & Seibold, D. R. (1999). The impact of formal procedures on group processes, members, and task outcomes. In L. R. Frey, D. S. Gouran, & M. S. Poole (Eds.), *The handbook of group communication theory and research* (pp. 395–431). Thousand Oaks, CA: SAGE.

Thomas, K. W. (1977). Toward multi-dimensional values in teaching: The examples of conflict behaviors. *Academy of Management Review, 2,* 484–490. doi:10.5465/AMR.1977.4281851

Thomas, K. W. (1992). Conflict and negotiation processes in organizations. In M. D. Dunnette & L. M. Hough (Eds.), *Handbook of industrial and organizational psychology* (pp. 651–717). Palo Alto, CA: Consulting Psychologists Press.

Timmerman, C. E., & Scott, C. R. (2006). Virtually working: Communicative and structural predictors of media use and key outcomes in virtual work teams. *Communication Monographs*, *73*, 108–136. doi:10.1080/03637750500534396

Tropman, J. E. (2003). *Making meetings work: Achieving high quality group decisions* (2nd ed.). Thousand Oaks, CA: SAGE.

Tse, H. H. M., & Dasborough, M. T. (2008). A study of exchange and emotions in team member relationships. *Group & Organization Management*, *33*, 194–215. doi:10.1177/1059601106293779

Türetgen, I. O., Unsal, P., & Erdem, I. (2008). The effects of sex, gender role, and personality traits on leader emergence: Does culture make a difference? *Small Group Research*, *39*, 588–615. doi:10.1177/1046496408319884

Turman, P. D. (2008). Coaches' immediacy behaviors as predictors of athletes' perceptions of satisfaction and team cohesion. *Western Journal of Communication*, *72*, 162–179. doi: 10.1080/10570310802038424

Van den Hooff, B., & de Ridder, J. A. (2004). Knowledge sharing in context: The influence of organizational commitment, communication climate and CMC use on knowledge sharing. *Journal of Knowledge Management*, *8*, 117–130. doi:10.1108/ 13673270410567675

Van de Ven, A. H., & Delbecq, A. L. (1974). The effectiveness of nominal, delphi, and interacting group decision-making processes. *Academy of Management Journal*, *17*, 605–621. doi:10.2307/255641

Van Mierlo, H., & Kleingeld, A. (2010). Goals, strategies, and group performance: Some limits of goal setting in groups. *Small Group Research*, *41*, 524–555. doi:10.1177/1046496410373628

Van Swol, L. M. (2009). Discussion and perception of information in groups and judge-advisor systems. *Communication Monographs*, *76*, 99–120. doi:10.1080/03637750802378781

Waldeck, J. H., Shepard, C. A., Teitelbaum, J., Farrar, W. J., & Seibold, D. R. (2002). New directions for functional, symbolic convergence, structuration, and bona fide group perspectives of group communication. In L. R. Frey (Ed.), *New directions in group communication* (pp. 3–23). Thousand Oaks, CA: SAGE.

Walker, R. C., & Aritz, J. (2015). Women doing leadership: Leadership styles and organizational culture. *International Journal of Business Communication*, *52*, 452–478. doi:10.1177/2329488415598429

Wall, V. D., Jr., & Galanes, G. J. (1986). The SYMLOG dimensions and small group conflict. *Communication Studies*, *37*, 61–78. doi:10.1080/10510978609368206

Wall, V. D., Jr., Galanes, G. J., & Love, S. B. (1987). Small, task-oriented groups: Conflict, conflict management, satisfaction, and decision quality. *Small Group Behavior*, *18*, 31–55. doi:10.1177/104649648701800102

Wall, V. D., & Nolan, L. L. (1986). Perceptions of inequity, satisfaction, and conflict in task-oriented groups. *Human Relations*, *39*, 1033–1052. doi:10.1177/001872678603901106

Walther, J. B. (2002). Time effects in computer-mediated groups: Past, present, and future. In P. Hinds & S. Kiesler (Eds.), *Distributed work* (pp. 235–257) Cambridge, MA: MIT Press.

Wang, L., Han, J., Fisher, C. M., & Pan, Y. (2017). Learning to share: Exploring temporality in shared leadership and team learning. *Small Group Research*, *48*, 165–189. doi:10.1177/1046496417690027

Warfield, J. N. (1993). Complexity and cognitive equilibrium: Experimental results and their implications. In D. J. D. Sandole & H. van der Merwe (Eds.), *Conflict resolution theory and practice: Integration and application* (pp. 65–77). New York, NY: Manchester University Press.

Watson, W. E., Johnson, L., & Merntt, D. (1998). Team orientation, self-orientation, and diversity in task groups: Their connection to team performance over time. *Group and Organization Management*, *23*, 161–188. doi:10.1177/1059601198232005

Watson, W. E., Kumar, K., & Michaelsen, L. K. (1993). Cultural diversity's impact on interaction process and performance: Comparing homogeneous and diverse task groups. *Academy of Management Journal*, *36*, 590–602. doi:10.2307/256593

Watzlawick, P., Beavin, J. H., & Jackson, D. D. (1967). *Pragmatics of human communication: A study of interactional patterns, pathologies, and paradoxes.* New York, NY: Norton.

Webber, S. S. (2008). Development of cognitive and affective trust in teams: A longitudinal study. *Small Group Research*, *6*, 746–769. doi:10.1177/1046496408323569

Weick, K. E. (1969). Laboratory organizations and unnoticed causes. *Administrative Science Quarterly*, *14*, 294-303. doi:10.2307/2391107

Wellman, B. (1988). Structural analysis: From method and metaphor to theory and substance. In B. Wellman & S. Berkowitz (Eds.), *Social structures: A network approach* (pp. 19–61). Cambridge, England: Cambridge University Press.

Wheelan, S. A. (2009). Group size, group development, and group productivity. *Small Group Research*, *40*, 247–262. doi:10.1177/1046496408328703

Wheelan, S. A., & McKeage, R. L. (1993). Developmental patterns in small and large groups. *Small Group Research*, *24*, 60–83. doi:10.1177/1046496493241005

Whitford, T., & Moss, S. A. (2009). Transformational leadership in distributed work groups: The moderating role of follower regulatory focus and goal orientation. *Communication Research*, *36*, 810–837. doi:10.1177/0093650209346800

Whitton, S. M., & Fletcher, R. B. (2014). The Group Environment Questionnaire: A multilevel confirmatory factor analysis. *Small Group Research*, *45*, 68–88. doi:10.1177/1046496413511121

Witteman, H. (1991). Group member satisfaction: A conflict-related account. *Small Group Research, 22*, 24–58. doi:10.1177/1046496491221003

Wittenbaum, G. M., Hollingshead, A. B., & Botero, I. C. (2004). From cooperative to motivated information sharing in groups: Moving beyond the hidden profile paradigm. *Communication Monographs*, *71*, 286–310. doi:10.1080/0363452042000299894

Wittenbaum, G. M., Hollingshead, A. B., Paulus, P. B., Hirokawa, R. Y. Ancona, D. G., Peterson, R. S., Jehn, K. A., & Yoon, K. (2004). The functional perspective as a lens for understanding groups. *Small Group Research*, *35*, 17–43. doi:10.1177/1046496403259459

Wittenberg-Lyles, E., Oliver, D. P., Kruse, R. L., Demiris, G., Gage, L. A., & Wagner, K. (2013). Family caregiver participation in hospice interdisciplinary team meetings: How does it affect the nature and content of communication. *Health Communication, 28*, 110–118. doi:10.1080/10410236.2011.652935

Wolfram, H.-J., & Gratton, L. (2014). Gender role self-concept, categorical gender, and transactional-transformational leadership: Implications for perceived workgroup performance. *Journal of Leadership & Organizational Studies*, *21*, 338–353. doi: 10.1177/1548051813498421

Wu, J. B., Tsui, A. S., & Kinicki, A. J. (2010). Consequences of differentiated leadership in groups. *Academy of Management Journal*, *53*, 90–106. doi:10.5465/AMJ.2010.48037079

Yong, K., Sauer, S. J., & Mannix, E. A. (2014). Conflict and creativity in interdisciplinary teams. *Small Group Research*, *45*, 266–289. doi:10.1177/1046496414530789

Yuan, Y. C., Fulk, J., Monge, P. R., & Contractor, N. (2010). Expertise director development, shared task interdependence, and strength of communication network ties as multilevel predictors of expertise exchange in transactive memory work groups. *Communication Research*, *37*, 20–47. doi:10.1177/009365020351469

Zanin, A. C., Hoelscher, C., & Kramer, M. W. (2016). Extending symbolic convergence theory: A shared identity perspective of a team's culture. *Small Group Research*, *47*, 438–472. doi:10.1177/1046496416658554

AUTHOR INDEX

A

Aaron, J. R., 167
Allison, B. B., 180
Alper, S., 132
Ancona, D. G., 71
Anderson, C.,156
Anderson, C. M., 107,109
Anthony, T., 101
Aritz, J., 150,152,154
Arrow, H., 19, 60, 107, 108
Asbury, M. B., 59
Aube, C., 21
Avolio, B. J., 153

B

Bailey, D. E., 99
Bakar, H. A., 99
Baker, D. C., 146
Bales, R. F., 25, 119
Ballard, D. I., 38
Baran, B. E., 164
Barge, J. K., 140
Barki, H., 79
Baron, N. S., 49
Baruah, J., 79
Bass, B. M., 143,152
Baxter, J., 152
Bazarova, N. N., 76
Beavin, J. H., 25
Beck, S. B., 59, 97, 164, 185
Behfar, K. J., 103, 121
Bell, B. S., 49, 50, 51
Bell, M. A., 199
Bell, M. P., 44
Berdahl, J. L., 107, 108, 156
Berg, D. N., 119, 120
Berry, G. R., 49, 51
Bettenhausen, K. L., 16
Bies, D. J., 104
Blight, M. G., 141, 142
Bonito, J. A., 17

C

Botero, I. C., 56, 57, 78
Bradley, P. H., 125
Brashers, D. E., 76
Brawley, L. R., 97
Brennan, M., 41
Brooks, A., 154
Brown, T. M., 63
Bruch, H., 153
Buchholz, R. A., 154
Burgoon, J. K., 123
Burke, C. S., 139
Burnfield, J. L., 172
Burtis, T. B., 43
Byrnes, K., 104

Canary, D. J., 127
Carini, B., 19
Carron, A. V., 97. 99, 101
Carson, J., 148
Carter, D. R., 140
Cartwright, D., 100
Chen, C. C., 157
Clegg, S., 123,125
Clifton, J., 142, 152
Cohen, A., 128
Cohen, S. G., 99, 107
Cohen, S. P., 119
Comer, D. R., 16
Contractor, N., 60, 65, 148
Cruz, M. G., 158
Cummings, J. N., 50, 51
Czienskowski, U., 57

D

Dabbs, J. M. Jr., 77
Dagosta, J., 140
Dailey, J. C., 78, 81
Dagosta, J., 140
Daniloski, K., 146
Darics, E., 49

SUBJECT INDEX

CPSIA information can be obtained at www.ICGtesting.com
Printed in the USA
LVIW01n0156141217
559632LV00005B/13

* 9 7 8 1 5 1 6 5 1 9 2 8 6 *